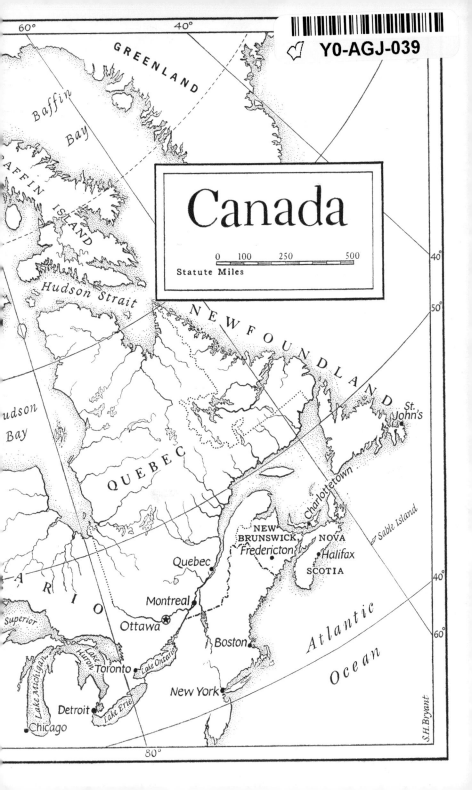

60°   40°

GREENLAND

Baffin Bay

AFFIN ISLAND

Hudson Strait

udson Bay

Canada

0   100   250   500

Statute Miles

40°

50°

NEWFOUNDLAND

St. John's

QUEBEC

Charlottetown

Sable Island

NEW BRUNSWICK

NOVA

Fredericton

Quebec

Halifax

SCOTIA

ARIO

40°

Montreal

Ottawa

Atlantic

60°

Superior

Boston

Ocean

Lake Huron

Toronto

Lake Ontario

New York

Lake Michigan

Detroit

Lake Erie

Chicago

S.H.Bryant

80°

Y0-AGJ-039

Pursuit in the Wilderness

Pursuit in the Wilderness

by

Charles Rivett-Carnac

LITTLE, BROWN AND COMPANY · BOSTON · TORONTO

Published simultaneously in Canada
by Little, Brown & Company (Canada) Limited

PRINTED IN THE UNITED STATES OF AMERICA

Foreword

WHEN it was first suggested that I write this book, I viewed the proposal with some doubt as I knew that it would have to be an autobiography or personal account of what one individual tried to find in life, and, bearing in mind the physical and metaphysical aspects of this problem, I wondered whether I could properly accomplish such a task. However, after considering the question and giving thought to the conflict in the world today, more particularly as it applies to youth, I felt that perhaps some purpose might be served by describing one man's journey toward the goal he searched for and the adventures, both of the body and of the spirit, he met with on the way.

While setting down the events as they occurred, I have had to change an occasional name here and there and, as I have had to depend almost entirely on my memory, there may be one or two minor errors in the earlier chapters; if there are they will be confined to detail and should in no way affect the chronicle itself. This, I suggest, is reasonable enough. Half a century is a long time to throw one's mind back to such things as the exactitudes of dialogue or to remember those particulars which, by reason of their unimportance, have, in the substance of the whole, no vital place or worth.

In the writing of this book, I would like to extend my sincere thanks to various people for different kinds of help:

To Mr. Reginald Bretnor, of Berkeley, California, for his interest and advice and for the suggestions he has made in regard to the manuscript, as well as for the editing and cutting he has done. To the British Red Cross for information it supplied covering the time I spent with the French Army. To Mrs. M. Moffett of Bird and Company, Calcutta, for certain details concerning the years I spent in India. And lastly, and beyond everything else, to my wife, who has spent many long and arduous hours in typing and retyping the innumerable pages — or so it must have seemed to her! — which go into the production of a book.

CHARLES RIVETT-CARNAC

Contents

Pursuit in the Wilderness

Prologue

~~~~~~~~~~~~

WHAT does man pursue? What is worthwhile — money, fame, wisdom, the things of the spirit, the roar of crowds in acclamation as one passes by? These are, I suppose, some of the things we seek in the wilderness of life, following the hidden trails we hope will bring us to that place where happiness is found and we can rest content, at last at peace.

Do we get there? It's very hard to say. If the gods smile we reach the forest's edge and see the valley stretching before us full of sunshine and bright meadows where the birds sing. But we do not pause there. Man, being what he is — a part of Nature's elemental strife — looks always onward, viewing the distant mountaintop, ranging the long horizon, breasting the battle and the storm and climbing higher, higher, to where the star he follows can be dimly seen, a diamond point within the dark and mist.

This is the story of such a search, and one that leads through far-off lands down vast canyons where the spirit failed and up great precipices toward the cresting light, until, after trials and adventures of no ordinary type, I came upon the thing I looked for in the end. The story has strange ingredients: war, elephants, dog teams, spies, a murder or so, incredible happenings and circumstances — and perhaps the overthrow of fear. These and the age-old search for understanding. A witch's brew.

3

Part I

which it would serve no purpose to mention here. A good deal of our history has always been linked with India, where one of my ancestors was Governor of Bombay and Chairman of the East India Company at the beginning of the nineteenth century. We are one of those loosely strung together tribal units which in the past used to spread from one country to another, playing a part in their development. India, however, was our special field and the one in which we were best known. Rudyard Kipling mentions the family in his story "The Tomb of his Ancestors," which has to do with a man's struggle against a phantom tiger — a tale that bears some metaphorical similarity to my own.

Soon after my birth, my father, who was a Deputy Inspector General of Police in India, on leave in England at the time, took us back to Assam, the frontier province bordering Burma in which he was stationed. I spent the first few years of my life in this area full of mountains and impenetrable jungles where every manner of wild beast made its home, and snakes ranging in size from the deadly pencil-length *krait* to great boa constrictors slipped quietly through the grass or hung suspended from the trees. It was intensely hot and humid, and when the rains came and the rivers burst their banks to form chains of inland seas, nearly everything was under water and native dugout canoes sailed over the grasslands and the flat, open valleys.

I have only vague recollections of that period, but there are one or two incidents that stand out, sharply etched like photographic plates. A crowd of men beating a python to death: unfortunate creature, it had dined not wisely but too well, having devoured a goat that stood out in its middle and made it look like one of those long balloons which, blown up, suddenly bulge in some unexpected place; heavy with food, it had been unable to get away. An earthquake when the house shook and the fan hanging from the ceiling swung slowly to and fro while the rope that ordinarily propelled it kept moving quietly up and down, untended and alone — and of my being grabbed by one of the native servants and rushed outside in case the house came down.

It was an interesting life for a young boy, though it had its dangers. Disease was prevalent, with little medical help available. Cholera, typhoid, enteric fever, and malaria abounded; and in the bazaars one could see the lepers begging for alms, their faces, arms and legs a mass of sores and their hands and feet slowly rotting off. I can remember this very well, for there were very few white children where we lived, and during the day I was often left to my own devices and would go running to the market in the native quarter near which all my small friends lived. They were, mostly, the children of the local merchants or of government clerks. They were dark, cheerfully dirty, and clad in practically nothing — just a small loincloth tied round their waists.

Barefooted and wearing only a pair of shorts, I would join them and their families in fascinating pursuits. In this manner I learned to speak Assamese fluently, and could converse easily with anyone around. Though we got into mischief we managed never to get hurt. Once, for example, I stole a revolver and a box of ammunition from my father's office, and my little friends and I had a fine time trying to load the weapon. This was very exciting at the age of four or five — and luckily the cartridges were of the wrong caliber. I remember it especially well because I found myself in a good deal of trouble after one of the native constables found us.

It seems remarkable that I remained untouched by any of the ailments, eating as I did all the foods and condiments handed to me, which immediately before had been a repository for every type of fly, and drinking any liquid that I could lay my hands on when I was thirsty without thought to its myriad germs. At my parents' house we were more particular; everything was filtered and most of it boiled.

Once in a while, my father would take my mother and

9

me on his journeys into the hills on police business, and there we would visit the villages where the savage tribes lived, great tall men who were almost naked and armed with broad-bladed, eight-foot spears. It was the smell, I think, that really made its mark upon my memory, and the sight of chickens, dogs and goats running between and under the grass-thatched houses built on platforms off the ground so that their occupants would be reasonably safe from wild animals. Not entirely safe, for some of the tigers were man-eaters and occasionally forced their way in.

When I was six I was taken back to England to be educated. It was considered unwise to expose children to the continued hazards of disease, and it was traditional that they should go to suitable English schools to prepare for their eventual careers. This had been done with my three older brothers, who were in due course to enter the Royal Military College at Sandhurst and join the Army and Indian Police later on. My sister, too, had left India and been sent to a girls' school on the south coast of England where young ladies were taught the requirements of behavior so that they could take their appropriate place in society. In my case, my future was in the hands of an uncle and aunt in England who undertook to bring me up.

It is tragic that until one reaches the age of comprehension one seldom appreciates the benefits conferred on one as a child. I know now that I was a reprobate of the first order when my aunt first took me under her control. As the youngest of the family, and used as I was to having my every wish granted by the native servants who surrounded me at all times in Assam, I found the strict rules of her house a most unwelcome change; and yet, if I had not been speedily disciplined by her and by the authorities of the school I attended, my future might not have been the same by any means. My aunt was a tall, regal woman, crowned with gray hair, and in the household her word was final. I soon learned to do what I was told — go to bed at an early hour of the evening, be polite and wash my face and hands before coming in to meals. If one failed in one of these things one heard about it very soon. My uncle, who was a retired colonel of the Indian Army, short and stocky and armed with the largest snowy-white buffalo moustaches I have ever seen, of course had similar ideas, and although it took me time to adjust to them I must say now how grateful I am for what I was taught. Ably seconded by Mrs. Wilkes, the wife of the principal of St. Cyprian's, the preparatory school to which I was sent, they taught me much which stood me in good stead in later years, when, despite risks and consequences, I had always to go on.

There were no modern comforts on the south coast of England at the turn of the century. The telephone had only recently come into existence, and occasionally one of those amazing new contrivances, a motor car, would come creaking, clanking and groaning up the street, the occupants wrapped in heavy coats and wearing knickerbockers, peering anxiously before them as they made their tortuous way. Street lighting by electricity had not made its appearance, and one aspect of beauty that I'll always remember was the lamplighter going from lamp to lamp on a foggy evening, and with his magic wand bursting them one by one into flame. The hurdy-gurdy or barrel organ was frequently heard, and there was enchantment not only in the music but in the sight of the usually swarthy, moustached individual from Italy who cranked his machine and then, when the tune was ended, sent his gaily bedecked monkey — generally wearing a colored waistcoat and small, round pillbox hat — climbing the walls to the upper windows to collect any offerings. The highlight, though, was when a German band made its appearance on the street and filled the neighborhood with its blaring and bleating, resonant notes thundering far and wide and penetrating into every cubicle and crevice. The musicians were always big, fat men, clothed in bright, gold-braided uniforms, and invariably cheerful and pleasant to the scores of children who followed them as they hauled their instruments on foot from one concert to another.

Those were the days, too, when the horse was a useful friend of the community and not regarded as almost a prehistoric beast. Once in a while there would be an exciting day when someone's house caught fire and four magnificent animals would come roaring up the street at full gallop, the red-painted fire engine swaying from side to side and the firemen hanging on grimly. Every small boy lucky enough to be in the vicinity cheered them on and waved his hat as the wild, careening juggernaut flashed by — why, it was something that everyone would talk about for a week!

My uncle's house was a big one that overlooked the street and had a large, spacious garden at the rear. In the winter it was very cold; the gales blew up the Channel continually and the open fireplaces were the sole source of heat. The kitchen was the warmest place, and whenever I could I spent spare hours there with the cook and the parlormaid, provided they allowed me to and I did not get in the way.

In that house I became aware of something which was to prove of inestimable value later on — that one *must* overcome fear however much one may be afraid.

The room I slept in was in the attic. To get there, I had to climb the stairs to the first landing, on which the main bedrooms were situated, and then another flight which made a steep, reverse turn before the attic floor was reached. Next to my bedroom, on the landing, stood the metal water cistern that supplied the house, and getting to bed meant going up the last flight of stairs in the dark. This I, like many other small boys, was always hesitant to do. Once on the landing, I had to enter my room in pitch darkness, cross to the head of the bed, and light the gas jet that stood out from the wall. It was always an ordeal — one never knew what horror might be lurking under the bed — but one night the cistern just beyond the door of my room began to knock and to pound. I must have been about ten years old at the time, and I started imagining all kinds of terrifying things. In my panic I could almost see some indescribable monster striking the cistern with sledgehammer blows, working itself into a frenzy of rage before coming after me into my room. I lay in bed, shivering and shaking, with the covers pulled over my head until, after what seemed hours, the noise stopped and I was able gradually to fall asleep.

Next day, in the bright light of the morning, the landing was empty of terror or threat as I ran down the stairs to have breakfast. It was the holiday season, and there were one or two young guests in the house who were considerably older than I. Discipline was strict, and ordinarily I was not allowed to speak at mealtimes except in response to a question. On this occasion I was so much in need of reassurance that during a lull in the conversation I decided to take a chance and break the recognized rule. "What was the noise in the cistern?" I asked.

There was a moment's silence, and then somebody said, "Oh, nothing to worry about. Probably only a dead man trying to get out!"

All day I waited to hear the knocking again, but the attic was quiet as a tomb. Every once in a while I would go to the foot of the stairs and listen, dreading the coming of night. No one seemed concerned about the dead man; presumably as long as he kept quiet there was no point in disturbing him!

Then that night, just as I was going upstairs to bed — *thump, thump, thump!* — there he was again beating the cistern with dull, hollow blows. On the first landing I waited, trying to summon up enough courage to take on the dark above. I had to reach an important decision: should I call down below for someone to help me or should I go up by myself? The pounding was getting louder, its staccato beat drumming faster and faster as the terror-filled minutes dragged by. I stood there waiting at the far end of the landing, my face in my hands. Then I made up my mind and crept up through the blackness. At the end of a journey which seemingly had no end I was at last in my room with the gas jet blazing — and the noise on the landing had stopped. I was still shaking with fear, but I'd learned that one must always go on. For the first time in my life I'd taken a gamble and won. It was to prove the first, faint whisper of knowledge.

I was always in trouble at school. St. Cyprian's was a couple of miles from our house and as I was not a boarder I had to walk the distance twice a day. Part of the route led me through an area where gangs of the young, rougher element had their assembly points. Generally they would leave me alone, but dressed in my school cap, jersey, and blazer I was a natural object for any mischief they could devise, and sometimes this would result in a running battle with stones. While I was always on the defensive due to the number of my attackers I developed a very accurate aim with a rock, and gradually I was left to continue my perambulations alone.

Alone. I think if I were given one word to describe my childhood that would be it. It was not that I was not surrounded by people at home or at school, but that I was always just outside the group, looking in. Nearly all the pupils at St. Cyprian's were boarders who came from well-to-do families and as such formed a closely knit clan. The few day students were exterior to the family life of the school, rather than an integral part of it. They received the same education, played on the various teams, were members of the Cadet Corps, took part in all physical and cultural activities, but when evening came they disappeared like small separate ghosts, leaving the others together. At home it was much the same; notwithstanding the kindness I received it was different from living with one's own parents, and it taught me to shift for myself. I developed a strong sense of independence, not always well directed and sometimes leading to retribution at home and at school. I had only two real interests — reading tales of adventure and going for long walks when I could to get away by myself.

When I was fourteen, I left St. Cyprian's and was sent to Eastbourne College, this time as a boarder. My preparatory school had been designed to train boys between seven and fourteen years old, and Eastbourne College took over from there until the student was ready to go on to Oxford or Cambridge or through the finishing academies of Sandhurst or Woolwich into the commissioned ranks of the Army. Some students, of course, went into business or civil affairs, but the main purpose of the college, like all similar institutions, was to prepare its inmates, academically or otherwise, to become useful citizens who would provide leadership in whatever career they subsequently chose to follow. In my case things did not work out quite as expected.

I cannot say that I enjoyed Eastbourne College, but that was my fault and not the fault of my tutors. Used to wandering around by myself, I could not fit myself into the pattern of the school. The control, of necessity, was strict, and much of the punishment — some of which came my way — was administered by the senior pupils who, as prefects, were authorized to belabor their juniors with canes for a variety of minor trangressions. Anything serious was dealt with by the masters themselves, and any such guilt would speedily put one in a bending position with consequent hurt to one's dignity and oneself. If the offense was one without hope of pardon, the headmaster would administer justice himself in the awful and gloomy precincts he occupied and from which he would emerge from time to time clad in his mortarboard and long, flowing robe. The college was an excellent one, a mold from which graduates were discharged scholastically accomplished. Everyone had much the same accent, the same ideas of behavior, and almost the same taste in clothes — but not necessarily the same degree of intelligence. The year I spent there did me a great deal of good, mainly, I think, because it taught me submission and continued the training in ethics I had learned at St. Cyprian's and at home, though academically I never got very far.

At this time, I met a girl of my own age whose real name doesn't matter but whom for purposes of this narrative I will call Deirdre. She was at a girls' school at Eastbourne where she spent the holidays, since her parents were in America as mine were in India. Being without any close family ties, we formed a brother-sister relationship and I spent much of my time with her during the off-term seasons when I was not at school. During this period I lacked anyone else to whom my affections could be applied, and we formed a friendship which was to run, strong and unbroken, through the years of our youth until we had grown to maturity and were separated from each other, half a world away.

Time was marching on. I was now fifteen years of age and the world was embroiled in war. There had been a lot of excitement about men going overseas, and at Eastbourne College some of the prefects joined up when they reached eighteen, a number in the Royal Flying Corps. I was, of course, thrilled by the exploits of the aces; the danger of flying and fighting people in the air was as appealing as winning the Victoria Cross for some heroic action on the ground. Many of the sons and relatives of persons one met were being killed, and I recall the apprehension with which the possibility of this news was constantly awaited. But I cannot honestly say that any of this made a great or lasting impression, at least not consciously, for at fifteen you don't think very much of other people's troubles and not very seriously of your own. Your concern is much more in what *you* want to do than in what may be happening outside the small orbit of your mind.

My father had retired on pension in India and, notwithstanding every sacrifice my parents could make, there was no money to pay the bills. As a result it was decided at the end of the Easter term that I would go to another aunt who lived in the suburbs of London and there continue my education at one of the local grammar schools, free of charge. This was a major change and it could not have been expected that I would adjust to it with ease. The mold was half set; now I would be poured out of it to start all over again in a totally different sphere. I was filled with dismay at the thought.

Something had to be done! It was the holiday season and when I reached the new environment in which I was to live I found that I could come and go as I pleased. My aunt in the London area was a widow who was not financially well off and had two young children of her own who occupied most of her time. Nobody seemed to mind what I did or where I went during the daytime, and in consequence I spent most of my time wandering the London streets, viewing the sights and considering my problem. In a few weeks the holidays would end, and unless I could find some solution I would have to go back to school. I hated the idea of beginning again.

Then one day, during one of my walks, I came across an advertisement asking for ambulance drivers for the British Red Cross and Order of St. John of Jerusalem in France. I thought it over. Perhaps it was only a dream, but if I could manage to be taken on my difficulties would be solved. It was as simple as that! But I could not drive a car. I then remembered a friend in London who had visited my aunt and uncle at Eastbourne and who seemed to take an interest in me. I got in touch with him in London and he loaned me the money to take a course of lessons in driving — perhaps because he was intrigued and even amused by my audacity — and I enrolled in the British School of Motoring, from which I graduated in due course, proficient enough to keep a car on the road under ordinary circumstances.

Now the crucial step was before me — would I be taken on? When I appeared at the headquarters of the British Red Cross and filled out the application form I was met by queer looks, and a good deal of discussion and whispering went on. However, it was early in 1918; tens of thousands of men had been killed or wounded; no one knew what the morrow would bring. There might have been a certain amount of sympathy, too, for a boy who wanted to take his part in the struggle. Whatever the reason, it was decided that no harm would be done if I was allowed to take the tests.

An appointment was made with a driving examiner the next day. When I arrived, the vehicle was there, waiting. It was an ambulance, and I had never seen anything that looked so big and wide; certainly it was a giant compared with the much smaller cars in which I had gained my instruction. My heart sank as I got behind the wheel.

At first, all went well. My examiner was a pleasant, cheerful young man who engaged me in conversation as we went along. I had to do all the usual things until he suddenly directed me into a narrow lane which made a tight circular turn. *Crash!* I had taken it too fast, jumped the sidewalk, and scraped the fender on the stone wall of a building that towered like a cliff overhead.

Everything had collapsed; my hopes of engaging in my new profession, of escaping my new school, had all vanished together! But my examiner, perturbed for only a moment, told me to back the ambulance out until it was free and then carry on. Another few hundred yards and we were at our destination. Dismayed I prepared to descend. My examiner was busily occupied marking up my score in a notebook he carried while I was opening the door of the ambulance to get out.

"Here, wait a moment," he said. "I think I can pass you — you'll get some practice as you go along." He looked at me, smiling. "You must be pretty keen to get to France if you want to do this at your age. Well, good luck — I'll send the papers along to the office."

I could hardly believe my ears. The impossible had come true! Within a few hours I was taken on, and shortly afterward I was bound for Boulogne. My aunt and uncle at Eastbourne, whom I had told of my intentions, had believed success to be out of the question. I slept happily in a big coil of rope on the Channel steamer that made the crossing from Dover. It was night and it was raining, but what did that matter? I was on my way! I was sixteen.

2

The Battlefields of France

BLOOD and rum are poor things to cut your teeth on, for they are likely to be indigestible at first. Then, after a while, one comes to accept them, and I was to taste a good deal of both in the months that followed.

When I arrived at Boulogne I found that I was to be a member of an ambulance unit comprising twenty or thirty cars and drivers. I had not thought very much about what I would have to do — all I knew was that I was going to the war as a driver for the Red Cross, and nobody had made clear exactly what this consisted of. The future was a great, blank book open at the first page. This seemed a very pleasant prospect, and if I had been asked at that time what it was that I was pursuing I would have shrugged my shoulders at the futility of the question. Certainly I had never seriously considered that I might be killed. But even at that age some subconscious idea of purpose must have been running round in my mind — I had to go and find out things for myself.

Boulogne was the main point of operations of the Red Cross and Order of St. John on the French coast, and I was issued a uniform similar to that worn by the British Army and a khaki cap with the emblem of the organization prominently displayed in white and scarlet enamel. I was given a mentor, a pleasant, gray-haired man of about fifty who in private life had been chauffeur to one of the great families of England. Though our association was short, I was able to increase both my self-confidence and proficiency at driving. I paid attention to his teaching, and with the help of his great experience I prospered.

Our machines in Boulogne were nearly all British — mostly Vauxhalls and Wolseleys — and at least one Model T Ford. They had pneumatic tires but no starters, and they had to be kept in first-class condition, with all the brass and metal work on the engines polished for inspection. Every so often one would have to be repainted, and all the old paint had to be chipped off by hand before the new coats were laid on. It was a dirty job lying underneath on one's back, hammering away with the chips falling down on one's face.

The actual work of the unit consisted of driving British wounded from the trains on which they arrived from the front, to the base hospitals at Boulogne, and then, when and if they recovered sufficiently, taking them to the docks where they embarked for further attention in England. This did not apply to all; those with comparatively minor wounds were returned to their units after treatment. Quite a few such trains arrived, and it was up to the drivers on duty to help load the wounded into the ambulances, which had room for four stretcher cases or twelve walking wounded. Two men formed each Red Cross crew. Once stretcher cases were on board, the ambulances would move off, crawling hesitantly along to the hospital, their drivers exercising every possible care to avoid any bump or hole in the road. Torture and agony were written sharp and clear on the white, harrowed faces of those who were seriously wounded, and as I helped load their motionless forms into the ambulance for the first time in my life the smell of death hung heavy in the air. It made a lasting impression on my mind.

Quite a number of the men driving the ambulances were over the age limit for active service or ineligible by reason of some minor disability. Most were from England, but one or two came from distant parts of what is now the Commonwealth. There were two categories: the salaried driver (of whom I was one), and those who had volunteered in an unpaid capacity. These latter were very much in the minority and, for the most part, performed the duties of officers and were treated accordingly. They lived separately in their own quarters, while those of us who were paid employees were accommodated in a long dormitory in an old stone building on the waterfront.

I had had almost no contact with adults except for a few relatives and schoolmasters, and, to me at least, some of the drivers seemed interesting types indeed. Among them were taxi drivers, chauffeurs, men who had been in various businesses, and others whose previous vocations remained mysterious and unknown. They were a strange assortment. In the dormitory directly across from me was an old taxi driver from London, a fat, gross old man with gray handlebar moustaches, a round, seamed face and small, deep-set eyes. Next to him was a tall, lanky Australian, always suave and debonair, a man of the world able to find his way around in any situation. On my side of the dormitory, I was flanked by two extremes. One was a blue-eyed truck driver about twenty-five years of age, a good-natured product of London's working mass. The other, a few years older, was called "Archie" by everyone and was universally popular. He was fair-haired, tall and round-shouldered, with very good manners and diction. Though Archie and the Australian took me under their wings in their off-duty journeys around Boulogne, I was never able to find out anything about their backgrounds.

Boulogne was a typical French city with — except for the main thoroughfares — narrow cobblestoned streets from which the tall, flat-fronted houses rose. Around the dormitory there were quite a number of estaminets which my two friends and I frequented, where I became acquainted with the carefree and volatile life of the inhabitants, a pleasing and welcome change from the more restrictive atmosphere in which I had been brought up. The girls especially were sparkling and warm-hearted, their conversation flowing around them in fast, rippling streams. It was like being thrown into the bright shining current of life after being held in some small, landlocked pool.

Far removed from the front as it was, Boulogne was ordinarily a peaceful place, but once in a while there would be an air raid and the city would be bombed. When this happened the ambulances not on duty would be taken out of town so that they would not be blown up. Sometimes, those of us who did not accompany them would take refuge in one of the deep cellars of the vicinity with the local citizens who had been caught on the streets. There we would wait, listening to the shriek of the bombs as they fell, estimating their distance by the roar of the explosions. Although afterwards I became used to shell-fire and occasionally being machine-gunned by a passing aircraft, I could never escape a feeling of anxiety in an air raid, for while one could hear the planes overhead one never knew where they were. Just when a series of explosions could be heard at the other end of the city, one or more aircraft might be right overhead, aiming directly at the place where we were packed closely together, men, women, and children, in the dark of the cellar. If one was going to be killed the open air seemed preferable, and accordingly, after one or two experiences of near misses, I formed the practice of going down to the end of the jetty close to our dormitory and watching the air raid from there. Pointing out to sea as it did and surrounded on three sides by water, the danger — except in the case of a direct hit —

was negligible. From there one could see the flash of the bombs as they exploded and watch their lightning split the black curtain of night.

Every time there was a raid there would be a few people killed, and sometimes a bomb would devastate a shelter, penetrating through the floors like an arrow and bringing the walls down in its wake. When this happened casualties were high, but for the most part little damage was done. The bombs were comparatively small in those days and had not reached the lethal capacity they were to attain in the Second World War. The number of planes available to the enemy was also very limited, and the majority had only a small fuel supply with which to reach their target and return. Generally, too, one could tell when an air raid was coming. During the morning a single plane would fly overhead, far out of range of the guns, to photograph ships in the harbor. Then, that night, if the visibility was clear and the moon shone brightly enough, the planes would arrive in force. The towns closer to the front had much more serious difficulties to contend with, and the damage was correspondingly higher.

I was not, however, to remain in Boulogne for long. The Red Cross had three ambulance units serving with the French Army at the front which were known as Section Sanitaire Anglaise 16, 17, and 18 respectively. Service in these units was on a volunteer basis and, as the prospect of getting closer to the front seemed much more interesting, I applied, despite the efforts of my friends to dissuade me. Although I was told that there was no hope because of my age, in due course I was accepted, and with three other reinforcements left Boulogne with two ambulances which were to replace damaged vehicles in the French sector of the line near Chalons-sur-Marne. I was filled with excitement. Now at last I would see the real thing and get away from what had become a somewhat monotonous routine at the edge of events.

It was a bright, sunny morning when we left Boulogne, traveling the tree-fringed highways that seemed to stretch endlessly without bend or curve toward the rumble of war. Here and there a house had been damaged, and some of the larger communities had suffered a great deal from bombs. From the coast on clear nights I had been able to see the reflections of the explosions in the sky when some city to the east was being attacked; now the results were there at first hand. Late in the evening, as we passed through a city which had suffered a large number of raids, we found the warning sounding and the inhabitants moving on foot or by whatever faster means they had available to safety in the hills on the outskirts.

Finally we reached the headquarters of S.S.A. 17 near Chalons-sur-Marne, to which I was to be attached. This unit was operating in aid of the 163rd Division of French Infantry, which comprised the 53rd, 142nd, and 415th regiments. Our ambulances would come as close as they could to the *poste de secours*, or first field dressing station, and we would take the wounded back from there to the nearest hospitals. In some cases the *poste de secours* was a mile or so from the trenches, but more often than not considerably less. Soon I was to achieve what I had set out to do — taste the full flavor of war.

S.S.A. 17 consisted of about twenty ambulances — some of them old, four-cylindered Buicks — manned by the same types of men I had met at Boulogne, except that a Frenchman or two formed part of its complement. The latter were engaged on liaison and commissariat duties, acting as interpreters as well when the occasion required. One man alone stands out in my memory — Colonel Barry, the officer in charge of the unit. He was a very fine Irish gentleman; well past fifty, he had had a tracheotomy and breathed through a hole in his throat. The rest were of various ages and sizes, but their personalities have receded into the routine business of what we were doing — going up to the line and bringing back the wounded.

The unit was mobile, setting up its headquarters wherever it could as the regiments moved from one part of the line to another or when they went into rest areas to recuperate after heavy casualties. Now, closer to the trenches, the life was totally different from that I had known at Boulogne. Nearly all the buildings and a greater part of the trees had been razed by shellfire. What roads there were twisted over the empty landscape, pockmarked by enemy fire and frequently broken by cavernous pits where great shells had landed, erupting the soil and forming small, shallow pools. Rain was with us continually, making what was left of the roads a quagmire of mud over which the ambulances skidded from side to side, their wheels either racing on the greasy surface or coming to a stop in one of the many holes which obstructed their way. Close to the *poste de secours* there was no road at all, and we would have to go over the open fields through deep rutted tracks. And just in front was the roar of the battle, the flash of explosions, the sharp woodpecker rattle of machine guns, and the shouting of shells overhead as the guns of the enemy fired and the French artillery in our rear barked in response.

S.S.A. 17 had to find its accommodation wherever it could. While our mustering point was always a few miles behind the line, one could never be certain where this would be. With the others of the unit, sometimes I was billeted with a French family in a village, sometimes on a farm, occasionally in some old building that had been left vacant when its occupants left. It made little difference, for most of the time the ambulances were on the road, their drivers catching sleep on a stretcher whenever they could, or at the *poste de secours* if the footing gave our wheels enough hold to get there. If this was possible, usually there was a dugout close by the post, and in it a number of bunks in which one could rest when one became used to the crash of guns overhead.

There had been no change in the uniform for service with the French Army except for the issue of a steel helmet such as the infantry wore, and a gas mask. This latter piece of equipment was essential in traveling the roads, especially at night when at any moment one might find oneself in an area where mustard gas or chlorine shells had been used. To come upon it suddenly and unwarned was always disastrous, and yet to take in the first breaths and then put the mask on was almost as bad. If the nauseous smell made you vomit, it was too late to take it off, for that would mean searing your lungs.

With the French Army we received what was known as "blood money" — a small sum each day in addition to what we were paid by the Red Cross. Allowed to accumulate, this extra amount was most useful on the infrequent occasions when we were allowed to go on leave. Besides the "blood money" we were issued free cigarettes and a liter of *pinard*, the coarse red wine of the French, and a small quantity of spirits. I never clearly learned what this latter concoction was made of, but while rum seemed its base there must have been other ingredients involved to supply its galvanic effect. In the wet and the cold, and with the gravely wounded and dying around us, it did much to dispel the horrors that came with the night.

Day by day I became used to the ghastliness of war, the sight of men bloodied and bandaged limping along helped by their comrades, the groaning and agonized figures gasping for life on the stretchers, the sudden rattle of breath in the throat as death came to take them away. Gradually I began to build a mental shield of armor around me — for to let oneself think about what it meant would have been to go mad. Sometimes I had to scrape a dead man's brains off a stretcher and sleep on its canvas, sodden with blood. At others the ambulance would get stuck in a shell hole with four seriously wounded French soldiers on board. Then we would have to get it moving again as fast as we could, chipping the frozen ground away as we lay on our bellies under the tailboard with our charges breathing their life out a foot or two over our heads. At night it was doubly difficult. Then we always moved very slowly, as we had no lights to help us since they might draw enemy fire. More often than not one man would have to walk on ahead, feeling for the shell holes and giving directions while the driver tried to avoid the sudden lurch that would mean we were stuck.

Except for this handicap, traveling by night was generally safer for the wounded. Usually, during the day, the highways were subjected to spasmodic shelling, not aimed directly at the ambulances but more in the hope of hitting anything that might be moving up to or back from the front. There were ammunition convoys, for instance, huge lumbering trucks filled with shells. When visibility allowed and the roads were good enough, they raced from far in the rear with fuel for the battle. When such a convoy was met it was wise to pull in to the side of the road and wait until it had passed. The drivers allowed nothing to hinder the task they were on, and any lesser vehicle would otherwise find itself in the ditch.

One night, halted at the side of the road as a convoy swept by, I watched the giant shapes plunge, one by one, from the shadows, and listened to their turmoil of sound as they passed. While their drivers could see the road by the half light of the stars, the square, boxlike shape of the ambulance became visible only a short distance away. All at once I felt a great crash that tipped us up on two wheels. There was a dreadful rending of canvas and wood. And then, slowly, the ambulance settled back on all fours. One of the trucks had left too little margin in passing, with disastrous results. I got down to inspect the amount of the damage and found that the truck had sheared one side of the ambulance off like a knife. Luckily there were no wounded within, but nobody stopped to ask if anyone had been hurt. The convoy rushed on and on, threatening never to end, until incredibly the night swallowed its tail and the noise of its passing grew fainter and at last, fading to a whisper, was gone.

Sometimes we found that the place where we had to wait for the wounded was close to an artillery unit of French seventy-fives. If the enemy was searching for its location, a stream of shells would criss-cross the position the guns were in, trying to find the range and exploding at various intervals close by. Generally we were safe enough at such times, as the pattern made by the falling shells was likely to remain in much the same place, either in front of or behind or to one side of the guns. Every so often, though, we would be taken by surprise as one of the enemy shells landed close to its mark. If two or three shells exploded close by, and it became obvious that the enemy had found what he was looking for, we would take cover underground until it was over. Sometimes there was a chance hit; one man was killed by a splinter from a shell that fell a quarter of a mile away, much too far ordinarily to do any harm.

It was largely the same on the roads. Most of the time one could see the shells exploding on the highway or in the adjacent fields a considerable distance ahead, and if we had wounded on board we would come to a stop and wait. When the shelling ceased, or moved on to some other target, we would continue our journey, and then repeat the process again when the next set of explosions took place. There was an element of doubt involved in this procedure, however, and every so often there would be a great bellow of sound as a chance missile came in and exploded close by, showering the ambulance and ourselves with dirty gray water and mud. Then we would sit up, shake ourselves, and move on a bit in case the gun that had fired might do so again without the enemy changing his sights. It was surprising, though, how few casualties there were and, apart from having large quantities of debris flying around, neither our ambulance nor the wounded in our charge were ever hit.

Then the influenza epidemic came upon us. This was a particularly vicious disease which turned as often as not to pneumonia. Those in the trenches had now two enemies, the guns of the enemy and the unseen, silent approach of this sickness. So many died that the Division was withdrawn from the line and replaced. S.S.A. 17 was moved to a village some distance behind the front, but even here the shells came whistling in, giving us little rest.

The accommodation was limited, and my particular bed was a heap of straw in a stable which I shared with a cow. It was here that I came down with influenza and lay tossing and moaning on the straw, half delirious and without medical help. Sometimes one or two of my friends would come to see how I was getting on, and early every morning the farmer arrived to persuade my stable companion to give up her milk.

The farmer was a tall, gaunt individual, unshaven, dirty and morose. His approach to his task was always the same, and very ill though I was I could not help being distracted by his performance. He never paid any attention to me, but relieved his feelings toward the world in general by shouting "Sacre chamou!" at the top of his voice at the cow, and followed this up with a well-aimed kick at her stomach. When my four-footed friend had recovered sufficiently from the attack on her person, the farmer would sit down on his stool, the bucket between his legs, and drain off the milk. Then without a look in my direction he would depart, eminently self-satisfied. As time went on, I began to feel very sympathetic toward the cow and grieved for the situation she was in, which must have been painful. She in her turn seemed to regard me with sisterly or maternal affection, whisking her tail vigorously to keep the flies moving and staring at me from time to time with her sad, brown, limpid eyes. Finally I recovered sufficiently to join S.S.A. 17 again as it moved up the line. This period had been comparatively peaceful, and for this, notwithstanding my illness, I was grateful.

Every four months we were given permission to go on furlough to Paris for two or three days, and there the bright, animated life of the city, the wide, open boulevards and the crowds were a welcome contrast to the carnage and destruction I'd seen. We made the most of our opportunities, taking in the shows and the Folies Bergères, and having a very gay time in a few short hours. When the time came to return, it was like entering some dark, gloomy cavern and leaving the sunshine and laughter behind. Perhaps we would never see it again. There was no sign of an end to the battle. "Big Bertha," the long-range gun of the Germans, was shelling Paris — though no one seemed to pay much attention — and what might happen before victory was won was still much a matter of doubt.

The war was, however, gradually ending. In an all-out effort, the Germans launched their last great offensive, and failed. Soon they were retreating, and the advance of the Allies began. S.S.A. 17 was continually on the move, following the troops. The dead were everywhere — by the roads, in the houses where the struggle had raged, on the barbed wire where the trenches had been — Frenchman and German alike. As we moved on, the bloated, decomposing bodies of horses killed a week or two earlier lay here and there, their ghastly smell polluting the air. Previously the war had been more or less static, the opposing forces facing each other from their trenches only a short distance apart. Now it became a battle of movement and continual advance on our part. As the main body of the Germans retreated, solitary machine-gunners would be left at short intervals across the front, each to destroy as many of the advancing French as he could. Then, at the last moment when our men were upon him, he would throw up his hands in surrender. Not many were taken prisoner; too many of the troops had seen friends killed at their hands.

The French had always been very good to the members of our ambulance section, and now, moving forward, we found those who had been in enemy-occupied territory especially so. There were not many houses left in which to take shelter, and for the most part we used dugouts which had only recently been the enemy's. Some were well constructed and comfortable, but we had at all times to be careful of booby-traps, not only in the dugouts but in the houses we occupied as we went on. These took the form of various devices — a fine German helmet left hanging on a nail on a wall, an automatic pistol that would make a good souvenir, or sometimes simply a door which when opened blew up the place together with anyone unfortunate enough to make his way in. In one house where we stayed overnight there was a large barrel of sauerkraut in a corner. We were used to French rations — often *la soupe*, a fragrant vegetable stew with sometimes a main base of horsemeat — so this looked singularly appetizing. Much to our disappointment, we had to refrain from eating it in case it was poisoned.

Finally, on November 11, 1918, the war came to an end. The Armistice was signed. Rumors of what was impending had reached us a short time before, and perhaps the same thought was in everyone's mind — would we be alive when the fighting had stopped? Life suddenly seemed all the more valuable, caught as we were with our heels still in the holocaust.

The fighting was to end at 11 A.M., and we were poised on the brink of a river over which one of the regiments was due to attack. The *poste de secours* was in a house on a hill overlooking the water, and in it were some women who had been in enemy hands and who were assisting the troops in any manner they could. There had been some heavy shelling and quite a few men had been killed and many more wounded. When they were brought in all the women were crying. I had seen desperation and agony all through the war, but never grief so intense. Another hour, and the men all would have been safe.

As soon as the hour of the Armistice arrived, firing stopped and we breathed in relief. Now at least we knew we could go on living. We celebrated, drinking anything we could find. We were like prisoners released out of darkness to the bright light of day.

Sometime afterwards our forward march was discontinued, and S.S.A. 17 was returned to Boulogne so that demobilization could take place.

I was now seventeen. I tried to assess my qualifications. I had all the outward requirements of social behavior learned during the first few years of my life, but these were only a covering to hide the creature within. I had seen all the viciousness of war, and now I could not return and continue my education. In some ways I was too old to begin all over again even if the money had been available, and in those days there was no system of organized grants to help those who wished to go on to higher spheres of learning and had been handicapped by taking part in the war. I knew something of Latin verbs and the French language, but my academic accomplishments in mathematics or anything practical were negligible and certainly much less than those of my friends who had continued their scholastic careers. All I could do was drive a car well, but even this gateway was closed, for no one would think of taking me on as a chauffeur because of my youthful appearance. Besides, I did not feel much like doing this kind of work. It would have been a dull way of earning my living after my experiences with the French Army. The truth is that I had become a hybrid — old in some respects, youthful in others — and as such I was finding it difficult to fit squarely into any fixed groove or pattern.

Back in England, I realized that it was time to take another plunge. I decided to go back to India. My parents were there, and it seemed probable that I could find something to do in that once familiar environment. I had some money saved, and managed to get some more for my purpose. I bought passage by boat to Calcutta. I arrived there on my eighteenth birthday, broke but confident that something would turn up.

3

~~~~~~~

Elephant Camp

THE feet of the elephants fell noiselessly on the path through the jungle. They came on, one by one, smelling the air, their long trunks caressing the trees and the pendulous vines that fell from their branches. Here and there the huge beasts broke off a few leaves and fanned themselves gently before thrusting the foliage into their cavernous mouths and chewing it slowly. Their bodies undulated gently from side to side as they pushed themselves forward. Upon each animal's neck a mahout sat astride, digging his toes into the loose skin at the back of the elephant's ears, urging it onward. In his hand, each mahout held a short iron goad, like a miniature boathook, to stick in the flesh of the elephant's head and enforce his commands. And behind every mahout, a long, heavy chain stretched from the mattress-like *gadi* on top of the elephant's back to the cottonwood log it pulled through the jungle. I was in charge of the Assam Sawmills and Timber Company forest operations for the Tezpur area near the Tibetan border, and it was my task to supply the sawmills with lumber. Our trees were different from the cottonwoods of the American continent. Known as *simul,* they were great and tall, often many feet wide at the base, with beautiful big red flowers when they bloomed. Tea boxes were made of them because their wood was soft and easily cut, and light enough to be rafted down the river.

This was a change indeed. In the jungle the silence closed in, broken only by the cries of the mahouts as they directed their charges. *"Doop . . . doop,"* and an elephant lowered its head to uproot a small sapling. *"Outow . . . outow,"* and it picked it up with its trunk to drop it gently aside as it heard the words *"Biri . . . biri."* Then, taking the strain again, it would move slowly onward, the log gouging a snakelike channel of black in the soft earth behind it. Here it seemed peaceful. The huge soaring trees moved gently in the breeze while below on the ground the scarlet flowers of the cottonwoods floated to earth, forming layer on layer of bright, shining carpet. But the scene was deceptive. Here in the jungle the battle for survival still raged. The camp was on the Bhareli River, a swift, turbulent stream that flowed from the foothills of the Himalaya Mountains, widening always as it rolled on to where it issued into the broad, turgid reaches of the Brahmaputra, a hundred miles away. Where I was, the Bhareli narrowed to its source, cutting its path in wild, cascading rapids through the dark canyons and gorges a few miles above. This was the back of beyond of the jungle.

To get there had meant a long journey, first by train from Calcutta, and then some days of travel by paddlewheel steamer up the Brahmaputra to Tezpur. Above Tezpur, the source of the Brahmaputra was far away in Tibet, and below the settlement the great river ebbed for countless hundreds of miles, eventually flowing into the Indian Ocean. Tezpur, the main settlement of the region, was one of the small hubs of civilization in this vast jungle territory, and there the local government had its offices. In addition to the officials, management and staff of the sawmills, there was the usual white and native community, and a neighborhood club which the tea planters visited when they came in to Tezpur to relax and enjoy themselves.

My parents, who lived at Shillong, a hill station several hundred miles to the south, were visiting Tezpur when I arrived, and after a short stay with them I began to look around for a job. One day in the club I was approached by the manager of the sawmills and offered employment in the elephant camps, and I gladly accepted. The work sounded exciting and consisted of getting logs out of the jungle, at different points where the camps were situated, down to the Bhareli River. As there was no other means of hauling them from jungle to river, elephants had to be used.

A day or so later I was driven in the manager's car to the spot where a rough dirt road ended in the heart of the jungle, and there deposited to make my way onward by elephant. One of these animals and its mahout were waiting. After loading myself and my few possessions aboard, with some gruntings and groanings we set off for our destination. Several hours afterwards the dank, dark forest opened up and, entering a clearing, we found ourselves on the banks of the Bhareli River, shining and sparkling in the light of the setting sun. A few hundred yards upstream some elephants were being given their evening bath in the current, and after another few minutes of ambling along I had reached my destination.

All at once I was removed from the comparative quiet of the jungle into the busy, chattering life of the camp. After hearing nothing for the last few hours except the chirping of birds and the occasional outcry of a monkey, the sound of human voices as the mahouts prepared their evening meals over their campfires seemed inordinately loud. They were a wild-looking crew wearing nothing but loincloths, their eyes inflamed and red from fever and the opium they were in the habit of eating.

Typical of them was Bangshidar Hazarika, head elephant *jemadar,* who was more or less Sergeant-Major over the others — if one can imagine a Sergeant-Major without any discipline. He was tall and thin and about fifty years old.

His draggly moustache fell down on each side of his mouth like a Chinaman's, and his full, baggy, dirty-white loincloth reached his knees. He wore a small turban and constantly chewed betelnut, first wrapping it in a leaf he found in the jungle, so that his lips and teeth were stained red. His opium-red eyes completed the picture. Naturally, he knew all there was to know about elephants, their maladies, and the native remedies.

In a semicircle to the bank of the river, never far away from each other, were the mahouts' thatch-and-bamboo houses, and in the center of the perimeter was a large open space. Here the elephants were fed packages of grain before being released for the night, their front legs hobbled, to forage for themselves in the jungle. In the early morning, at first light, the mahouts would go into the jungle to find them and, after removing their hobbles, ride them back to camp preparatory to the day's work.

The people who did the actual felling and cutting, before the elephants and mahouts took over, were a tribe of Miris, a water people whose villages were scattered along the river. Their houses were all built on *chungs* — stilts to keep them dry when floods came — and often they would come to work in their dugout canoes. They had their own language, which I never learned, and seemed very uncivilized in comparison with the Assamese of the towns and tea gardens. But they were remarkably skilled with the axes which were their sole tools.

I had not seen elephants since I was a child. The great, gray beasts, moving so deliberately, lifting their trunks high in the air before inserting each grass-wrapped package of grain in their mouths, their little eyes wandering from side to side, their tails swinging and smacking their vast hindquarters to dislodge the swarms of flies that continually pestered them, filled me with pleasure. Against the background of river and jungle, they seemed an integral part of their setting, and the human, unkempt mahouts merely trespassers in their wilderness kingdom. The light of the fires and the sharp, pungent smell of the smoke as it rose in the air served only to stress this impression. Occasionally one of the elephants would tap its trunk sharply on the ground, expelling the air from its lungs and at the moment of impact creating a noise like a drum. Another would lift its tusks and, with raised head and trunk curled in an arc high above, emit a piercing scream.

My hut, like the others, was made of grass and bamboo. It had a dirt floor, a camp bed and wash basin, a few knives, forks and spoons, some dishes and glasses. These and a rough wooden table and cash box in which the mahouts' wages were kept made up its essentials. It was close to the edge of the river, and at night a paraffin lamp lighted the hut. It had no bathroom or other facilities, the nearby jungle and river taking the place of such luxuries. Apart from my shotgun, rifle and pistol, the most important item in the place was the mosquito net that, raised on four poles at night, shielded my vulnerable form from the insects. It had another purpose too — when the rains came and the river overflowed its banks, the snakes made for the higher ground on which the camp was situated and a mosquito net firmly tucked in at the sides was an effective deterrent to any unwelcome partner. Once in a while a snake would climb to the ridge pole and, losing its grip, fall with a thud on top of the net, where it would remain writhing and struggling until it dropped to the floor. There were many snakes near the camp during the wet season, some of the tree snakes being the most poisonous. In the morning one had to be especially careful, since one never knew when some small but nevertheless deadly reptile might be curled underfoot. Then, in the daytime, traveling by elephant could also be dangerous. A snake twined around a branch was hard to see against the green background; and if the elephant was careless enough to dislodge a hornet's nest — and there were many — one was in for bad trouble, for they could sting one to death in short order.

The heat and humidity, too, were intense, causing clouds of mist to rise here and there as the damp trees and undergrowth steamed in the warmth of the cloud-covered sun. In the rainy season there was a never-ending deluge, the water swelling the river and streams and forming great, shallow lakes. The leeches were everywhere, fixing their voracious mouths to one's body, sucking blood and growing larger and rounder as they filled themselves. It was useless to wear boots; the leeches simply crawled through the eye-holes or over the edges, and when I removed my footwear there were twenty or thirty short, stubby pencils, bloated to many times their normal size. It was simpler to wear only shorts, a hat and shirt, as then when they fastened to feet, legs or body they could be picked off and thrown back, squashed delicately between finger and thumb, into the jungle. You had to be particularly careful that they did not crawl up round your thighs.

Besides being a nuisance, those leech bites had one especially distressing feature. Each mouth was armed with a very sharp set of invisible teeth, and after each blood-thirsty creature was disposed of, the minute wound it had made would itch frantically. Unless restraint was used — and at times the impulse to scratch was almost uncontrollable — blood poisoning could always set in.

Such inconveniences were annoying but never fatal. At worst, your legs might swell after a very bad day in the swamps of the jungle, but that was of minor importance. There were other, worse hazards — snakes, wild elephants, tigers and disease. One could not worry about snakes, since it was in the hands of fate. If one was unlucky enough to step on one of the poisonous varieties and was bitten, one died. It was as simple as that, the same kind of chance that elsewhere might exist when lightning coursed down the sky in a storm.

Wild elephants were a different proposition, since one could, given a chance, either escape or destroy them, and this applied equally to the tigers. In the unexplored depths of the jungle on the upper Bhareli, elephants roamed the forest in large numbers, and from time to time were encountered. Tigers were seldom seen; they belonged to the night carnivores, and in common with panthers or leopards sought seclusion by day in some hidden and shady retreat. As in everything else there were, however, exceptions.

The wild elephants were always around us. Every day the huge imprints of their feet could be seen where they had passed in the night seeking companionship with our tame ones. While usually they kept their distance, occasionally they would overrun the camp singly or in groups. This happened most often when, knowing that they were close, we had chained one or more of our male tuskers close by in order to avoid an encounter. Ours were at a disadvantage with their front legs hobbled and, unless they were kept either in the center of the camp or at least within its periphery, there would be a screeching, trumpeting and general uproar only a quarter or a half mile away as battle was joined. In such an event, while we knew that our tuskers would in all probability be injured, we could never go to their rescue; to do so in the dark would simply be courting disaster.

When the camp was attacked, the well-being of all required a swift, organized system of retreat. Then we knew that a fight was unavoidable. As we heard the wild elephants approaching and the crash of their progress grew louder, we would let loose the chains on our tuskers and abjectly run as fast as we could for the boats. Out in midstream, from the dugout canoes we would watch the fierce battle.

It made an unforgettable sight in the moonlight, the great beasts shrieking and screaming, their shrill trumpetings of rage shattering the silence as they circled about for position, their long, sharp tusks thrusting and stabbing against the black backdrop of the forest. All we could do was to fire off our guns in the air in the hope of frightening our assailants away, but usually without any result; they were far too busily occupied to pay much attention. Generally the struggle ended when our tuskers — handicapped by the fact that the ends of their tusks had been blunted as a safety precaution for humans — made off in haste to the jungle, while the marauders remained to destroy our possessions and houses and consume any bags of grain they could find. It was only then that I could take aim and fire without risk of hitting our tuskers, and this would agitate the attackers enough to cause their departure. Then off they would go, crashing back through the jungle, bellowing their defiance, while we edged back again to the bank and, after repairing what damage we could, resumed our night's interrupted rest.

One day I got tired of this. We had been enduring a series of raids, and due to wounds suffered by our elephants and the general disruption in our work the supply of logs was getting behind. Soon, unless the situation was rectified, we might not have enough lumber to send down to the mills. For nearly a week, one wild elephant had been in the vicinity, coming closer and closer each day and frightening the mahouts. They were obviously disinclined to ride into the jungle while this hazard was present, for there was no knowing what he might do. Some of them had seen the beast, and described him as being "as big as a mountain," with long, sharp tusks and very ferocious. They said that when they had come upon him while hauling logs he had blocked their paths, tossing his head as if threatening to charge, and as their opportunity for escaping in a hurry was impeded by the heavy obstruction at the end of each chain, they were thoroughly frightened.

Something had to be done, and the mahouts plainly expected me to do it. I armed myself with a double-barreled .577 rifle — not a high-velocity weapon but one of the older models — and got astride the neck of the elephant I usually rode on my tours through the jungles, and went in search of the enemy. As a safety precaution, I had Bangshidar Hazarika armed with an old muzzle-loader on an elephant on one side of me, and another mahout with nothing but a machete in his hand on the other. I had no real idea of what I intended to do, and vaguely thought that if we encountered this menace to our welfare it might be psychologically subdued by the sight of the opposition and make off farther afield if a few rounds were discharged in the air from our weapons. Somewhat foolishly I had discounted what I had been told about the unpleasant disposition of this particular animal, feeling that the reports I had received were exaggerated, perhaps because the mahouts were always ready enough to think up some reason why they could not go to work. I had never seen the elephant personally as I went about the jungle.

At first all went well. We pushed the elephants in the direction where our quarry had last been reported. It was an eerie business, peering from one side to the other through the green, tangled undergrowth, expecting at any minute to see the monstrous gray bulk — if he was there he might be standing close by, watching us, motionless. A great blanket of silence overlay everything, broken only by the occasional cry of a bird and the rustle of leaves on the branches as our elephants pushed them aside.

We had only gone a quarter of a mile or so in this manner when we came upon a new set of elephant tracks, diagonally crossing our path. We stopped to examine them closely; they might have been made by one of our own elephants in the course of its work. But the mahout on my left knew better. Bending down from his perch he pointed at the wide foot marks with his machete. Then he straightened himself and turned sideways to me.

"Wild elephant," he said. "Very big!" He pointed his knife in the direction the tracks disappeared, where the animal's body had plowed through the brush. Neither of the mahouts seemed anxious to go on, and they waited, watching to see what I'd do. I was just as uneasy, but having come so far I couldn't turn back — it might mean losing the authority I held in the camp. Stirring my elephant behind its ears with my toes, I pushed it slowly along the wild elephant's tracks, the two mahouts following a short distance behind.

We reached the middle of a small glade about fifty yards long and the same distance across when suddenly from outside its perimeter, at the right of the trail we were following, came the sound of branches being broken.

Before we had time to move and face the sound, the curtain of green on our right exploded — and all at once the elephant was there in the clearing, head and tusks raised, trunk curled in a circle between them, prepared to assume the offensive. Obviously, he was in the first quick steps of his charge, and in the position I was in would catch my animal broadside. The two mahouts and their elephants lagged a short distance behind as we entered the clearing and I was alone in the path of the thundering colossus.

Screaming with rage, the wild elephant raced across the clearing. I could see that his course would bring him to where his tusks would slash through my animal's stomach halfway between legs and shoulders. As my elephant started to wheel in order to face its oncoming adversary, I managed to twist my body to the right and let the attacker have one barrel of my rifle in his head. Striking solid bone,

44

the bullet only staggered him. He still came on, changing his course by about thirty degrees. My elephant, turning as fast as it could, had now reached a point where the wild elephant *might* pass, head to head, at a foot's distance or so — but there was still a good chance that they would meet in a head-on collision. With my legs hanging down each side of my elephant's head I felt very squeamish.

He brushed past my elephant's head a scant twelve inches away. In the excitement of the moment, I must have possessed more than my usual strength. I raised the heavy rifle with one hand — there was no time to take aim — and thrusting the muzzle close to the wild elephant's ear as it swept past, pulled the other trigger. He crashed sideways, turning over and over and smashing down the jungle in his path with his weight. By this time my elephant had completed its turn and was facing back the way we had come; having had quite enough, it made off in the direction of home with me hanging on for dear life to its back. Holding on while the creepers and branches lashed at my face and body as my panicky charger made its headlong way through the trees, I looked in vain for the two elephants and mahouts who should have stood by in support — they were nowhere to be seen! Far ahead in the distance, the sound of crashing branches told me that they had been much faster than I in their flight. As soon as I could, I looked back anxiously, hoping the wild elephant was not on my trail. Through the screen of the trees I could see him getting up on his feet, quite obviously groggy, before making up his mind to move off.

I had no desire to return and find out more about his condition; after this narrow escape it was well to put as much distance between us as possible. In any event, my own elephant had only one single idea, one that closely paralleled mine — to find some peaceful place and settle its tottering nerves. It was uncontrollable. When shortly afterwards we found ourselves back in the camp again, there were the two mahouts and elephants which had accompanied me, waiting.

I was still feeling edgy. "That's a fine thing!" I exclaimed. "What happened to you?"

Hazarika grinned, a nasty smirk that fell down each side of his mouth behind the long black moustache. "Our elephants were frightened," he replied. "They ran away." Then, shrugging his shoulders and holding his hands palms upward, expressively, "What could we do?"

There was no point in arguing, but I had strong ideas of my own; certainly I had heard no sounds of remonstrance from their riders as the elephants beat a retreat. I was alive, that was the main thing, and the hypothetical problem of whether the elephants or the mahouts were alarmed was one that could never be definitely solved. I felt very shaky as, catching my elephant's ear, I slid down its side. I patted its trunk gratefully; if it had been a fraction of a second slower in turning in that mad scramble of action I would not have been there.

About a month later, two inhabitants of the jungle arrived in camp with the tusks. They had found the wild elephant dead in the jungle a considerable distance away, by following the smell of decomposition which, over a wide area, covered the ground like a fog. I was unable to find out exactly how far it had traveled — ideas of distance to the natives were unimportant and vague — but they said it had fallen "one day" away, from which I estimated it had gone thirty miles. After the destruction of this animal the wild elephants kept away.

The leopards and tigers caused us less difficulty, though we saw them occasionally. Once, passing under a large branch on a path through the jungle, I looked up — and there, three or four feet overhead, a big spotted leopard was reclining, watching me. If it had stretched out its paw as I went by underneath it could almost have touched me, and with very little exertion indeed it could have been on my shoulders. I had a rifle in my hand, but did nothing about it. The leopard lay there as I stopped on the trail a few feet away and looked back; it seemed to be making up its mind whether or not to attack. In a sense it had spared my life, and it seemed only fair in return to let it go. Besides, it was in an advantageous position overhead on the branch and would certainly kill me unless my aim was sufficiently straight to put it right out of business at the first shot. I went on — after all, one was used to leopards. They could be heard continually round the camp at night, and except for stealing a stray goat or chicken were reasonably inoffensive and did no harm. One could always tell they were there by their short, rasping breath, and once in a while their eyes could be seen in the dark, two small gleaming lights.

Tigers too were comparatively harmless unless one annoyed them. This was not the case with man-eating tigers, which, in areas where food was short, had learned to stalk humans. Sometimes, too, one would become a man-eater when either old age or some injury made it incapable of overtaking deer or pulling down wild buffalo. When this happened it would become a scourge, entering villages to drag away humans or lying in wait on the paths. On the Bhareli River, presumably because game was so plentiful, we had none. The tigers were a nuisance, however, as sometimes one of them would kill a tame water buffalo kept by the villagers and, catching the neck in its mouth, drag it into the jungle to eat in seclusion.

One night I saw one of these animals pass by in the moonlight with its cub, playing a few feet away on the edge of the river while I lay on my bed, pistol in hand, watching it through the open door and fervently hoping that it would not come inside. I always slept with a .455 Webley and Scott automatic pistol at full cock close by my head for such an occasion, for to move and pick up a rifle might focus

47

attention and lead to attack. I thought that if a tiger actually thrust its head in, at a foot's distance or so I could not miss its brain, and although the shocking power of the weapon was comparatively low, at that range it would at least give one a chance. Luckily on this occasion the tigress went on. The two moving along nuzzling each other, the black stripes on their sides vivid in the moonlight, made a pretty sight though it was a bit spoiled by a certain measure of apprehension.

I never harmed any of these animals except in self-defense, although the opportunity for indiscriminate slaughter was everywhere. Besides the larger beasts of prey the jungle abounded in wild buffalo, *mithun* or bison, boars, and various species of deer. I would sometimes kill the latter when meat was required for the pot. Each of these animals had its own peculiarities when confronted by humans. The buffalo, if wounded, would circle back on its pursuer, unseen in the jungle, charging him unawares from the side or rear. The bison, a huge, massive beast with formidable forequarters and horns, would charge at sight with the crashing roar of an avalanche, and then if it missed would usually continue on through the jungle and vanish. The wild boar was probably the most aggressive of all; if it crossed a path a human was on, it would turn and charge racing up the trail, intent only on eviscerating its enemy with its tusks. The only thing to do if one was unarmed in such circumstances was to throw oneself at full length on the ground in the hope that in its first head-long charge it might miss. If its aim was bad and one had a chance, one then might escape in a tree.

Bears, too, were dangerous to meet in the path — they had a nasty habit of taking a swipe at one's face with their claws. When they stood up on their hind legs to attack, their long sharp nails could tear away flesh and eyes with one single stroke. The natives, I was told, had an ingenious method of defending themselves. They carried a long sharp knife resembling a miniature sword in a bamboo sheath, and when the bear attacked they struck at its head without drawing the weapon. Then when the bear put up its paws to grasp the knife the sheath would come off and leave the weapon free to deliver the second stroke at its neck. Quite a number of villagers up and down the river had been marred by the claws of a bear.

It was strange, though, how few persons were bitten by snakes. For the most part, like the other denizens of the jungle, they would avoid molesting anyone unless they were actually stepped on. Even in situations dangerous to themselves they would attempt to slither quietly away without doing harm. The one exception to this was the hamadryad or king cobra, which, according to the natives, sometimes grew to be seventeen feet long and would attack anyone on sight. If unsuccessful in its first attempt, it would follow until, overtaking its victim, it could sink its deadly fangs in. One favorite story that made the rounds of the Club at Tezpur was about a man who protected himself from a pursuing hamadryad by taking off his sun helmet and turning to face the snake with this shield before him; as he did so, he kept backing toward the door of his bungalow. Every time the hamadryad struck it fastened its fangs in the cork of the helmet. Finally the man got inside the door and closed it. The snake, frustrated by this unorthodox behavior, went away. While undoubtedly there were hamadryads loose in the jungle on the Bhareli River, they must have been comparatively rare, for I never came across one — much to my relief.

Life in the elephant camps was fascinating. Soon, I shed the ways of a white man and became one with my associates, riding my own elephant like a mahout and wandering barefooted through the forest wearing only a hat and a pair of shorts. Assamese, which I had learned as a child, began to come back to me and I was able to converse familiarly with the mahouts and with those villagers who understood the language. Besides these things I also mastered the difficult art of standing upright in a dugout canoe and poling it against the fast current upstream toward the farther reaches of the river, where it issued from the hills. There I would fish and hunt completely alone in this area entirely unspoiled by the presence of man. On such occasions I was enchanted by the mystery of the river and jungle and the hidden things that might be found around every bend. Sometimes a *mithun* might be seen standing fearless on the bank, or a wild elephant bathing in the water. The water was crystal clear, and in its depths fish moved freely. Overhead the sun shone and birds of every variety wheeled gracefully about their affairs. At dawn when the mist was rising from the river it was particularly beautiful. It was then that the wild animals came down to the banks in numbers, and as the mist drifted away they would stand disclosed in all their majesty, the creatures of this unknown kingdom. Then when the time came I would return downriver paddling, standing up in the canoe as it drifted down the riffles, passing over the quiet places, taking on the surge of the current in the rapids, until, as night came, I would pull in to the bank at camp again and take up my life with the mahouts where I had left off.

I seldom saw a white man and for weeks at a time never heard my own language spoken. There were breaks in this routine, though, for when I had a chance I would go to Tezpur, either walking by short cuts through the forest or riding by elephant to where the tea plantations began. Then, if one of the tea planters was driving on the dirt road that led to the settlement, one could sometimes get transportation by car. While I spent many pleasant evenings at the homes of my tea planter friends I was always glad to get back to my hut in the jungle. There was something there which is hard to explain, the freedom I had and the unknown things that seemed always to beckon from behind the mysterious foothills.

From almost anywhere on the Bhareli, one could see the great peaks lifting their heads into the sky, enigmatic, far beyond this hidden corner of the world, chaste, unconquerable. In the dawn one could distinguish a single colossus standing apart behind the others in majestic loneliness, its white dome tinted by the first pink rays of the sun. To each side the mountains fell away veiled in obscurity, the mists rising from the valleys to embrace them, while down below the foothills swept to the river. And yet one could not even cross those foothills. The path was barred and miles of crawling jungle sealed the way.

What was in the mountains? Life was there I knew, for on a clear day one could see smoke from the villages of the headhunters who lived within their kingdom in the hills and seldom ventured down. There were many strange tales told about these savages — how their houses were decorated with the heads of their enemies on poles, how occasionally in the past they had raided a tea garden and returned with prisoners to their hills. It was even said that years before a white child had been abducted and raised in their villages, and that when she was finally found she was to all intents and purposes a savage like themselves. I came across them on only one occasion when a small group were on a hunting trip, and I was on one of my solitary excursions. Though they were armed with spears and bows and arrows they seemed inoffensive enough. We sat down on our haunches and conversed, and to impress them I suggested by sign language that we hold a shooting competition, their bows and arrows against my rifle, at some predetermined mark. One old man placed a reed against a tree stump and at a distance of thirty paces pierced it through with his first and only shot. When after taking careful aim I fired, the black bullet hole stood a finger's breadth away. Everyone thought this a great joke and presently, after sitting and smoking a while, they departed to their mountain fastnesses, as I watched them from the river's edge.

The camps moved from time to time as the supply of cotton trees close enough to the water became depleted. There were half a dozen or so Miri villages along the river. The Miris were rather small men, with a distinctly Mongolian cast of countenance, and some of them suffered badly from a disease that swelled their legs to the size of vegetable marrows. They wore loincloths only and nothing on their heads, but they were good-natured enough except when their tempers were up, and some of the girls were remarkably pretty. Originally, I suppose, they must have drifted down from Tibet or China.

These river folk felled the trees and cut them into lengths our elephants could pull. The large trees, three or four feet in diameter, were cut into much shorter lengths than the slender ones. Then they notched the logs at each end so that they could be tied together in rafts at the river's edge. All the work was done with axes, which were especially effective against the soft wood. We waited till the rains came, the river rose, and there was sufficient water for the rafts to be set free on the current. Each was steered by two or more men with long sweeps, to avoid the innumerable snags that always stood in the way. Sometimes the raft would stick on a sand bar, and then it would take the united strength of those on board to get it going again.

At the mouth of the Bhareli there were many crocodiles, which ordinarily inhabited the warmer waters of the Brahmaputra, and these I would sometimes shoot as the rafts drifted past and they could be seen sunning themselves on the sand bars. It was almost impossible to recover the bodies — the belly skins made useful suitcases if sent to Calcutta to be made up — as the bullet had to strike them in the head to render them immobile. If hit in the body, they invariably had sufficient strength left to slide into the water and vanish.

Things were catching up with me, though. There was one danger which I could not avoid — disease. The jungle swarmed on all sides with mosquitoes, many of them the deadly anopheles. For some time past, I had found myself intermittently in the grip of malaria, which always presaged its coming with long spells of shivering that turned, as the day wore on, into burning fever. Then I would lie on my bed incapable of anything, swallowing quinine and large draughts of water, the sweat running in streams all over my body. After a few hours, the attack would be gone, and I would return to normal, though a little bit weaker each time. If it reached its worst stages, I knew it would turn into blackwater fever, something for which at that time there was no treatment or cure. It was not uncommon among the tea planting fraternity, and such was its on-slaught that sometimes a man who was well enough in the morning was stretched out dead by night.

The time had come for me to go. I did not ask for a change, but the authorities of the mill at Tezpur had seen my condition and knew what would happen if nothing was done; I had to leave the hot, humid jungle. The head office of Bird and Company, the parent firm, had many other interests besides the Assam Sawmills and Timber Company, and one of these was the making of lime in the dry belt, approximately a thousand miles southwest, at Bisra. There the climate was good and an assistant manager's position was vacant. I said good-bye to Hazarika and the elephants and, putting together my belongings, left for Tezpur. A few days afterwards I was on the river steamer bound for the junction point at Gauhati, from which I went on by rail. Finally, after a stopover at Calcutta and another long journey by train, toward the center of India, I arrived at my destination, the Bisra Stone Lime Company. As I descended to the platform and saw the flat arid country around me, the heat seared at my lungs like a torch.

4

The Dancing Men

THE lime kilns were long, and mighty, and rectangular, throwing off thick, black coal smoke sixty feet above the earth. Miniature-gauge rails ran to the very rim of these volcanoes, and along them coolies pushed their trucks, first coal, then limestone, emptying them one by one into the multiple inferno. First coal, then limestone, each truckload burned at white heat in the kilns; then coal and stone were wedded there, and finally lime was extracted from the bottom of the pits, red-hot and incandescent. It was a never-ending process.

Away from the kilns it was almost as hot. The sun moved across the sky, delicate pink in the first light of dawn but quickly changing to a blowtorch of red as it crept slowly upward. Then, the shadows of the buildings and the long, dark shadow of the kilns gathered themselves slowly together and retreated step by step until they disappeared like children hiding in their mothers' skirts. The land lay bare and flat. The trees, short and sparse, standing singly or in small clusters, formed outposts of green around the central perimeter and were scattered here and there in the scorched, arid levels. Farther out, the country went to the horizon in soft, rolling hills in the sweltering haze. They did not even break the sense of the land's immensity.

After the northern jungles, where the damp, clinging undergrowth had coiled mile on mile through the forest, my first impression of Bisra was that here men walked to and fro like insects on a burning plate. There, on the Bhareli, one always had the feeling of encroachment. Wherever one went it had been push, cut and struggle to get through. Here, at Bisra, the land wandered away supine and empty, drifting to nothingness. It almost seemed that one could walk in any direction and, if one had the strength, go on forever. Except for the sun.

Bisra at this time was the largest lime manufactory in that area of India. The village, a way-spot on the Bengal Nagpur railway,* consisted of a jumble of buildings, native stores and houses, and a bazaar. It lay on the other side of the tracks from the kilns, dwarfed and forgotten in the seething commotion that flared at the feet and heads of the gray, belching giants. The town slept quietly in the heat, its occupants accepting the kilns as one of the evils of progress. The kilns gave work to the men, provided food for the women and children, and were thus important in the economy of the district. Men sweated and labored at their top, pouring the stone and coal into their maws, while others below hauled out the product that glowed deep in the pits at the end of the burning. When this had cooled, it was shipped in the railway cars that stood on the siding to points near and far where, still biting and poisonous, it could be put to good use. Some of the quicklime, however, was slaked by spraying it with water in flat, narrow bins, and then in its powdered form, sacked for shipment.

At one side of the kilns away from the town were the administrative buildings. Only one was of consequence, the main office where the affairs of the kilns were considered and decided upon. This was where Alexander, the manager, pondered his problems with the help of a *babu* clerical staff which kept the books and the ledgers. Now, aged

* Now the South Eastern Railway.

nineteen, I was his right-hand man, helping in general with the work of the company, overseeing the activity of the kilns, and taking his place when he was absent, as he frequently was, elsewhere in the district. For while Bisra was the main operating center of the company, there was another important project in view about fifty miles distant. This was the erection of a larger and more up-to-date group of kilns at a place having no name on the map but known to us as Raipura.* As this undertaking required continual supervision, from time to time either Alexander or I would have to travel, first on the main line and then on a thirteen-mile spur built for the purpose, to Raipura to see how the work was getting on under its engineers and builders.

The bungalow that Alexander and I shared at Bisra was set back a quarter of a mile or so to the north of the kilns. By comparison with the standards I had been accustomed to in the jungles, it was sumptuous. Fans moved in the ceilings; Indian servants came at each nod and call; the food was prepared by a capable cook; and, even though the diet was largely similar, consisting of chickens, eggs, and rice with an occasional change to fish or something locally available, it was set out on gleaming white table-cloths, the knives and forks polished and shining and the dishes deftly served by a turbaned Indian. Alexander, a stocky young Scotsman about thirty years old, was a pleasant companion with whom I got along very well and, except for the never-ending heat, I was really in clover. There was even a bathroom, though without running water! But on the other side of the scale there was always malaria.

Malaria is a queer kind of disease and its attack is in-sidious. In time, when its mosquito-borne germs have multiplied in its victim's bloodstream, the effect becomes noticeable. Chills afflict him during which his temperature drops far below normal, his teeth chatter and he shivers uncontrollably. After a few hours, the temperature rises,

* Later named Birmitrapur.

57

sometimes to as much as 105 degrees, the chills depart and instead the patient sweats profusely, the perspiration running off him in streams. He is consumed by thirst, and while the attack is on feels very ill indeed. Then it is over — and next day the victim is to all intents and purposes back to normal, though he feels weaker.

At first my attacks came fairly far apart, but as the germs became more belligerent the chills and fever repeated themselves at shorter intervals, gaining severity as they did so. Quinine, in 1920, was the only known palliative, and in my case it certainly was no cure. Whiskey was also said to be good as a preventive — although, judging from the amounts I consumed with no appreciable result, I later came to the conclusion that it was just another excuse for making the best of a bad situation. However, it deadened the senses, and perhaps had the same effect on the germs swarming inside. At all events, I was now falling victim to the disease every ten days or two weeks. At most, an occasional month would elapse in which I would be left in peace, and day by day I became weaker. In youth, fortunately, the body's resistance is stronger, and once an attack had passed I was able to go about my duties until the next time.

Quite often these duties took me to Raipura. At the junction point on the main line some distance from Bisra a spur left the railway and traveled, always ascending, through a country of low-lying hills to where an outcrop of limestone rose high in the air — a sharp, jutting ridge a hundred feet high and some four hundred yards long. This was pure limestone, its base descending deep into the hollows of the earth. The story of its discovery, as it was told me, may be of some interest.

Gordon Duff, the General Manager of the Bisra Stone Lime Company, was prospecting one day in the Raipura area when he came upon a small outcropping of rock on some land belonging to one of the local inhabitants. As he was taking some samples of stone, the owner expressed interest in what he was doing, no doubt alarmed by the white man's curiosity about what his land contained. Being an illiterate farmer living far from any kind of civilization, he naturally had no knowledge of the use to which limestone could be put or any idea of its value. The outcropping was small and of poor quality, and, when Gordon Duff showed him a sample, he asked that it be left alone and said that he knew where a virtual mountain of the same kind of rock was available. Gordon Duff agreed readily and, following the farmer's directions, sure enough some twenty miles distant he discovered the large deposit of high-grade stone. From it came the great kilns, which were now being built in its vicinity.

The approach to the kilns on the railway spur at Raipura was by a broad-gauge track which, close to the junction point, crossed a river by means of a long bridge built at the cost of hundreds of thousands of rupees. While every precaution had been taken to make it strong enough to withstand the floods that swept down when the rains came, something essential must have been left out of the computations — for a short time after its completion a torrent of mud, water and debris destroyed it, leaving only the pylons close to the shore standing. The bridge had been built with a good deal of help from the native labor of the surrounding district. Most of these people were superstitious, and they got the idea that a *boudh* or ghost who was said to live on a low hill on the farther side of the river had become displeased by this encroachment on its sanctuary; to show its anger, it had taken steps to remove the sacrilege and so impede the building of the railway. When it came to replacing the spans, therefore, there was considerable difficulty in finding enough local labor to carry out the task. It could never be done, they said; the "old man of the mountain" would not allow it, and if the white man was foolish enough to rebuild the bridge it would simply be swept away again as on the previous occasion. Nevertheless, in time the spans were replaced, trains ran over them, the line was completed, and the *boudh* presumably rested and considered in a calm, detached manner what sort of retaliation it would take.

From the main line the spur gradually ascended in a series of ups and downs toward the place where the new kilns were being built, the overall gradient rising slowly all the time. Sometimes passage could be had on one of the engines from the riverbank where the bridge lay broken, but more often than not transport was by trolley car, a flat wooden contrivance mounted on four railway wheels and pushed by two natives. On the upgrades the natives would walk, grunting and straining, forcing the trolley up the slopes, and then when there was a downgrade they would jump on the back and move to the front as the trolley gathered speed, each taking hold of a short plank which he held vertically in his hands, the broad bottom edge close to and at right angles to the rails. The trolleys had no brakes, and sometimes on the longer downhill grades an approximate speed of fifty miles an hour would be reached. The purpose of the planks was to knock stones and rocks off the rails, placed there by small boys tending goats in the nearby fields in the hope of relieving the monotony of their lives!

To us on the trolley it was by no means humorous to see a small pile of stones interrupting the smooth flow of the steel down which we roared with no hope of stopping. Excited cries would rise from the natives, the plank would be lowered perpendicularly from the front of the trolley until its broad base was flush with the rails, the plank would heave and jerk as it struck the rocks and sent them flying — and the obstacle would vanish, scattered in the rush of our passing. It was exciting work; we as passengers could only hold on and hope for the best, praying that the trolley man's hand would be steady. There were frequent sharp turns on the downgrades, and as the small hills obstructed the view, one never knew what lay round the next corner. Very occasionally an engine and freight cars were met coming up the track, but as their time of departure was generally known allowances could be made and care taken. On the occasions when a train was known to be coming, the men on the trolley would run behind on the downgrades, holding on so that it could not gain momentum.

But one had to take a chance sometimes and Gordon Duff was no exception. It was said that he hit an engine head on not far from the *boudh's* personal mountain.

At Raipura there was another bungalow very well furnished by bachelor standards. This was kept for the use of anyone visiting the new kilns from Bisra or elsewhere in the vicinity, or for an occasional visitor from Calcutta. It was an attractive place, nestling among the small foothills that broke the bare landscape. Diminutive trees and shrubs grew in the rocky, dry earth and gave refuge to various beasts and birds, not the least of which were peacocks. They could be seen and heard everywhere, their raucous cries sounding across the heat-laden silence. Only a shotgun was necessary to have one for dinner; they were excellent eating, their flesh soft and white, a cross between chicken and turkey. Once in a while a deer could be seen, and pigeons of various types flew about in profusion. Below, the new kilns rose, squat and huge down in the hollow, awaiting completion.

One day, one of the overseers happened to ask me if I would like to see the dance of the aboriginals who lived in the district. I had heard of them, but their villages were mainly in the untraveled parts surrounding Raipura and the inhabitants were seldom seen. Now, said the overseer, it was some festive occasion of theirs, and if I was agreeable they would come in to perform for some small gift or consideration. The time would be the next night if I agreed. I said I was willing.

It was after dark when I went to the appointed place, down the slope from the bungalow. A long line of small fires had been lit, and at their edges, standing back in the shadows, were about two hundred men. Once in a while one would come forward to lay another stick on a fire and then return to his companions. They were all tall and lithe, clothed in not much of anything, with their long hair tied in a bunch at the back of their necks. Soon, at a signal, they took up positions facing the fires and the dance began, slow at first and then gathering speed. There was no music or accompaniment, only the bronzed arms and legs swinging in the light of the flames as each man kept perfect time with those on the right and the left of him in one synchronized movement, their shadows dancing behind them as the flames rose and fell. Except for the sound of their feet on the ground and their breathing, not a sound could be heard.

The symmetry of their motion was such that I found myself staring, wrapped in the smooth flow of the long line of men. There was something here if I could just understand it. Some influence seemed to hover about, touching the dancers, clothing them with light, and making them one with the night that shadowed them and a part of the dark ceiling of sky overhead. The stars blazed down, the flames flickered and fell, the smoke billowed and rose in the still air of evening, the arms and legs going faster and faster, everything part of one motion. Suddenly, when the dance had reached its crescendo of movement, it stopped. The dancers stayed motionless, each one a carved copper statue. Then they broke up into groups again and slid to the edge of the shadows; the performance was over.

I came to with a start; whatever had been there was now gone. The dancers sat around talking among themselves for a while and then made their departure. I walked slowly back up the slope to the bungalow. What was it? Perhaps I had been hypnotized by the mass movement of the men's bodies and the atmosphere created by the smoke and the light? But it had lasted a long time — or had it? At all events, things were now back to normal. Wondering about the effect the dance had made on my mind and my senses, I went to bed. Undoubtedly, I told myself then, it had been nothing but imagination. But this, I think, was where I may quite unknowingly have started on the pursuit which shaped my life.

One night I had occasion to get out of bed in the dark, and as I put my foot to the ground I felt an agonizing pain as though I had stepped on a knife. Quite apart from the torture I suffered I was considerably alarmed, for I thought that a snake might have bitten me. If so, I knew that I had to find out what kind it was — and how poisonous.

Jumping around on one foot, I lit the coal-oil lamp on a table close to my bed, and with it commenced to hunt round the floor of the room. I couldn't see a snake, and wondered apprehensively if, in some way, it had managed to get out. In that case I would not be able to find out whether it was one of the poisonous or nonpoisonous kinds — and already in my imagination I could see myself dead on the floor by the morning. Then by an almost miraculous chance I saw a scorpion edged into a corner of the long, black room, the shine of its body reflecting the light of the lamp in my hand. Well, at least I now knew what it was that had stung me; the pain would be bad, but as far as I knew there was little chance that the effects would be fatal. The scorpion was still full of fight, raising its tail ready to strike. I killed it and went and sat on the bed, inspecting the sole of my foot, on which a hardly discernible mark had raised a small bump. It was beginning to swell, the pain a red-hot stiletto thrusting gradually upward past my ankle into my leg. Soon this began to swell too, and I tied a tourniquet round it to try to stop the poison invading the rest of my system. I sat with my knees hunched close together, groaning. Every so often as the swelling grew larger I had to move the tourniquet upward until at last it was tied close to my thigh. The night went on, the blood surged and pounded in my head and veins, and then after a period of eight or ten hours the pain gradually came to an end. The ordeal was over. Not long afterwards the swelling disappeared and that afternoon I went back to work.

Now it came time for Alexander, the manager, to go on six months' leave to England. Who would take over? I was just twenty years old by this time and there were large-scale responsibilities involved; besides the kilns at Bisra there were the new ones at Raipura, and there was another area still, where the main quarries were situated and a large labor force was employed mining the limestone for the kilns until Raipura got under way. A good deal of this work was performed on contract and did not need close personal supervision, as a large, competent native staff was there to watch over details, but still there were close to a thousand men employed and property values which were considerable. I was told by the head office at Calcutta that I had been appointed to take over during the manager's absence and I faced the task with considerable trepidation, visualizing all the difficulties I could get into and the damage that might be caused if I failed to live up to the obligations that were now square on my shoulders.

But everything proceeded much as usual; as far as I could make out there wasn't much difference except that, for the first time, I found the chains of large-scale responsibility galling. When everything was running smoothly nothing was more pleasant, but always lurking at the back of my mind was the possibility — the probability — of making a mistake. There were plenty to be made, too, if a close watch was not kept.

All this, however, lasted only a few short months, for my old enemy was at my throat again and my health was steadily deteriorating from malaria. Finally it was decided that I should be moved to the head office of Bird and Company at

Calcutta, where medical facilities were more readily available, and on Alexander's return I was sent there.

Bird and Company was at that time one of the great commercial organizations in India,* and its business enterprises included such things as lumber, lime, coal, jute, and many others. It consisted of a block of offices in central Calcutta which was split up into various branches, each unit dealing with a particular industry. Due to the experience I had gained at Bisra, I was made assistant to Mr. Burbidge, who managed the affairs of the Bisra Stone Lime Company.

The life in Calcutta was very different from anything I had previously known. After the French Army and the elephant camps and the lime kilns at Bisra it was like entering some vast pleasure garden where all one needed was to have a good time. It was true that every day one had to spend a few short hours at the office, but by four o'clock one's labors were over and one was free to engage in any one of a number of delightful pursuits. Then, too, one of the partners of the firm, the father of one of my contemporaries at St. Cyprian's School at Eastbourne, took me into his house in the capacity of social secretary, a position which was pleasant in the extreme and called for no arduous application of one's faculties. It was an imposing mansion situated in one of the best districts in Calcutta. It had among other things a small square lake in the garden and a tennis court of its own surrounded by trees. There was a native staff consisting of a butler, a cook, various house servants and gardeners, and a chauffeur. All I had to do was to look after the accounts, write a few letters, and generally make myself useful. I was regarded as a member of the family, taking part in all social engagements.

While Calcutta was perfection insofar as the comforts of living were concerned, it also had its dangers and pitfalls. The social round was smooth, rapid and gay, and a good deal

* It is even larger now and known as the Bird-Heilgers Group.

of the evening life of the city was to be found in the Clubs, of which there were many. I soon found myself enrolled in two or three of these meeting places where the younger set met after the day's work was ended. By five o'clock in the afternoon most of my age group and some of their elders were to be found in some such resort as the Saturday Club, drinking and dancing on those occasions when there was an orchestra present, or around the bar when there wasn't. Then there were the continual parties at the houses of friends at night, when one either sat listening to the sound of soft music from the verandah overlooking the garden or simply sat and talked until the small hours of the morning over whiskeys and soda. It was a gay but very empty life, and not the best type of existence to find oneself in when one was still crowding twenty-one. While there was a great deal of stability among the older members of the business community, most of whom were married, among some of the younger element there was not. We danced and drank, played golf and tennis, occasionally went riding in the early morning or evening, and then as the night bore down were swept into the social whirl of activity.

Pretty girls, married and unmarried, were in Calcutta in profusion during the cold weather months, but as the rains came with their damp, clinging, sticky heat, most of them departed for one or more of the hill stations such as Shillong or Darjeeling, which were reasonably close to Calcutta by rail. The men followed them on those occasions when brief leaves of absence could be obtained. In consequence, in the hill stations the girls — a general term embracing those young and innocent and also those considerably older and greatly experienced — were much in preponderance, and visiting males by reason of their comparative scarcity were much in demand for every sort of occasion. It was certainly a relief to get away from Calcutta — where one sat at one's desk in the office, with the sweat dripping from one's forehead onto the paper — to the cool upper levels where pine trees shaded the hillsides and the cool air filtered down from the mountains, fresh, keen and invigorating. On the occasions when I went to Shillong it was pretty much a repetition of the life in Calcutta in more pleasant surroundings. But the war had ended only two years before; we were all of us young; and the privations of one kind or another that most of us had experienced no doubt had some bearing on the life we led in seeking enjoyment.

I did not thrive in this kind of environment. True, if I had accepted it for what it was worth and been content to grow in that particular pattern, I would have found a prosperous future before me: I was doing as well as my contemporaries in the business field; the life was all one could wish for where material pleasures were concerned; one was waited upon hand and foot in every direction; and there was every promise that as the years went by, if I did not die of disease or meet with some accident, I would end up with a sizable bank account. But the deck seemed stacked against me; it was much more likely that I would never attain this happy situation, for my malaria was now getting continually worse, necessitating large amounts of quinine every morning and injections into my stomach muscles three times a week. Soon I was in bed at my employer's house, shivering and shaking, and then on another occasion in the hospital. I well remember the fat elderly nurse who ministered to my wants, bathing my back with force and devotion while the perspiration dripped from her face on my unclad form like a tap slowly running. And then, one day, the doctor showed me a slide of a recent blood sample under a microscope.

"There it is," he said. "That's what's causing your trouble!"

Fixing my eye to the glass, I peered down at a number of little red circles. Most of them were clear, but in others, smaller still but quite obviously present, were minute dark objects, harmless-looking and motionless, but for all their stillness as purposeful and malignant as a slow-acting poison.

I had never seen malaria germs before, and the sight of these pulled me up sharp in my tracks.

"Do you think I can get rid of them?" I asked.

The doctor was noncommittal; apparently he could form no conclusion; sometimes they went, sometimes they stayed — but it was clear that I was not in any favorable position. Something had to be done. But what? That was the question. There was no answer except to go on as before unless I left India, and then to what land would I travel? The war, elephants, lime, the round of engagements in Calcutta — what use would they be in any foreign environment? Besides, I had no money.

There is no doubt that about this time I began to slide down the scale. Malaria is deadening, depressing. At all events I began to care less and less about what the future might hold; I could do nothing about it. And I was becoming reckless. I began getting myself mixed up in minor troubles, a fight here and there, a ride on a motorcycle at two in the morning down the main street of Calcutta, standing on the saddle — all more or less innocent escapades of youth, but none of them likely to lend weight toward a good reputation. But nobody seemed to care; generally speaking, while there was a frown here and there, these little peccadillos were passed off with amusement.

About this time I was stung on the foot by another scorpion on getting out of a bathtub, and this incident will serve perhaps to illustrate the state of my mind. As I was going to a dance with a very pretty girl, I cut the side out of my shoe and went on with the engagement. Everyone thought it a great joke to waltz with a foot like a pumpkin — no one had ever done it before. "How does it feel, old man?" they'd ask, peering at the patent leather shoe, its outer edge empty and staring. "Nothing at all, nothing at all, old boy, just a mere pinprick!" But as the evening wore on the torment was awful, and it was without any regret that I finally relinquished my partner to the arms of another and went home, there to nurse my leg sitting up in bed all the rest of the night, sleepless and tortured.

Then a letter arrived from Deirdre, with whom I'd been corresponding through the years, saying that she was engaged to be married, and unaccountable though it seems, suddenly it became important that I should go home and see her just once before the chain that bound us together was broken off. It was dated August 9, 1922.

But travel costs a lot. There is no doubt that I was in a bad way, physically, financially, and in things of the spirit. Suddenly I was sick of Calcutta. The chances weren't good — if I stayed I would probably die of malaria or of blackwater fever, and if I didn't I would still grope along for years, sweating, shivering and shaking at indeterminate intervals; it would mean just running along with the mob, growing older and more decrepit each year, and even if I lived, retiring in some small English town, worn out after two or three decades of the climate and life of the tropics.

I had to get out! But where would I go? Well, there'd have to be a temporary solution — perhaps if I went back to the elephant camps I could save some money. Then after a time, if the disease made no overwhelming attack, I would have enough to pay my passage to England. And after that it would be in the lap of the gods. When I'd seen Deirdre I could go back across the Channel and join the French Foreign Legion. But I had another thought in mind, too. There was another land — Canada. If I could possibly get there.

I had quite a time persuading my superiors to fall in with my wishes. My employer, with whom I resided, was firmly opposed to the idea. What about the malaria? Well, it couldn't be worse anywhere else than it was in Calcutta. Finally he agreed but said that he would not help me; if I was determined to go I would have to do it on my own.

Ultimately they did decide to send me to another location, north of where I had been before, on the upper reaches of the Brahmaputra near Dibrugarh. I packed up what be-

6 9

longings I had, said good-bye to my friends, had another gay party or two, and a week or so afterwards was on the great wide river again, the paddle-wheel steamer plowing through the muddy brown water to Sadiya, not far from the borders of China.

5

Farther Back of Beyond

S ADIYA was even farther back of beyond than the Bhareli. There were no airplanes at the head of the Brahmaputra in those days, but even if there had been the place could never have been seen by any pilot, so crowded in were its few buildings, huddled under the emerald green jungle. And yet, twenty years later, the air was to swarm with aircraft as they flew from close by in this northeastern pocket of India over the Himalayan hump into China, and the blanket of silence that had covered the land since time began was to be split by the hammering roar of tractors up and down the precipitous forest slopes of the Ledo Road. But in 1922 nothing moved. The jungle slept, dark, impenetrable and mysterious, its few human inhabitants moving almost without identity, the shrouding frieze of branches reaching to the sky and cloaking them, it seemed, from the very eye of God. So thick was the jungle that one seldom saw the sun. And yet there was life there; monkeys swung chattering through the trees; wild beasts moved silently on their excursions, slowly, almost hesitantly, a paw raised from time to time in question, a head turned to peer suspiciously around a bamboo clump or tangled growth of vines, ready at an instant's notice either to attack the prey they stalked or vanish in a streaking, jumbled flash of color when danger threatened. Snakes, coiled, winding through the labyrinth, their forked tongues licking the air as they slid noiselessly past the mounds and depressions of the ground and thrust their blunt, triangular noses inquiringly before them, searching every dip or hillock, hole or corner, with hard, diamond eyes. Birds flew everywhere, some brilliantly colored, seen only for a moment, a wingtip streaking through the leaves, while others in muted shades of greens and grays darted, a flash of movement only, into the hanging backdrop of the trees. For, as on the Bhareli, the jungle stretched mile on mile bordering the vast, snow-crested mountains. And covering every leaf, branch, twig, and vine was the vampire army of the leeches, waiting, standing on their tails, their gray, threadlike bodies gyrating in the light-flecked misty atmosphere and smelling for approaching blood on which to feed.

To reach Sadiya one must go to where the Brahmaputra twists outward like some great serpent from the hills: after it merges with two other rivers and forms the massive trident of the forks. It streams on southward, brown and broad — miles wide sometimes when the rains come — island-studded and crocodile-infested, past immeasurable leagues of flatlands to its mouth. Northward through the mountain wall it has another name — the Dihang — and lost to sight deep within the canyons, its thunder a whisper in the peaks above, it throws itself, boiling, cascading, through the Himalayan cleft. This it has done for a million years, its origin somewhere secret beyond the Tibetan crags, its course winding for nearly a thousand miles beyond the mountains — where it is known as the Tsangpo — almost to the Chinese border. In Tibet it turns sharply to the mountain wall, stabbing it, and then in a dagger flash of white meets the somber trees and flows through the lower reaches to the light. Here, just south of Sadiya, the other rivers join it, and the mighty torrent for the first time gets its name — Brahmaputra!

Sadiya hides a few miles in the jungle, a nightmare place of blood and death. Not far distant live the headhunters along the Himalayan brink, their presence known by drifting smoke among the hills. Brave and ruthless, they keep their borders closed. Sometimes in those years one or another of those bands would send a hunting party onto British soil; then, at night when you were asleep in some grass hut you might wake to see the shadow of a man standing beside your bed, his form silhouetted, his knife raised ready to stab downward if you moved. A soft rustling would reveal the presence of another as he crept stealthily about the darkness in search of food or anything you had. If you were wise, you closed your eyes and lay quite still pretending sleep until they left.

I had been sent to Sadiya to organize the setting up of camp so that timber-cutting operations could commence in a new area. Below Sadiya, Dibrugarh — another settlement somewhat similar to Tezpur — crowned the Brahmaputra's bank and was the headquarters of the tea industry, a last pinpoint of civilization before the land rose northward, sloping to the sky. I had passed through Dibrugarh on my journey up the Brahmaputra, staying a day or two and seeing that the town provided the usual amenities — the Club, white women, drinks, clean clothes, and all the comforts which especially in that distant place did much to make life bearable.

It was the last time I was to see anything of civilization for some time, as a week or so later I was a hundred miles northward, living like a native again in the forest west of Sadiya. Here I had a grass hut on the bank of a small stream that joined the main river. As I had a camp bed and chair but no table, every night before going to sleep I would push my loaded Webley Scott automatic pistol, the hammer at full cock, through the grass wall close to my head where it would be held suspended near at hand if I was disturbed in the night by either prowling animal or man. Some distance

73

away — a third of a mile or so — was the main camp where the woodcutters lived, and from there the tributary flowed on.

The inhabitants of Sadiya were an Army officer, a white man, in command of a small group of sepoys of the Assam Rifles, an Indian doctor, a native police post comprising four or five men, and a few resident natives engaged in various matters of business or administration. The whole village added up to eight or ten houses in all. Occasionally I would walk through the jungle from my hut to talk to the Army officer, who led an isolated life but one not quite so solitary as my own. At least he had a small bungalow and a servant to help him live in something approaching a civilized way. In contrast, I walked barefoot, most of the time wearing only a hat, shirt, and shorts. And always on these journeys one had to be careful not to get lost. This had happened to me once in the Tezpur area and for two or three hours I had been searching frantically, not knowing which way to go. Finally I had come out at a woodcutter's cabin and had been able to find the trail home from there. Near Sadiya, though, two sepoys had not been so fortunate; they had become lost while out hunting and their whereabouts had not been discovered for a week or ten days. They were both dead, their bodies hardly recognizable under the writhing blanket of leeches which covered them from head to toe.

I was soon in difficulties at Sadiya. Where I was on the tributary there were no elephants; they were to come later from a different area in which they were working pulling logs from the jungle. On the tributary we were simply cutting the trees so that all would be in readiness when the elephants arrived. As labor was hard to get because there were few people around, it was part of my job to find enough men to deal with the preliminary work.

Except for a handful who had been recruited from around Sadiya itself there was no one else present when the camp was set up, and all it consisted of was a huddle of grass-and-bamboo buildings on the edge of the stream. Although there was a rough forest trail between my hut and the camp, the intervening jungle was still a formidable barrier. In the other direction, to reach Sadiya, it was necessary to walk through the jungle for seven or eight miles, so to all intents and purposes I was cut off. All travel on the tributary was by dugout canoe, and it was my hope that I would be able to obtain sufficient men from the Miri villages that were to be found, widely separated, up and down the local watercourses. My success was very much in doubt, as the Miris were a lazy lot. I knew this from my months on the Bhareli, where on one occasion when I had been unable to get them to work I had taken an axe and had personally commenced felling the trees. Next day the Miris were out in force, and it was explained to me by one very old native that — because a white man could not possibly do this kind of work — all their wives were laughing at them and so, although it was most annoying, they had been forced to come to my help!

Ordinarily, if the small rice crops they planted were poor or if fish were hard to catch, they would condescend to fell a few trees, but as long as their stomachs were full they were well content to sit around their houses built on stilts at the water's edge, discussing the affairs of their world and fortifying themselves with whatever opium they were able to obtain. When, therefore, five men of the tribe made their appearance one day and offered to work I was considerably surprised and gladly accepted their services. They had traveled a long distance by canoe from their village, they said, were very hungry, and requested an advance payment of food. They were not a prepossessing group, being short and squat and surly of countenance, but as I had to depend on anyone I could get I complied with their wishes. I gave them enough rice, salt, and other minor essentials to last for a few days and, getting into my own dugout, accompanied them down to the sandspit at the mouth of the creek where it joined the main stream. At the sandspit, on one side was the broad expanse of the river while on the other was the creek down which we had come. The base of the triangle of sand was formed by the jungle in which were the trees that the Miris were to cut down. After showing them what they had to do, I poled my canoe back to my hut, carrying their assurance that they would commence work the next day.

Due to my having to supervise the affairs of the main camp, more than forty-eight hours passed before I was able to visit the sandspit again. There I found that nothing at all had been done; the Miris, in fact, were all comfortably ensconced on the sand, lounging about and totally unconcerned about earning their pay. Having given them a considerable advance of food, I was naturally upset at what appeared to be a breach of good faith, but when I gave voice to my views I was met with nothing but savage, belligerent looks. It was plain that the men had no intention of fulfilling their obligations now they had what they wanted — the food — and that the next thing they would do would be to take off in their dugouts for home.

After some argument one of the party scrambled toward me and a scuffle took place that finally ended in blows. At once the whole group was upon me, and in a moment I was hit on the head from behind while dealing with those who came at me from in front. Although I did not lose consciousness I felt my knees sag and was considerably staggered by the blow, which raised a bad bump.

Things were getting very warm indeed, and with the odds against me it seemed that discretion might be the better part of valor, as there was no doubt at all I'd be killed if I stayed. My path was barred by the Miris, two of whom had now armed themselves with axes and another with a long split-bamboo pole, razor-edged, while the others tore at me with their hands, clawing at my eyes and throat. For some reason no one thought of picking up a knife or *dao,* of which there were quite a number around. Practically everything I'd been wearing had been torn off in the fight — it was definitely time to find some other place fast!

I ran for the creek, a distance of two or three yards, and waded in. At first there was a shelving beach where the water was as transparent as glass, and then after quite a number of yards the bottom suddenly vanished. I was up to my chest by this time and, intent only on getting to the other side, had not looked around to see what the Miris were doing. Now I turned to see them launching a big canoe in pursuit. They were standing up, paddling the dugout furiously toward me. The man at the bow was armed with a long poling paddle, while another at the stern was similarly equipped; the others in between still carried the axes and split-bamboo pole with which they'd armed themselves. As the dugout gained speed they all leaned forward, straining like dogs at their leashes, screaming and shouting with rage.

There wasn't much time; certainly if I started swimming that would be the last of me, I thought, and my head would be split before I'd gone more than one or two yards. As the bow of the dugout tore through the water toward me I waited, and then, as the nearest man lifted his paddle and struck, jumped aside, letting the vessel pass by. Immediately there was a great scurry as my assailants tried to bring their craft to a stop while the savage with the split-bamboo pole was able to rain several blows at my head. Fortunately the men with the axes could not reach me. Blows fell thick and fast for a minute or so, but luckily the aim of my attackers was bad and most of them missed. The split-bamboo pole, however, was another matter. I saw it coming down straight at my head and in the excitement of the moment put up my hand to stop it; although I felt no pain at the time it almost severed my thumb. I leaped at the legs of one of the men who carried the paddles and pitched him out of the canoe. Diving underneath the dugout, I wrestled the paddle away and, holding him with my injured left hand, chopped him hard on the jaw. He released the paddle and at last I had a weapon of my own in my hands.

The battle was still a dead heat, but now things began to work out in my favor. I swung the paddle at the occupants of the canoe; they were standing up and it was like taking a sweep at a row of sticks with a scythe. I connected with one of the men who had an axe, and the force of the blow threw him into the water. I jumped for him, holding his head under, and picked up the axe as he began to lose consciousness and let go. Now I was all right. The Miris, uncertain of the outcome, made for the beach.

I waded out, curiously enough finding myself laughing and singing. The Miris grouped themselves together, watching while I sang and danced, whirling the axe around my head, the blood from my wounded hand pouring over my body. I was undoubtedly an unpleasant spectacle and they probably thought I was mad. At all events, after some hesitation they all came and knelt down, begging for mercy. I kept the dance going and the axe swinging for quite a while to wipe out any further feelings of hostility they might have, and then told them to get into the dugout canoe. They obeyed meekly, and I sat down in the stern, still holding the axe in one hand while the other trailed in the water beside me, leaving a path of crimson behind. I told the Miris to paddle, and threatened, if one of them even looked round, to crack his skull open.

I was determined to hand my assailants over to justice at Sadiya and, on getting back to my hut where the trail through the jungle began, made them form a single file while I brought up the rear with the axe. By this time my charges were thoroughly scared and gave no trouble at all. On arriving at Sadiya, I handed them over to the native police, had my hand stitched and bandaged by the Indian doctor, and then made my way to the house of my friend the Army officer for a rest. A week or so afterwards I was transferred to the sawmills at Murkong Selek so that I could get treatment for my hand. I was not a bit sorry. Notwithstanding the attention it had been given at Sadiya, it was very painful indeed, and I found it not at all easy to pole a canoe or cook my food in the jungle with only one arm.

Murkong Selek was another bad place, in some ways the equal of Sadiya. Set back a few hundred yards from the Brahmaputra River, the sawmills were in an open plain, a couple of square miles in size. The scream of circular saws thrust the silence outward and back to the forest's dark rim. A sea of elephant grass six to eight feet in height covered the clearing, and driven straight through it was a narrow-gauge railway line that crept to the edge of the trees and disappeared. There, changing its course, it turned at an angle and came to its destination a mile or so farther on in the woods. This was the point where the elephants came one by one to the railroad, each hauling a log at the end of its chain to be loaded on flatcars and taken to the mill.

The camp was an eerie place, lost to every whisper of noise save the bleat of the whistle at the mills which sounded the hour of noon and, at evening, the end of the working day. Deep in the forest the trees crowded in, leaning together over the thin cleft of the railroad until their tops shut out the light of the sky, except where an occasional spear of gold transfixed the dark-green, leafy ceiling and stood there rigid and bright. When the rain came the heavens emptied, cascading in sheets of drifting, glimmering silver onto the jungle below; thunder echoed with vast drumbeats of sound, rumbling and dying, crashing again suddenly, splitting the world as the firmament opened in another inferno of flame. Then the trees stood etched for a second, every leaf and branch pearly, ashen in torment as they lashed themselves from side to side under the driving force of the wind. Sometimes a forest giant would slide, bending earthwards slowly, submitting, as some wild blast of the gale blew it down and it fell, defeated and dead, upon the railway line, there to remain, black roots probing upward like gnarled clutching fingers seeking the thrust of the rain. The line was a tunnel of darkness, a shaft dug deep in the jungle where human moles and their charges came soundlessly, one by one, with their loads.

At the mills, on the other hand, even in still weather one could hardly hear oneself speak; the sharp, keening voice of the saws assailed one's ears. Here, it seemed, was the anarchist foe of the jungle around, a man-made pinpoint redoubt that was shouting defiance against the great octopus circling it in. There was a feeling of waiting. "Get back, get back!" the mills screeched, the saws whining and buzzing, the engines that gave them force thumping and pounding, shaking themselves in impotent fury. But the jungle simply stood there, moving a slow inch or two forward, knowing that it was only a matter of time before its tentacles would encompass all this, the tendrils and vines wind themselves over and round, the great trees shoot up — and it would be gone, lost and forgotten under the healing carpet of green.

As my hand got better I was put to work at the mills. At Tezpur the logs had been cut into planks, shaped to size, and nailed together, forming strong square boxes good enough for tea but otherwise quite undistinguished. At Murkong Selek we were vastly superior — we were making three-ply veneer. First the logs were dumped in a vat of hot water and then, soaking and steaming, rolled to the oversize lathes. As these revolved, a thin slice of wood moved continually forward, a wafer peeled off by the sharp blade. Then it was cut into squares, glued, placed one square on top of another in piles, and fed to the presses; in due course, they would come out thin and firm, each middle section cemented to the top and bottom pieces of wood. Sometimes for special purposes five- and even seven-ply veneer was made.

There were six white men employed at Murkong Selek

including myself; Hind, the general manager, who was in charge of the overall work of the company up and down the river; a manager who looked after the output of the mill; an engineer who took care of the machines that powered the lathes, presses and saws; an assistant manager; and the jungle manager. I was the odd-job man who filled in when anything extra had to be done. Sometimes I would act in some general capacity, sometimes oversee the stamping of the plywood squares — each had to be inspected and the flawed ones discarded — and occasionally assist Needham, the jungle manager, whose business it was to see that the logs were loaded at the railway terminal so that the mill would never run short.

Two persons stand out as reflecting this stage of my career — Hind and Needham. Hind was stocky, about five foot eight, and immensely strong. He was pleasant, had a very rough sense of humor, was extremely tough and very brave. On one occasion when there was a riot at the mill at Tezpur he drove out from the Club in his car, confronted a mob of more than a hundred natives quite alone and, walking up to the leader, who was more than six feet in height, struck him such a blow that he was catapulted along the ground and the remainder fled. He was held in such awe that the riot was over. For a while, though, it had been touch and go whether the rioters would set fire to the manager's bungalow — he was seeking safety inside, having barricaded the doors — but Hind's opportune arrival soon set the situation to rights. No one knew much about his past, but it was understood that at one time he had been in the Merchant Navy and had worked his way up. For some reason he was always very good to me, and although he was more than double my age we got along very well.

Needham was different entirely. He was extremely good-looking, a fair, Viking type of man, slightly taller than Hind and very well educated. He was a renowned hunter who took impossible chances, but so sure was his aim that he never got hurt. He had killed charging wild elephants standing alone in their path, and tigers and buffalo with which the jungle abounded. It was said that one of his methods was to prowl barefoot through the forest at night with a bottle filled with fireflies at his belt, so that when he saw a tiger's eyes gleam in the dark he could take a firefly out of the bottle, stick it on the front sight of his rifle, another on the back sight, line the two up, and pull the trigger with these two pinpoints of light guiding his aim to the tiger's head. Common gossip had it that he had killed eight of these beasts in this way, and although the idea seemed quite unbelievable such was his reputation that I gradually came to think it might be true. Among his various weapons he had a twelve-bore rifle loaded with black powder, and when a buffalo charged him he would fire one barrel; there would be a great flash and cloud of smoke, and as the animal was upon him he would jump aside and fire the second barrel into its side as it passed, blinded, into the gray thunderhead which had suddenly raised itself in its path! He never spoke of these exploits himself, but he had no need to; they were the kind of thing that men talked about when they gathered together and the subject of hunting came up.

There is no doubt at all that Hind and Needham made quite an impression on me — I was just at the age when such types would have the most impact. There were others, of course, whom I'd known to take chances — one tea planter named Farley used to get his amusement by chasing cobras to their holes and then, as they descended, grasping them by the tail, hauling them out, and cracking them like a whip overhead so that their spines were broken and they died — but I was more closely associated with these two, and their attitude toward life set me thinking. I had heard of the same kind of thing elsewhere, in the war, and had met quite a lot of unusual characters at much too early an age, but whatever it was, the ordinary individual now began to look very pale by comparison. I enjoyed nothing more than helping Needham with his work at the elephant camp when for some reason or other my assistance was wanted. When after a while he went away temporarily, I took over in his absence.

Up to this time I had lived with the assistant manager, a good-natured Scotsman, while my hand slowly healed. Conditions were very comfortable as a cook and native servant were available, but my job in the mill was exceedingly boring, a routine of walking around and seeing that the proper quota of work was performed. Most of the labor had been recruited from central India, the men's transportation being paid by the company on the understanding that they would work for a specified number of years. They were much darker in color than the Assamese or Miris and were accommodated in rows of huts called the "coolie lines." The majority had their wives and families with them and were not discontented, despite the unaccustomed climate and surroundings. Their wives also worked in the mills, so they were doubly secure financially and always able to provide for their wants, something very doubtful indeed in the areas they came from, where they were in danger of famine and drought. They were well trained in the work of the mill and required little supervision. However, someone in authority always had to be around, as left to themselves they were prone to relax and slow down.

I was glad, therefore, when I was sent back to the jungle to take over from Needham, even though it was understood that this was to be only for a short time until he reassumed charge of the camp. Again I was my own master, moving about the forest with the same sense of freedom I had enjoyed on the Bhareli and at Sadiya. There was always a fascination in feeling that one was quite by oneself in the mysterious kingdom of the trees and, although the living conditions were as primitive as ever, I felt more at home. Malaria, though, was to be my undoing again and it was not long before I was racked by fever, shivering, shaking and sweating in the small grass hut I occupied at the elephant camp. Curiously enough, before this latest attack my health had been better, and this I put down to the amount of quinine I had absorbed under the care of the doctors at Calcutta. Now the disease had returned in full force and it seemed likely that my condition would grow worse.

All this time, the one thought I had was that if I lived, somehow, by some manner of means, I'd get back to England. After all, returning to the jungle had been the first step toward this, but while there was not much on which to spend my salary, it would still take a long time to save enough money for my passage. The return of malaria now heightened the odds. Besides, after Needham returned and I was sent back to the mill the days were filled with monotony. What did the future hold? I asked myself. Gradually the gates were closing; I had imprisoned myself in a cage having no visible walls, but walled nonetheless — and what was worse, by walls at least partly of my own making. If I remained, ill as I was, there was little chance of any kind of advancement at Murkong Selek. Yet I could not go back to Calcutta, for the head office, having reluctantly allowed me to return to the jungle, would be justified in refusing any such request. In Calcutta, anyway, there would only be the same old business routine again, and I could not see myself fitting into it when I already knew what it meant. There was no doubt that I was very confused. Partly it was youth. But mainly, back behind everything there was something else — I had to get back and see Deirdre again.

One day I could bear the situation no longer and sent in my resignation. If I could make my way back to the seaboard, from there I decided I'd place my luck in the lap of the gods. I'd try to get a job on a tramp steamer at Calcutta, and once there would just have to wait and see what turned up. Vaguely I had the idea of going to Canada if I could, or if this were not possible since it was half way across the world, I'd have a try at joining the French Foreign Legion.

These were the two most difficult realms I could think of in which to find some sense of achievement, and however great the gamble both seemed filled with excitement. Anyway I had nothing to lose. It was a one-sided wager, for if I remained malaria would inevitably get me down.

Then a strange thing happened. Bird and Company came to my help and offered to pay for my passage to Canada!

I suppose that Hind must have made the suggestion. At all events, it happened that one of the partners of the firm came from Calcutta to make an inspection, a custom observed only at very long intervals. There had been one at Tezpur when I was on the Bhareli; now an important official of the firm came to Murkong Selek and I was sent for. As I entered the office he stopped discussing some subject with Hind which I felt uncomfortably was quite possibly me. His next words confirmed it.

I cannot remember all the details of the conversation but it went something like this.

"I see that you want to leave your work here," he said. "I want you to understand that if you do it's difficult to find any other opening to which you can be moved."

"I'm not asking for a transfer, sir," I replied. "All I want is to get away from this climate — that's why I put in my resignation — this malaria is getting me down."

"Yes, I know you've been ill," he said, "but what do you intend to do with yourself if you leave here?"

"I don't know, sir. I'll have to decide that when I get to Calcutta — I was thinking of going to Canada if I could get passage on a boat. Maybe I can ship on some tramp."

He got up and went to the window while I waited.

"That might be a good idea," he said quietly. "Perhaps you could do well there — anyway it might be worth giving it a try."

He paused, looking at me.

"Well, I'll tell you what we'll do — we'll pay your passage to Canada if you like, and then, once you get there, it will be entirely up to you. Mind you," he continued, "it will only be the cheapest way possible — I would think not more than third class. What do you say to that?" He stood waiting, wondering perhaps what my reaction would be.

"Thank you very much, sir," I said. "I'll be very glad indeed to accept." I was astounded at the generosity of the offer he had made — it was more than good of Bird and Company!

He nodded. The discussion was over and I left the office, grateful that a door was opening from the dilemma I'd been in and from which I could now find my way out.

Canada! I knew nothing about it — it was a land of mystery somewhere at the edge of the world. None of the people I knew had a much wider knowledge. "You'll have to use your fists there!" said one when he heard I was going. It was a remark showing the general idea of my destination — apparently, according to the customary conception, one was thrown into some headlong fight as soon as one stepped off the boat! And somewhere farther west, they had read, there were always red Indians — and snow! I gave some appropriate reply and sat thinking about it — perhaps things might be tough but that was no cause for alarm. I doubted that they could be worse than the life I had known. The main thing was to get there and see England and Deirdre on the way!

I had been told to leave Murkong Selek when the next river steamer arrived, and then, after spending a short time with my parents at Shillong, to go on by train to Calcutta so as to arrive the day before the ship sailed. Ill and without means, I had no wish to spend any time there, for this would add to expenses and cut into my very meager resources. Once I was on the ship, however, my board and lodging would be assured, and after that it would be up to chance.

A week or so later the river steamer arrived at Murkong Selek and I embarked. I looked back from the deck of the vessel to the buildings and mill without any trace of regret;

it was not the fault of the place, but rather of its climate, that I had not made better progress. The past three years had been a climb and a descent; it had been something to have been in charge of one of the largest lime manufactories in India before I was twenty-one, and — leaving some of the minor turbulences of youth aside — I had done quite well in Calcutta. Now I was without money, resources, or job, and still racked from time to time by malaria.

Transferring from the steamer to a bus near Gauhati, I continued my journey to Shillong. There, my parents were concerned about my departure, and suggested that I stay with them until something acceptable in the way of a position came along. But my mind was made up. I said good-bye, returned to Gauhati, and from there took the train for the overnight trip to the south. It would get me to Calcutta just in time to catch the boat on which passage had been booked.

Every other time I had traveled by rail between Calcutta and Shillong it had been by first class. This was different. Now I made my way to what was known as an "intermediate" carriage, and the attendant looked at my ticket with curiosity as he knew me from other trips I had made. He was good enough to show me to an empty compartment, however, suggesting that if I was temporarily short of funds I could travel in style in one of the better carriages and make the difference good at the end of the line. This I could never do and so, after thanking him for his interest in my welfare, I settled down with a book. As the train made its way out of the station, the change in my circumstances for the first time brought itself forcibly home, and I felt that at last all the old ties really were cut and I was off to something new again on my own.

When I reached Calcutta I saw one or two of my friends, and finally I was on the ship — leaving India. As the shoreline faded, I passed over the events of the last three years in my mind. They had not been without incident, I thought, and while my prospects now seemed dim at least I had gained some valuable experience at considerable risk to my neck. The curious thing, too, was that now the malaria seemed better; at least I'd suffered no further attack since leaving the jungle. Things were looking up temporarily, but there still seemed every chance they'd get worse. That was the great gamble that I'd taken, and I'd have to abide by the results. It was pleasant to know that while I might be down at the moment I still wasn't out!

6

~~~~~~~~

Hail and Farewell

THERE was no third class on the ship or I would have been on it. As it was, I joined the dozen second class passengers with a feeling of freedom. I had climbed out of the box I'd been in, and even though my prospects weren't bright the walls surrounding me were now gone. After seeing the purser and finding my cabin, I went on deck and made my way forward to the bow of the vessel. There the damp soft wind of the tropics breathed softly past, fresh and pure from the sea, the long horizon of white, wave-crested green stretching wide as the skies above to where the world ended. Below, the knife-edge of steel cut through the water, the sunshine lighting the few white clouds that sailed in the blue bowl of heaven. Free! Here on the sea the boundaries were limitless, the road to the future cloaked in obscurity, but at last I'd got away from the close, clinging grip of the jungle. I felt oddly excited. I'd burned all my bridges behind; now nothing was left but to go on.

The ship plowed through the Indian Ocean. Soon we came to Aden and Perim at the foot of the Red Sea, where the heat was unbearable and where we stopped to refuel. Then after the Suez Canal, we crept slowly at first but soon gathered speed, into the Mediterranean. I had made friends with the other passengers on board and was enjoying myself;

what made me particularly thankful was that since leaving the East I'd not suffered any further attacks of malaria. The feeling of weakness and depression had gone, the amenities of civilized life and the climate of the south coast of France were beginning to have their effect, and things were looking much better. At Marseilles, the ship stopped for a day and I spent some time making inquiries about the French Foreign Legion. Canada was still a very long way off and I wondered if I'd ever *really* get there. It might be as well to have another string on one's bow and there'd be no harm in finding out about conditions of service. Then if anything raised its head to interfere with my reaching the goal I'd set my mind on, I could come back from England by some cross-Channel port and perhaps enlist in the Legion. It was highly unlikely but one never could tell, and as I had very little money, this kind of information might later be useful. What I was told at the French Army headquarters was by no means encouraging. Apparently, if I joined, part of my service would be spent in French Indo-China. The malaria bug, I knew, would be just as deadly there as it had been on Bhareli and in the back of beyond of the jungle. It was curious, I thought, that so small a thing could prove such a mountainous obstacle.

Another week went by and the vessel, after traveling along the west coasts of Spain and France, forged into the Channel. A day or so more and we reached Tilbury, from where I took the train on to London. The first part of the journey was over and now, after a few days in England, I'd be embarking again on another. There was a hotel nearby and I went in. It would be better to use the telephone there than one in the noise of the station.

I had written to Deirdre telling her I was coming home, so she was not surprised when I phoned.

"Charles! How nice to hear your voice again," she said, once the questions and delays of the long distance call had been disposed of. "When are you coming down? I'm dying to see you!"

"Today?"

"Yes, today. There's a train gets in here about five o'clock. We'll send the car to meet you. It'll be such fun to hear all your news. It's been simply years, hasn't it?"

"Quite a few. Well, I'll be there . . . see you around five, then . . . good-bye."

I leaned against the wall, the figures passing in the lounge suddenly drifting off in a blur of misty vapor. It had been a dark night and raining when she had seen me off on the long voyage to India three years before, with Harris the chauffeur standing in the background, the foggy lights on the platform turning the passersby into ghosts without substance as the train pulled away in the dark. Now for a few short days I'd see her again, and then it would be the same old story and I'd be going on somewhere else. To her I played the role of a brother, nothing more.

Later that afternoon I arrived at the station. It was a small place far out in the country, and the single old porter who carried my baggage was quite overshadowed by the chauffeur and car that were waiting.

"Hullo," I said, "don't remember seeing you before. What happened to Harris?" I had half expected Harris to be at the station to meet me. He had driven Deirdre and me around London when I came home from the French Army on furlough, and so was an old friend. I was disappointed; his absence seemed, obscurely, to prove that the present had overtaken the past.

"Good afternoon, sir," the new man replied. "Name of Robbins — been with her ladyship for a couple of years — took over from Harris —" He named the family for whom Harris was now working, and relieved the old porter of my suitcase.

I got into the back seat of the car. I knew, of course, whom Deirdre had married, but beyond that had not thought much about it; now I wondered what I would find at the end of this journey. Whatever it was would be quite different from the old days when we'd been together.

The car purred along for several miles and, passing through a large iron gate, entered a driveway. Great trees stood here and there in the park land, the sun shining on their leaves, turning them golden. In the distance the woods grouped themselves closely together by long, emerald-green vales that ran off to nowhere. A few cows, chewing contemplatively, watched us in silence. After a while the house rose up, huge as a mountain.

A manservant opened the door while Robbins handled my suitcase. Within, a great hall extended, its walls covered with pictures, a winding staircase ascending on one side to the rooms above. Somewhere, not far away, I could hear a fire crackling. I gave the manservant my hat and made my way to the drawing room, waiting.

There was a slight flurry of sound on the stairs, and all at once she was there. We shook hands.

"Hullo, Deirdre," I said. "It's so lovely to see you. You haven't changed much — you're as beautiful as ever!"

"Charles, don't talk such nonsense. What fun to see you again! I'm sorry I was upstairs when you arrived. Did the car meet you all right at the station?"

It was the usual exchange of mixed-up banalities, entirely suitable for the occasion. We were old friends meeting after a long absence, that was all.

I stayed three days while time went all too quickly. I still had about fifteen pounds in my pocket and all I had to do was to go to Southampton and go on board — steerage.

The night before I left we had a family party, just Deirdre and I and her husband. There was a lot of gold plate and silver and quiet lights and chatter. Looking round, I couldn't help thinking that it was quite a change from the jungle — or the war. It was a haven of peace, a place of loveliness where for a moment in time one could forget the things one had seen, the leeches and blood and the never-ending fight for survival.

When the time came to leave, tipping the staff made quite a hole in my finances, and now the equivalent of about forty-five dollars was left. This, I thought, was the least I could do with when I reached Canada, but there was still one more to look after, Robbins, the chauffeur. Driving down in the Rolls-Royce — it was an open sports model, red and black with a long, silver bonnet — I took up the subject.

"Look, Robbins," I said, "I'm afraid I've no money to tip you."

"That's all right, sir." He took his eyes off the road for a moment and smiled. "I know how it is."

When we arrived at the docks I was almost engulfed by the crowd of porters and stewards who came forward. "First class, sir? First class?" they chorused, viewing the Rolls as it came to a stop.

Robbins got out and opened the door.

"Good-bye," I said. "Thanks very much for bringing me down."

We smiled at each other; I hadn't realized that the car would make such a sensation, and felt mildly amused at what would probably follow.

"No, third, thanks."

All at once most of the stewards found they had other pressing engagements, but a few stuck around, obviously disconcerted by this unexpected turn of events and probably wondering whether the size of the gratuity would justify standing by.

"Good luck, sir," said Robbins. "I hope we'll see you back, some time or other."

"Good-bye!"

Well, now it was really farewell! It was a relief to know that in a moment or so the door to the past would close irrevocably, leaving only the unexplored future. One steward remained, an old man who seemed to have a bright sense of humor. Grinning, he picked up my suitcase and together we turned, made our way up the gangplank and then into the ultimate depths of the vessel.

There were only about fifteen English-speaking passengers in the part of the vessel I was in; the remainder were Central Europeans with little or no knowledge of the language. In my cabin, somewhere below the waterline, there were three other occupants, one a mechanic from London, another a farm boy from the country, and a third whose characteristics I have forgotten. After a while we all made friends and got on well together; they were emigrating as I was, hoping to better their circumstances in the new land that now lay before them. The cabin without portholes was cramped and stuffy. As nobody thought about having a bath — perhaps there were no facilities or no one took the trouble to look for them — it was not long before our quarters began to get smelly, and while the days could be spent in the open air on deck, at night the atmosphere became very heavy. Fortunately, at twenty-one one can sleep quickly and soundly, so this was only a minor disadvantage.

The food in the dining saloon was nothing to be enthusiastic about either. As far as I can remember its basic element was stew in a large metal container in the middle of a long table, from which we all helped ourselves individually. There was enough of this mysterious mixture, however, to look after the wants of the third class passengers, and if one was not too fastidious there was no need to go hungry. Some of my fellow travelers — those from Central Europe, more particularly the women — went around in bare feet, and some did not seem accustomed to knives and forks. The contrast between conditions in the house in which I'd been staying and my present circumstances struck me quite forcibly; at one moment I had been up in the heights as far as material comforts were concerned, at the next I was down in the depths. But this was the beginning of the new life and conditions to which I had to become accustomed, and fortunately — youth being what it is — I found in it a challenge instead of frustration.

The voyage passed without incident except for a fight with knives — I missed this — in the recreation room between two of my new-found companions from Europe; it ended with honor being satisfied without blood being drawn. And then one morning instead of the never-ending drift of the ocean toward us, there in its place was a faint, hardly distinguishable line.

Canada!

As we came closer the land took on shape and substance, its outermost boundaries opening in fissures and channels until at last the banks of the St. Lawrence sloped inward and narrowed as we followed its course to the west, to Quebec. We watched the country slide past with its farms, villages and towns, a panorama of green that stretched to the skyline, dotted with homes in a profusion of colors, red-roofed and white-walled, with gray in between. Well, there it was! Slowly the land had emerged from the ocean to meet us. Now it was a living entity on which we would step when the journey's last hours had gone by and of which — as the seasons passed, days ending, each week beginning, months going by, years treading each in the track of the other — we'd be a part.

A few more hours and we reached Montreal. The ship nosed into the dock. The voyage was over. There was a hustle-bustle of confusion as the passengers sorted themselves into groups prior to landing. On every side a hubbub of foreign languages arose as each family gathered its possessions together and prepared to disembark. I said good-bye to my cabin companions, the last few words lingering on the air as they turned to wave down the gangplank.

I watched my friends disappear, and then followed. The sun was shining and it must have been nine or ten o'clock in the morning toward the middle of July 1923. I put my suitcase down and looked around, but there was nothing to see except the wall of the dock to the front and the side of the vessel behind.

There was a gate in the wall through which, slowly and hesitantly, my fellow passengers were filing. I joined the procession. I don't remember feeling particularly excited; I know I felt rather numb. Now I was like a log being swept through a sluice gate, a piece of flotsam that, having no will, must drift with the current till it reaches the shore. But under everything else was exhilaration. Somewhere nearby I knew was the city, its noise muted by barriers that I still must pass through. It was fascinating! What was going to happen?

The procession moved along. There were some small, blue-coated figures in the distance which gradually grew closer, and soon I was to find myself in conversation with the first Canadian I'd encountered since landing. It was an immigration officer — a woman.

I had made it! What had seemed almost impossible a year ago and half a world away had now come true; the door was open and I was on the threshold of the new life that I'd been seeking. It reminded me of the extraordinary luck I had had when I applied to join the British Red Cross five years previously. Since then a lot of water had flowed under the bridge and in experience at least I was considerably older. But I still had a great deal to learn, and here before me was the proving ground on which I was either to succeed or fall by the way.

Canada! The word had a magic sound, echoing the music of distant things and all that was unknown. Canada! The name grew from a whisper to a great sound that filled all my senses as I went slowly forward toward the blue-coated figures, waiting now only a few steps away.

There were others behind and in front of me in the procession, but I wondered if any of them could be feeling more insignificant than I was, more lost, or more utterly alone!

Part II

7

The New Country

P EOPLE are largely the product of their own environ-
ments. Take away the patterns and customs they have
known and they are left fleshless, mere skeleton outlines of
their complete selves. An aboriginal transplanted from his
native land would find himself lost and bereft on any distant shore. Then, slowly, as the years passed, he would become a product of his new surroundings, similar — except
perhaps in color — to those with whom he made his life from
day to day. At first, though, it would take all his time just
learning to exist.

That was my own position when I disembarked — apart
from my outward semblance to the inhabitants, I was not
much better off; England, the French Army, the elephant
camps, were very different from this new land where I now
found myself. I was a foreigner knowing nothing — almost
as lost as any creature of the wilds. But I had learned to
stand alone, and that was invaluable.

We must have passed Quebec during the hours of darkness as I have no recollection of the city, but I shall never
forget the woman, the immigration officer at Montreal, for
she was the first obstacle I had to surmount an hour or so
after I landed. She was standing at a gateway and was about
thirty-five years of age, slim, with light brown hair which,

for the most part, hid itself under a dark-blue uniform cap. Brown-eyed and plain, she used no makeup and, while the overall impression she gave was not obviously severe, her uniform clothed her in all the panoply of rank and official dignity. However, notwithstanding her firm and resolute air, there was about her some atmosphere of sympathy and understanding that seemed to belie her purpose there. Off duty, she was probably the mother of a young family, happily married and an adornment of her home. But now she was the other half of her personality, the functionary of government whose job it was to weigh and assess the qualifications of those who, after trials and tribulations of one kind and another, came hoping to enter this new country.

There were the preliminary questions:

"How old are you?"

"Twenty-one."

"Have you got a job to go to?"

"No."

"What are you going to do?"

"I don't know — get some kind of work, I suppose."

The brown eyes looked at me more closely. There was a pause — she was weighing something in her mind.

"Have you ever been sick?"

Had I ever been sick? Yes, I had. There was only one answer to that.

"I was ill for a while in the Far East — India, to be exact. Malaria. I'm quite all right now, though."

She passed it off. Malaria, I could see, meant very little to her.

"Nothing else?"

I searched my memory rapidly. I'd had two or three of the usual childhood diseases but this was presumably not what she was after — probably she was on the trail of some communicable disease.

"No, nothing of importance. I was sick once or twice as a kid — measles, chicken pox, that sort of thing."

"Are you sure?"

I couldn't make out why she was so interested in my health. Perhaps she was just holding me there, sizing up my possibilities. It did not occur to me that three years in India and a good part of them in the jungle might have left their mark. She kept looking me straight in the eye, obviously considering.

"Yes, quite sure."

She went off on another tangent. "How much money have you got?"

I knew so little about the requirements of entering a new country that I had not expected this question. Probably I should have asked or somebody should have told me before leaving England that some specified amount of money was necessary, but I doubt if it would have made any difference; I'd still have taken a chance. There had been some minor expenses on the ship, mostly for cigarettes, and I now had about thirty-five dollars left. I told her.

"You're supposed to have fifty!"

Well, I hadn't. Anyway it was no good worrying about it at this stage of the proceedings, though fifteen dollars did seem a small amount on which so much could hinge. It was quite obvious that my answer had bothered her; probably she was thinking that I might become a public charge. The brown eyes were puzzled, undecided.

"Have you any friends or relatives in Canada to whom you can go?"

The interview was going badly. Suddenly I saw myself as a possible candidate for deportation back to England. I was panic-stricken. If this happened, I had no place to go. It would mean starting all over again with practically nothing to fall back on. What on earth would I do?

Her last question had made me think quickly. No, I hadn't any friends or relatives that I knew of who lived in Canada, but my eldest brother was somewhere to the south, touring in the United States while on furlough. He was traveling by car, and had said that if I contacted him by letter at a prearranged address, he would look me up on his return through the eastern part of Canada. But it was a very vague arrangement and I had no idea at all when he would be passing through Montreal.

"Well, I have a brother . . . He's not in Canada at the moment but he's coming here . . ."

"Where is he now?"

I would have given a lot to get away from this cross-examination. My brother's possible arrival seemed a weak peg on which to hang my future, but I gave her the facts. Her eyes, which had lost their sternness momentarily at the mention of my brother, again were filled with doubt. I waited. There was a pause that seemed to stretch on forever as she stood there making up her mind. Finally she motioned me past with her head, saying nothing. I picked up my suitcase and hurried as fast as I could through the gate. After I had gone what I thought was a safe distance, I looked back over my shoulder. She was still following me with her eyes, and I hastened on, trying as hard as I could not to give the appearance of doing so, in case she called me back. I have many things to be grateful for, and not the least of these is the kindness and consideration of that immigration officer who, at that crucial moment of my career, decided to give me the benefit of the doubt and not to turn me back.

The next thing to find was a place where I could stay for the night. Walking up one of the streets near the docks I came upon a store window in which was a sign that read, *Beds, 25 cents a night*. While the exterior of the premises did not look very prepossessing, the charge seemed reasonable, so I pushed the door open and went in. The proprietor showed me upstairs to where, in a long dormitory, stood a considerable number of beds; somewhat to my surprise the place looked clean and respectable. Blankets and a pillow were provided, and although the room was very stark and bare it was at least a shelter from the elements and a place to lay my head. In fact, after living in the jungle, the dormitory seemed quite a pleasant place to be. There were at least doors and windows and walls and no mosquitoes, snakes, leopards, tigers or rampaging wild elephants to disturb one in one's sleep! Although there were about twenty beds in the room, only four were occupied, one at one end and three at the other. I sat down and wondered what I should do next. I was glad to have a roof over my head so soon after arrival, and while this may seem a small thing in itself it was something for which I was thankful.

Because of the low cost of living, I had enough money to look after the immediate needs of the future; but food at a dollar a day and twenty-five cents for my lodging would soon cut into the very small assets I had, and no time could be lost in getting some kind of temporary job which would improve my financial position. Only then, when I had established myself safely, could I look around and see what the prospects were of getting anything better. For quite a long time, I'd had an idea in my head which had first had its birth before I left India. The Royal Northwest Mounted Police! If I only could enlist, it might be the answer — even the name seemed to smack of adventure! I knew little about it, though; not even that, in 1920, it had become the Royal Canadian Mounted Police. I had no idea when I might have to apply to join, or whether there would be a waiting list of prospective recruits. Besides, there was always the question, if men were being taken on, would I be suitable. It would take time to find out and even then there was no guarantee that the results would be fruitful. Only by feeling my way could I get at the answers.

I went downstairs and, having obtained the address of the nearest employment office from the proprietor of the "flophouse" I was in, made my way there. It was not far away, and soon I found myself a member of a small group of men in a large, squalid room facing off the street, into which the light trickled through dirty windows that looked as though they had not been washed for at least a decade. All my companions were on the same mission and were inspecting the blackboards that hung round the walls, on which various job openings were chalked up. They were a rough-looking crowd, most of whom ordinarily would be found wielding a pick and shovel as their means of existence. I must have been conspicuous in my blue suit, neatly dressed with collar and tie, but nobody paid attention except a short, stocky man who struck up a conversation and invited me to accompany him into the woods. He was a logger who was returning to his camp after a few days in Montreal, and he offered to initiate me into all the skills of his craft if I would place myself under his wing. While his approach seemed to be in good faith I turned down his offer, since there was no way of knowing what one might be letting oneself in for accompanying a stranger into the forest. Besides, although it was agreeable to have someone take an interest in one's welfare, to do what he suggested would interfere with my getting into the Mounted Police. I thanked him politely and said no.

After my lumberjack friend made his departure, I wandered around reading the notices and found that among the openings for men with specialized skills — which I, of course, did not have — there was a demand for laborers in the docks. This did not seem very promising but at least it was a job, and I was in no position to pick and choose. If I could not get into the Mounted Police within a few days, it might at least be a beginning from which I could work up. At a desk in the room was a man who appeared to be taking applications, and, walking over to him, I pointed to the board. "I'd like one of those laboring jobs," I said.

There was hardly any conversation. He gave me a sharp glance, took my name, and after telling me the time and place at which I was to report, wrote something down. I was agreeably surprised for I had half expected to be questioned regarding my qualifications; my appearance must have made me seem ill-equipped for the work. It was a twelve-hour shift from six in the evening to six A.M. the next day; the pay was thirty-five cents an hour. It was not very much, but I had the satisfaction of knowing that at least I had found a job within a few hours of landing. All I had to do now was learn what to do and stay with it until something better turned up.

Going back up the street, I stopped to look at some of the sights in the great city around me. I had seen nothing like it for a long time except for the brief stopover in Calcutta and half a day or so in London where I had been too busy and preoccupied to do justice to my surroundings. In Montreal it was different. I had done what I had set out to do; it was something to have reached Canada after so many vicissitudes; the sun was shining and, by and large, the world seemed a reasonably good place. Listening to the roar of the traffic as it flowed by, traversing the canyons of stone formed on either side by tall buildings of innumerable shapes and sizes, the Brahmaputra and its headwaters seemed very far away. All around, the life of the city pursued its noisy way, the men and women intent on their own affairs, chattering in French but with a recognizable touch of English here and there. I had a feeling of loss that I had no one to talk to, but fortunately my life in the jungle had made me accustomed to that and it did not mean so much as it might have. With the exception of Deirdre, I had not spoken to a white woman for quite a long time, but I was content to watch them pass by, sometimes solitary, with some mysterious feminine purpose in mind as they hurried along, or as members of groups conversing in quick outbursts of words dotted with laughter. It gave one the feeling of being an inanimate object on the bank of a river, watching the current flow by — something exterior to the life of the everyday world, cut off by an invisible wall from all that went on.

Back in my lodgings, for the first time I found myself in contact with my four fellow roomers; they had been out on affairs of their own when I had first arrived in the morning but now had returned. On my left, stretched full length on his bed, was a tall, dark Irishman, while at the other end of the dormitory were three others of the same nationality forming a small, tight group and earnestly engaged in discussing some matter of moment of their own. They looked around, throwing a brief glance in my direction, and then continued, their heads close together. From the dark looks they cast from time to time at the occupant of the bed next to my own, it was clear that he formed the main subject of the conversation and that the results boded him no good. On his part he lay on his bed, puffing his pipe in an attitude of supreme indifference, seemingly without a care in the world. As I got to know him better during the course of the next few days, I found that he had recently arrived from Ireland, where he had been employed in maintaining law and order during the disturbances that shook the country at the end of the war, as a result of which independence was finally gained. The others at the end of the room came from the southern part of the country and had all been actively engaged on the Sinn Fein side, and for this reason it was very plain indeed that no love was lost between them. "Begorrah!" one said when I became better acquainted with them all. "If we ever get that so-and-so out in one of the dark alleys at night, it's going to be just too bad for him when we've finished!"

But I wasn't involved in the aftermath of the fight for independence in Ireland and, apart from warning my friend on the next bed to be on the lookout, preserved a diplomatic, neutral attitude and, as time went on, came to be on very friendly terms not only with him but with the three other Irishmen as well. The general atmosphere in the dormitory was, however, a difficult one, and I was relieved when I saw my neighbor pack up his belongings and go.

The afternoon of the first day had gone by, evening was coming on, and soon I would have to go to work. I left the dormitory early so as to find the place in the docks to which I had been told to report and found when I got there that I would be one of a group mixing cement. Nearby, close to a grain elevator that was being built, a huge revolving drum turned continually, disturbing the quiet of the night with its grinding roar. Next to it were two large heaps of material which, as I came closer, turned out to be gravel and sand. Two or three men with long-handled shovels were reducing these piles, while others waited to take over the night shift when six o'clock came. They were the usual types of the laboring fraternity, used to this sort of work, with muscles and hands hardened to iron through the years. A mixture of various nationalities, they spoke mostly English and French although one or two conversed in some other language unfamiliar to me, which from the appearance of its speakers I assumed was of central European origin. High above, the uncompleted grain elevator rose to the sky, a great mass of concrete, tall and tubular.

When six o'clock came the foreman, who I found later could curse with equal fluency in either English or French and inspire the same degree of terror with one or the other, motioned to one of the shovels just now discarded and told me to get to work. At the same time someone handed me a pair of heavy gauntlets to put on, well-used and dirty. At first I did not find the labor too difficult as there were frequent pauses while the machine chugged and churned, but as the hours went by my back started to ache until it was indescribable torture to dig in and pick up a heavy shovelful of gravel. Dark had come on and now the scene was lit by the glare of arc-lights. The men working at the elevator's foot took on the semblance of gnomes toiling in hell. Above the bulk of the elevator blocked out the stars while below the men moved around, some clear-cut in the foreground of light, others hovering half seen at the edge of the darkness. I worked on, pain shooting through my arms and tearing at my muscles, which were flabby and soft and of no use at this task. In spite of the gloves, my hands began to form blisters. I envied the men who were shoveling sand from the other pile — its substance was softer and much more easily penetrated by a shovel than the mass of stone which the foreman had assigned to me. Sweat poured from my face, which became dirtier and dirtier as I stopped to wipe it with my gloves. As the hours passed by I thought I would fall down and die before morning came, but gradually the first light of dawn made its appearance and then the night's work was done. I dragged myself off, lurching and stumbling. I was so tired I could hardly stand up, but I'd earned my first night's pay in the country I'd come to and I hadn't given up.

After a few hours' sleep in the dormitory, I awoke feeling greatly refreshed, though when I first moved I suffered the agony of the damned. However, after a while my muscles seemed to be in somewhat better shape, and making my way downstairs I found a telephone book and got the address of the Royal Canadian Mounted Police. I made myself as tidy as possible and, after having something to eat, found my way there. It was on one of the main streets of the city, and — such is the resilience of youth — as I walked along I found that the pain had eased until it was only a dull ache.

The headquarters was in a weather-beaten stone building that, by the look of it, had been there a good many years. There was a flight of steps and, inside, a passageway in which two or three doors faced each other. There was a sound of voices and some kind of activity going on, and I waited in the passage for someone to appear. Soon a man carrying a folder of papers came out of one of the doorways and, seeing me standing there, asked me my business.

"I was wondering if I could be taken on in the Mounted Police . . . " I said.

Apparently he had seen lots of prospective applicants, for he did not waste any time. "Wait here," he replied, and turned back into the office from which he had come.

There was a delay of a few minutes and he appeared again, beckoning for me to go in. I followed. The office had one occupant, a man about thirty-five years of age dressed in plain clothes, who was seated behind a desk. Sharp blue eyes took in my appearance, weighing me while the fingers of one hand moved restlessly on the surface before him. He had a small dark moustache and brown hair, and his general grim expression gave the impression that he had been around a lot. There was a cold hard atmosphere of latent power about him which, I was sure, could spring into life with startling suddenness. Subsequently, I learned that he was Staff-Sergeant Salt, already celebrated as a criminal investigator in eastern Canada, particularly Quebec, and later destined to retire with the rank of Superintendent after many years of distinguished service.

"So you want to join the Force?" he asked, fingers beating out a soft rat-a-tat-tat on top of a file which he pushed to one side as he spoke. Immediately, by his accent and manner, I could tell that here was another Englishman like myself with much the same background.

"Yes, sir," I replied. "I was wondering if I could get in."

"Well, we're not taking on any recruits at present. We're full up and have all the men we can handle."

He paused, looking down momentarily at the desk, and his words were like a knell of doom in my ears. Then after a brief second's thought he raised his eyes to study me more closely.

"Tell me about yourself — just arrived in Canada, haven't you? What have you been doing since you got here?"

I told him that I had arrived the day before and was living in some kind of boardinghouse near the docks.

He got up, and I thought that the interview was ended and turned to leave.

"Hold on," he said. "Wait here for a moment — I'll be right back." He picked up some papers, left the room, and disappeared in the direction of the passage. Presently he came back.

"Come with me — we'll see what we can do with you." He led the way out into the hall, giving me no indication of what was in store. After a few steps we came to a closed door where a voice replied unintelligibly to his knock. We went in.

Another man, clean-shaven and with a round, good-natured face, was seated behind another, almost identical desk but less cluttered with papers and documents. He too was dressed in civilian clothes, but from the furnishings of the office and his attitude and manner he seemed to be someone in a position of considerable authority. As I crossed the floor to stand in front of him he gave me a close, careful scrutiny.

"This is the man I mentioned to you, sir," Salt said. He placed the papers he carried in a filing basket on the desk and stood back, a little behind me to the left. My spirits brightened. The Inspector — for this I eventually found out he was —asked me much the same questions as those I had already answered: name, age, what I was doing, how long I'd been in Canada, and what my reason was for wanting to join the Royal Canadian Mounted Police. When I told him that I had been with the French Army I sensed a glimmer of interest from his eyes. At last the questions were done with, and I held my breath in anticipation.

"We've had a lot of applications lately," he said, "and I'm afraid we're full up and not taking on any recruits." He stopped speaking while he took out a handkerchief and wiped his nose. He had turned away and now looked back at me as I waited, again despairing. "That is with one exception, I should say," he continued. "There's still a vacancy or two left for men who can speak French. How does that apply to you?"

The question took me by surprise. This was no time for hesitation though my knowledge of French was very rudimentary. I had learned something of the language at school and had added to it a knowledge of the poilu French spoken in the trenches, but that was quite a time before and I had forgotten nearly everything. However, he had not asked me how well I spoke French — only *whether* I could speak it. I could truthfully answer in the affirmative, and obviously nothing would be gained by retreating in the face of the question with everything hanging in the balance.

"Yes, sir, I can speak French."

He turned to the Staff-Sergeant. "Send someone in who speaks French," he said. "We'll find out just how much this fellow knows!"

Well, here it is, I thought — this is where everything stops. How could I hope to hold my own with someone fully versed in the language, who would soon show up my obvious shortcomings?

Salt disappeared and two or three silent minutes passed by. Then he returned, accompanied by another man dressed in a brown uniform jacket, blue breeches with a yellow stripe on each side, and knee-high brown boots and spurs. He was about twenty-five years of age, dark complexioned, with a closely trimmed head of black hair. From others I'd seen in the last twenty-four hours I concluded that he had lived a good deal of his life in the Montreal area and had been born and brought up in Quebec. There was no doubt that he would make mincemeat of me as soon as we started the test. He looked at me briefly as he entered the room, then turned and stood at attention in front of the desk.

"I want you to speak French to this man to see what he knows," the Inspector told him. "Here, take a chair, Corporal. Sit down and go ahead." He motioned me to another seat that was vacant. "There's no point in keeping you," he said to the Staff-Sergeant. "I'll get in touch with you in due course."

"Very good, sir." I heard feet on the carpet behind me as Salt made his way to the door. The knob turned and it closed softly behind him, leaving the three of us alone. The Inspector picked up some papers and commenced reading them while I prepared for the struggle. *At least,* I thought, *he can't know very much French or he would have handled this on his own.* It was a straw to clutch at — he would not know the full extent of the verbal massacre to come! The Corporal let loose a babble of words. By concentrating as hard as I could I'd catch a familiar word here and there — enough to get the drift of the machine-gun bursts of vernacular that flew by. Fortunately, as the Corporal went on, he monopolized most of the conversation, contenting himself by ending each rattle of words on a questioning note to which I'd reply *"Oui"* or *"Non."* Things did not seem to be going too badly; I'd got most of the answers right, I thought, and as, at long last, the interview seemed to be coming to an end, I might as well try to make an impression if I was to pass. Cautiously working out the words in my mind as my French Canadian friend went on talking, I decided to wager everything I had on a single throw of the dice. When he came to a stop, I asked him some simple but very carefully articulated question of my own to which he replied with a further flourish of words. The Inspector looked up, sensing that the time for judgment had come.

"Well, can he speak French?" he inquired. I waited, holding my breath.

"He speaks very good French, sir, but with a Parisian accent!"

The words seemed to float through a cloud, half heard, penetrating the senses dully, having some meaning not quite understood. It was the Corporal speaking, but surely I hadn't heard right. It couldn't be! And then as full realization struck me suddenly it was as though a great weight had lifted, opening the way once again.

Silence settled down on the office while the Inspector tried to brush a wandering fly off his desk with his hand. Then, losing patience, he picked up a sheaf of papers and, rolling it up, brought it sharply down. The fly jumped aside and made its escape. It flew round the room, winging its way to the window, where it remained buzzing from side to side of the glass. I looked at it with sympathy as I stood fixing my gaze a foot or so over the Inspector's head, my hands stiffly at my sides, scarcely breathing while I waited for what he would say. The fly must feel rather as I do, I thought. Having momentarily escaped the most recent hazard to its life, it was now barred by the thin, flat surface before it from making its way out to freedom — unless in the course of its frantic rushes it could find the six-inch open space at the top of the window, the pathway to the open air.

My mind was in chaos as a result of my interrogator's words. He stared steadily before him. The Inspector sat watching the fly in the window. Suddenly, without moving his eyes, he spoke. "Thank you, Corporal, that will be all. You may go."

"Very good, sir."

The Corporal made a smart right turn and went out through the door. As he departed, the Inspector turned his attention from the prisoner on the window and looked at me steadily.

"You can fill in an application form if you like," he said. "If they're still taking on French-speaking recruits when it gets to Ottawa and if you can pass the medical, you'll have a good chance of getting in. I'll tell the Staff-Sergeant."

He looked down at the blotter on his desk, bringing the interview to an end. I left the office, my thoughts in confusion but filled with rejoicing, and made my way back to the office to which I'd been first directed, remembering too late that I'd forgotten to express my thanks.

"Well, how did you get on?"

There might have been a faint smile on the Staff-Sergeant's lips, but I put it down to the feeling of elation I had at having passed the test. "He said I can fill in an application form to join up," I said.

Then, just as he was on the point of replying, a buzzer sounded and he had to go out. When after a few minutes he returned, he went to a filing cabinet and drew out a form. "Here you are," he remarked, passing it over the desk. "Fill this in — you'll need a couple of references. I suppose there's no one you know in Canada who would do?"

"No, sir, I don't, but I've got a couple of letters from people I worked for in France and in India. Would they be all right to send on with the form?"

He nodded assent and I filled in the answers to the questions asked. There weren't very many — name, age, height, weight, previous employment, etc. When I came to "Do you understand the care and management of horses?" I played it safe and put down "No." I'd been more than lucky to pass the French language test and nothing would be gained by taking another chance, and that applied too to the next question innocent at first glance but filled with dynamite. "Can you ride?"

"Can ride a little," I wrote, keeping my fingers crossed, knowing full well that I was applying to join an organization world famous for horsemanship. Visions of hard-boiled riding instructors pointing with scorn to the small but potent "Yes" on the form if I answered in the affirmative crossed my mind. It was better to put my faith in the letters I'd attach, which spoke well of my past and might be of more help.

Staff-Sergeant Salt glanced briefly at the form when the replies were completed. He ran his eye quickly through my letters and attached them to the application. Then he laid the papers aside.

"Well, we'll let you know when we hear from headquarters. It'll take a little while, about a week or ten days. Where can we get in touch with you?"

A week or ten days! It seemed endless. There'd be nothing to do except to go back to the docks until the reply came. All at once my spirits fell. However, I explained that I had temporary accommodation but I couldn't be sure for how long. A letter might miss me. Would it be all right if I phoned in?

He could see that I was anxious about the result and raised no objection. As I made my way into the street I realized that it was mid-afternoon and before long I'd have to go back to work. But nothing really mattered — I was treading on air. I'd done all that I had attempted to do and now with a little bit of luck I'd be on safe ground with a future and a goal.

While the pain had gone from my back and from the muscles of my arms, I knew that my hands would not last very long. They were sore enough already from the unaccustomed work and another night's labor, hauling and straining at the shovel, would not improve their condition. But there was no other choice. After supper I made my way through the streets and alleyways to the grain elevator.

We slaved for four or five hours, the shovel getting heavier with each successive load of stone, and I had reached a point of desperation through exhaustion and the damage the handle was doing to my hands. As the night went on dust and grit got in where the blisters had broken and blood had started to flow down the fingers; my knees began to give way and every time I bent to my task a wave of nausea engulfed me, causing my head to swim and my guts to turn over. Finally I came to a stage where my body felt that it simply could not go on, and I leaned on the shovel, knees sagging, thinking that if I removed its support I would fall down. And yet I could not give up; it was my first venture in Canada and it would be an admission of defeat if I did not literally stay with it till I dropped. Summoning every effort of will I worked on, staggering as I thrust the shovel into what seemed the never-lessening pile of gravel before me, my face and body soaked in sweat, my back and legs a single groaning ache that stretched from my ankles to my neck and tore at my muscles as I moved. Almost when I was at my last gasp, the foreman — who for some time had been busy supervising the work at the elevator top — came down. It was midnight, halfway through the shift, and time for a short rest while everyone sat down to eat the lunch he had brought.

I do not know what motivated the foreman, but at the end of the lunch break he came over to exchange a few words. Perhaps he was curious to find out how a novice — for one quick glance when I reported the previous evening must have revealed this — was getting on. Whatever it was, after a few moments' conversation during which he ran his eye over me from the soles of my shoes to the top of my head — his gaze halting an instant when it came to my hands — he squatted down on his heels.

"Maybe you find this kind of tough — not done much of it before, I guess," he said, carefully inspecting the ground at his feet while he picked up a couple of small stones and rolled them around in his hand. Notwithstanding his ferociousness when I'd heard him yelling at some of my working companions, he seemed curiously peaceable.

"Oh, I'm all right," I replied. "Just takes a bit of getting used to — first time I've had to handle a shovel like this." I nodded at the instrument of torture I'd discarded, now lying on the stones. I met his eye as he looked up, forcing a smile. I was very apprehensive indeed that his pleasant manner masked something else and that at the end of what he had to say I'd be summarily dismissed. It was almost more than I could bear — to be sacked from the first job I'd had, in the middle of the second night's work.

He got up, shouting something in French to the men standing by the mixer, and picked up the shovel. When one of them came over he handed it to him and motioned toward the pile of stone with his hand. The man took it, saying nothing.

"There's another job you can try," the foreman said, turning his attention to me again. "You can take over from that fellow I was talking to." He pointed in the direction of the elevator, where there was a small hole large enough to admit a man at its base. "All you have to do is attach the rope to the bucket so that they can haul it up." He grinned encouragingly. "Maybe you won't find it so hard."

As nothing could be worse than working with the shovel for another six hours I summoned what energy I had left and stumbled through the hole into the base of the elevator. The interior was dark, with only a very faint glow thrown by the glare of the outside lights. I attached the hook to the handle of the bucket which, filled with cement, was passed through the hole from time to time, and at a tug on the rope was pulled up. The tunnel rose vertically, and I could hear the occasional sound of a voice drifting down from far above, where other humans were engaged in the mysteries of their craft. I had a distinct feeling that here at the base of this well I was cut off from the world and that my situation was not unlike being buried alive — all I needed to complete the impression was a load or two of earth dropped on my head. The noise of the mixer and the remarks of the men working with the shovels filtered in, and at intervals a ghostly hand clutching a bucket of cement would appear. I could not stand erect, for the floor of the shaft sloped inward forming a conical funnel of stone. This, splashed from time to time with cement due to the tilt of my bucket, formed a very poor base for my feet. It had the advantage, though, that once the bucket had began its ascent I could sit down; in fact there wasn't much choice in the matter, as otherwise I would have had to stand at the bottom of the cone with my feet in the ultimate depth of the pit and my head and shoulders trying to make contact with the wall. It was very uncomfortable, but as I inspected my hands, which by now had a protective coating of wet cement, I was thankful indeed that the shovel was no longer in their grip.

The hours passed, the buckets of cement appeared at the

hole and disappeared up the wall in a continuous chain, and it was now four o'clock in the morning. Except for the fact that my thighs were cold from reclining against the wall as each bucket ascended, I was getting on well enough. However, I must have been half asleep from exhaustion — for I hardly heard the sudden shout from the rim of the pit before something descended with the impact of what seemed to be a ton of bricks on my skull. I keeled over in the muck, wondering what had hit me. In the course of this floundering and groping, my hand came in contact with a foreign substance, a two-foot-long piece of lumber. Someone up above had kicked it over the edge by mistake and it had dropped like a javelin, until it connected in a glancing blow with my head and bounced off. I had been sitting on the edge of the funnel, leaning forward and smoking the one cigarette I had left, and now, semiconscious, my first thought was one of annoyance that I'd lost it.

Others had heard the shout and, no doubt, the sound of the blow, for there was a sudden silence outside and then one of the men came to the aperture at my side and called in. I was only able to moan faintly in reply, and seeing me doubled up, my body curved in a bow in the funnel, he shouted for help. There was a rush of feet and quickly the hole was filled with faces peering in. However, once the first shock of the blow had passed I recovered sufficiently to make my way out under my own steam, with the assistance of several willing hands that grasped my shoulders and arms as I emerged and laid me down on the ground as my legs gave way under me. For the first time I ran my fingers carefully over my skull and found a considerable bump there, and the flesh badly cut. Indeed, had the plank struck me directly I almost certainly would have been killed.

The foreman came over, full of concern, and asked what had happened. He felt my head and then, when he had assured himself of the extent of my injuries, told two or three of the men to move me over to his hut, where I was placed in a chair to relax.

The foreman was most solicitous. He may have been motivated partly by sympathy, and partly by the thought that as someone must have been negligent he might be held responsible. At all events, he arranged for a car to take me to the hospital and personally escorted me to the vehicle when it came, supporting my weight with his arm.

"Come back when you're okay," was his parting injunction. "We'll give you some other job, maybe helping out with the time sheets or something . . ."

It was a considerate gesture, and in spite of my head I was rational enough to be surprised and encouraged by the offer, for ever since I'd been hurt I had been thinking that this was the end of trying to justify myself in the docks. He sent one of the men with me in the car and I was admitted for emergency treatment and afterwards put to bed. It was about five o'clock in the morning and the dawn was beginning to show a faint tissue of light against the black sky.

They did not keep me long at the hospital. Later that morning I was out, my trousers sponged off the best way I could, my coat which I had placed aside while working forming an effective contrast in cleanliness to the cement-striped pants. A large white bandage was wound round my head, in the manner of some Oriental potentate wearing a turban, but apart from a minor drumbeat of pain every time the blood pulsed through my skull, I felt considerably better. When I reached the dormitory again, my Irish friends besieged me with questions. What had happened? Was I badly hurt? Well, I said, someone had lowered a plank on my head in the docks. All were profuse in expressions of sympathy. Quite possibly my friends had a record of violence and slaughter behind them — the struggle for independence in Ireland had been savage and long — but the fact remained that they were very kind to me. When one has nothing, small mercies are of vast consequence.

I was not particularly concerned about money, for my immediate expenses were low. Even had I wanted to, I could not have gone back to the docks, for it was to be several days before I would be sufficiently recovered.

Finally, after several days of lying on my bed, I got in touch with the Mounted Police headquarters and learned that my application had been approved. My relief was inexpressible. From this point the road was clear — I went to the headquarters and was issued with a transportation warrant to take me to Ottawa that same afternoon. There was a word or two with Staff-Sergeant Salt, a few curious stares at the bandage on my head from persons passing by in the office, but eventually I was back again in the dormitory, prepared to pack my few odds and ends and take my departure. Three of the Irishmen were there. In concert, they announced that they would accompany me to the station and see me off on the train.

When we arrived at the station there was a few minutes' delay and a last exchange of words with my friends while the train waited to pull out for Ottawa. I swung myself on board as the wheels began to gather momentum. On the platform the three Irishmen waved farewell and then vanished as the cars moved out of the depot. Walking down the corridors I found a seat and, placing my suitcase in the rack, sat down to relax. As I looked out of the window the clacking wheels gradually accelerated their tempo until it was lost in a muffled torrent of sound, and the city disappeared by degrees, giving way at last to the green of the fields and the blue and white sky where it sloped to the hills in the distance.

The ride lasted about three hours, though it seemed much shorter. As I walked into the street from the station the tall, stately buildings rose on each side of the square, the Houses of Parliament gracing a rise in the foreground. From their center the clock tower, a long slender pinnacle, stretched like a pointing finger toward the sky. It made a pleasant picture, clear and sharp against the light, filled with quiet beauty.

It was near suppertime and I was hungry — if I hurried I might make it in time to the barracks. The thought of a good meal filled me with pleasure. I smiled to myself; it was odd that even a commonplace thing such as food should seem so attractive and of so great a consequence. But then, before, I'd never had to think where the next meal was coming from; when there was a doubt it changed one's perspective. There was no question about it, the evening was golden and next day and every day in succession there'd be breakfast, lunch, and then dinner!

8

~~~~~~~~

The Red Serge

I WONDER sometimes what my reaction would have been if I had joined the Mounted Police straight from the comforts of home; I suppose that I might have questioned the bare, stark existence, the hard beds, the rigid discipline and the rough, boisterous ways of some of my companions. As it was I had been broken in, and therefore fitted like a finger in a glove into my surroundings. Certainly I would have doubted the sense of getting up every morning at 6 A.M. to attend stables, and then after a hurried breakfast working the rest of the day at various tasks — some of them extremely frustrating to the ego — under the stern eyes of various non-commissioned officers, none of whom had any great opinion of my abilities. Even the salary of $60 a month would, in all probability, have seemed insufficient to make up for the invective that was, from time to time, hurled in my direction. But $60 a month seemed quite a lot after licking the bottom of the pot and finding it empty, and the general atmosphere of the barrack room was not much different from life in the French Army — my bed was at least dry, and not a wet, bloodstained stretcher. Hard though the training was and unappreciated at the time, it was due only to my first mentors and those who afterwards took their place that eventually I came to know something about what had to be done, and, when I look back at them now, I am very grateful indeed for what I was taught.

The barracks were on the banks of the Rideau Canal about a mile and a half from the depot where the train had dropped me, and consisted of a long, low single-story building that looked rather like a large warehouse made of planking — the stables, rather smaller structures, being in close proximity nearby. The buildings made up the headquarters of "N" Division, situated at that time at Lansdowne Park. The main headquarters of the Force was some distance away, on Rideau Street, in downtown Ottawa.

Behind the barracks was a big open space, a long sweep of turf, and in the distance a huge semicircular amphitheater where, tier by tier, rose the wooden seats of the Exhibition Grounds. On three sides the houses of the city cut the blue of the sky in a broken line of rooftops, and on the fourth trees glinted in the sunshine, stretching away on each side of the canal. Where the green, grassy field swept away to the left in front of the amphitheater and met one of the main thoroughfares that bisected the city, a massive stone bridge ascended in an arch over the canal, its farther end disappearing in a wooded grove that verged on the water. In front of the barracks, a few steps away, the calm, shadowy canal shone like a ribbon of glass right and left, reflecting the pink and gold of the clouds as they rolled by overhead. Then it passed out of sight, under the bridge on the one hand, and on the other through the locks close by the Parliament buildings to lose itself in the Ottawa River.

It was a place of peace after the strain and sweat of the Montreal docks. The sun sank lower, creeping toward the roof of the barracks, the flame of its passage slowly fading to end in a surge of deep crimson, a background of red that would be somehow symbolical. The scarlet jacket! As evening came on the sky would become the color of the Force's famous tunic, the symbol that exactly fifty years before had moved quietly into the vast plains of the West and there, slowly but surely, had opened the land for the broad wheels of progress. At the time this was all I knew about the Royal Canadian Mounted Police, but what I had read was firmly etched on my mind — flat, open country with here and there a solitary hill, campfires and Indians, and superimposed on the canvas a big, shadowy figure on horseback that stood clad in its red coat, alone, self-sufficient, a sentinel guarding a world that stretched into limbo. It was not much in the way of knowledge perhaps but it was enough to introduce a stranger such as I. The years to come would fill in the picture.

This is not the story of the Mounted Police but of something far less important, one man's career. Much has been written about the Force, and to do justice to its heritage would require a long and separate journey. Even then it would be one that has been extensively traveled already; its much trodden path is well known. But for those in other lands who, like myself at that time, know little about it, the design of those past years should be brushed in quickly.

The Force has a history that spreads from a small drop of scarlet — small, that is, in the immensity of its surroundings — that tinted the soil in the vicinity of what is now Winnipeg, midway across Canada, in May 1873. From there as time passed it spread without fanfare across the length and breadth of the nation until, diffused by time and the always growing scope of its responsibilities, it stretched from sea to sea; east and west to the Pacific and Atlantic oceans, north to the far reaches of the Polar sea, south to the international boundary between Canada and the United States, until it became, as it is in the present day and age, the main instrument of justice in Canada as a whole and the national law enforcement agency. From that first faint spot on the map marking its birthplace, and from the initial contingent of approximately three hundred men who, in 1874, rode into the uncharted territory of the Canadian West, then empty of civilization and inhabited only by hostile Indian bands and desperate, lawless elements, the Northwest Mounted Police grew until it now numbers — as the Royal Canadian Mounted Police — about six thousand five hundred uniformed officers and men with more than two thousand office and other civilian staff. In the area it looks after — as large as the United States of America and about twice the size of Europe — it is charged with the enforcement of all Federal laws, the policing of eight of the ten provinces of Canada insofar as the Criminal Code and local statutes are concerned, the patrolling of the far North and Arctic areas to the margins of the Pole, the administration of justice in a great many cities, towns and villages over all Canada, and the safeguarding of internal security and the investigation of espionage activities on the part of foreign powers.

To single out any one of these duties as more important than another would be as difficult as to select one man's name and say that he alone was of supreme importance in leading it to its present distinction. Rather, it is the work of each component unit which to this day has set the standard of the whole. The red serge! It was something even to see it, much more to wear it, a scarlet talisman to cover one along all the strange paths of adventure of the body and spirit — the distant trails of the far North with their challenge of endurance, the long roads of loneliness that seemed to lead into nowhere, the faint approaches to understanding as one traversed the highways and byways, the weight of the effort as this thing bound itself to one, becoming heavier and heavier, until one emerged in the end strong and sure at the last. It was one thing to wear the red serge and quite another to fill it. It took a long time.

I was to learn all this later though; that first day the door was beckoning and I went in. After passing down a short corridor I found myself in a large room about seventy-five feet in length and nearly half as broad, in which a number of men were taking their ease. There were about fifteen beds on each side of the room — and after reporting to the Corporal in charge, I was assigned to one of them. A number of lights without shades hung down from the ceiling. It was very much like the dormitory I'd occupied in Montreal, except that it was on a larger scale with items of uniform neatly folded on shelves and different types of equipment, such as rifles, Sam Browne belts and revolvers, giving it a distinctly military look which was emphasized by the fact that it was scrupulously clean. To right and left of the uniforms, which I saw on closer inspection consisted of tunics, one red and one brown, were a pair of long brown leather boots with spurs on their heels and, fitting snugly between them on top of the tunics, a pointed Stetson hat which was circled with a narrow brown leather band. At the edge of each shelf a white cardboard square was tacked which supplied information regarding the occupant of the bed — name, regimental number and rank — and from two pegs below it a uniform belt and revolver hung down. At the foot of the bed a leather rifle scabbard was attached to its frame with the butt of a Lee-Enfield carbine sticking out.

There were about twenty men in the room, and later I was to find that they came from all sectors of the community — some were adventurers from different parts of the world, others from nearer home — mechanics, office workers, truck drivers, farm hands. A few had held commissions in the war and after being demobilized had, like myself, found their way to the Mounted Police, the flotsam and jetsam of those difficult years. Quite a few were ex-soldiers or sailors, a tough hard-bitten bunch with a good deal of life already behind them and well able to handle the stresses and strains of the new life they'd chosen. I soon found myself at home in their midst.

About fifteen minutes after my arrival suppertime came and I followed the others to another large, bare room containing a big mushroom stove and some long tables and benches. On the tables places were set out containing knives and forks, mugs and plates, but except for an occasional salt or pepper pot they were otherwise devoid of decoration. Doing as the others did, I picked up a plate and made my way to an opening in the wall — the door to the kitchen — from which food was being handed out, and then having received my share made my way back to the table. My meal that first night was very welcome, due to the uncertainties of the last several days. Later that evening as I crawled between the blankets — there were no sheets on the bed — I had this same sense of deep pleasure, a feeling that I'd at last found a place in which I could sink my roots and at least for a time find haven.

I'd been more fortunate than I knew in having been accepted as a member of the Force. In 1923 the Royal Canadian Mounted Police was in a transition stage between the old and the new, and there could not have been many recruits who were being taken on. Up until six years before it had been responsible for the policing of the old West — those Northwest Territories which, in 1905, became the provinces of Saskatchewan and Alberta — and that was where its reputation had been gained on the vast stretches of prairie that swept, broad, flat and unpeopled except for roving Indians and the occasional white settler, to the foothills of the Rocky Mountains close to where British Columbia begins. Then, during the war, with its strength depleted by drafts from its ranks sent as reinforcements to France and Siberia and by men leaving individually for the fighting overseas, the strength fell from about six hundred and fifty in 1917 to approximately three hundred the next year. In 1923, following various fluctuations, it had again risen to slightly more than eleven hundred men — now acting on a federal basis across Canada, its previous responsibilities in Saskatchewan and Alberta having been taken over by the provincial police forces which had been formed in 1917. The old days had gone but the Royal Canadian Mounted Police was at the dawn of a new and mechanized era in which it would increase in stature and size and gain added renown.

The horse, destined to be retained for ceremonial duties and for training purposes, was soon to fade into oblivion as a means of conveyance in the field, giving way to the swifter cars and planes of the modern world. However, when I joined in 1923, horses were still very much a part of our life. We groomed them when we got up in the morning, rode them during the day, groomed them again at noon and evening, bedded them down at night, and from time to time dreamed of them when we tossed and turned in fitful slumber as the snow came down outside. It was very cold in the winter. The heating arrangements were quite inadequate; the freezing breath of the frost seeped in through various chinks and openings, and unless one had been fortunate enough to get a bed close to one of the black iron stoves it was difficult to keep warm. A bottle of ink froze in my suitcase and broke, spilling its contents on the few articles of clothing I possessed when the liquid thawed with the coming of spring.

The morning after my arrival we were awakened by the night guard at reveille and, crawling out of bed, assembled outside the building twenty-five minutes later for our names to be called by the duty N.C.O., and then to make our way to the stables to attend to the horses. As I had no uniform I was told to fall in behind the parade and remain there after it had marched off. As the men disappeared in the early morning light, a broom was handed to me and I was informed that until further notice I was to perform the duties of Room Orderly, which I soon found to consist of sweeping the barrack room and keeping it clean, a task requiring no great amount of energy or exertion.

The next thing was to report to the Sergeant-Major so that my presence could be officially recognized. I had not seen any of the senior non-commissioned officers up to this point and wondered what to expect. I found him sitting in his office, an aristocratic-looking individual wearing the same uniform that I'd seen on the Corporal at Montreal except that he had a blue coat. There was a string of decorations on his chest, among which I recognized the Military Cross — obviously he was an ex-officer from the war.

He asked me my name and what I'd been doing, and I gave him a brief account of how I'd got there.

"Well, we'll have to get you some kit so that you can make yourself useful — what have you done to your head?"

I was still wearing the bandage.

"Plank hit me on the head, sir, in Montreal docks — busted it open."

He had a finely chiseled, patrician nose, and looked down it at the table.

"Well, I suppose you're all right — you'll have to have a medical as soon as we can arrange it," he said, "and after that you'll have to go to headquarters so that you can be sworn in. That's all for the time being, I'll see that someone gets in touch with you once we've fixed it up with the doctor."

"Thank you, sir."

I turned about and went out. The interview hadn't been very rewarding but the Sergeant-Major had impressed me, and at least it was a sign that someone knew I was there; up to that moment I had been feeling like a dog that had sneaked in but was not quite sure of its reception or whether it would be given a home. The broom was waiting for me when I got back to the barrack room and I was given a quantity of wet tea leaves to keep the dust on the floor. While the men were out exercising the horses I swept the room industriously, hoping to make a satisfactory impression if anyone came in. It was a pleasant interlude — almost a holiday after the last week or two — and I found myself singing. After a while, as I seemed to be making considerable headway with the broom and there did not seem to be much point in completing my task and then having nothing to do, I decided that a rest would do me no harm, and I sat down to read a newspaper and to contemplate my lot.

Just as I did so there was the sound of approaching footsteps in the passage outside and before I could pick up the broom and stand up the door was flung open by the Sergeant-Major to make way for the Medical Officer, who was engaged on one of his periodical tours of inspection. Although I had no idea who the officer was, the sudden appearance of the Sergeant-Major was sufficient to galvanize me into action. Leaping smartly to my feet, I commenced wielding the broom again with a degree of industry that caused the end of the room I was in to be enveloped in dust until it took on all the worst aspects of a London fog. I had forgotten all about the tea leaves. The Sergeant-Major and the Medical Officer had passed by exchanging remarks, and I was under the impression that I was doing well and would, no doubt, merit a word of praise as they went by on their return. But it was not to be. They stopped, turned, and no doubt clenching their teeth against the cloud of dust that billowed toward them, made their way back. In the meantime, seeing that I was now under observation, I redoubled my efforts until I must have looked like a dancing dust dervish to their startled eyes. My dense fog halted the Medical Officer, but the Sergeant-Major gallantly tried to make his way on.

"Here, wait a minute, Sergeant-Major," the Medical Officer said. "Who's this you've got here?"

"New recruit, sir — came in last night."

"Well, you'd better show him how to use a broom. He'll have us all dead with disease if he goes on like that!" Then, turning to me, "Give the Sergeant-Major your broom, young man, we can't have you kicking up all those germs!"

The Sergeant-Major advanced in my direction, an expression of acute displeasure on his face, his lips turned down, the high-bridged nose that had so impressed me wrinkling in disgust. I had stopped my labors and the storm I had created was settling and forming a light gray film on his highly polished boots. Obviously he was someone who took great care of his personal appearance, for he brushed at his coat and breeches with his hands as he made his way forward to where I was standing, externally shrouded in dust and internally sunk in deep gloom at the unexpected reaction my well-meaning industry had caused.

The Sergeant-Major deprived me of the broom and waved it gently like a wand in the air.

"Here, I'll show you," he said, fixing me with a cold, baleful look. "You do it like this — first spread the tea leaves on the floor, then gently sweep them up." He suited his actions to his words while the Medical Officer watched him admiringly, each movement of the broom filled with grace as it described a series of slow arcs in the air, its extremity hardly touching the floor as it descended and rose at the end of each stroke. There was something in his eye, though, that boded no good for my future and brought me back to reality very quickly indeed.

"You see, that's the way." He handed the broom back to me. "Now, carry on . . ." Taking no further notice, he accompanied the Medical Officer to the door and went out.

I was abashed. The Medical Officer had either simply failed to respect the dignity of so senior a non-commissioned officer or had such a mischievous sense of humor that it amused him to see the Sergeant-Major sweeping the floor. One thing that I had learned, though, was that the Sergeant-Major could stoop from his exalted position without losing face. He was certainly someone to respect, and at twenty-one this made quite an impression on me.

The work at "N" Division was routine. The place was a training depot, and also a reserve of manpower from which one might be sent elsewhere on duty. Much of the time was spent in teaching us to ride and in exercising the horses with periods of fatigue duty in between. The day began with early morning stables during which the straw that had been used for bedding was cleaned out and the horses groomed until they were spotless and shining, taken to water, and fed. Then came breakfast and afterwards the morning exercise ride through the streets of the city for those skilled in the handling of horses, while recruits like myself who knew little or nothing about riding had to learn the rudiments of the art in the vicinity of the stables. Our tutor was a rough-riding Staff-Sergeant who had been in one of the famous English cavalry regiments. The rest of the day was filled in with lectures on criminal investigation and first aid and drill. This last caused me no difficulty. I'd had some of it in the Officer's Training Corps at school and was able to hold my own.

There was no doubt that the course of riding instruction was an arduous one, necessitating a good deal of bareback jumping, and most of us took many falls. However this was led up to by degrees and as time went on we learned two things — how to stick on a horse, and that if one fell off one had to get up and try again, whatever the hurt to oneself. After a while we came to accept bruises and strains as a natural thing and to take pride in passing them off. It was excellent training, and later, when we went out into active police work, it was destined to bear fruit. Whether so designed or not, it served another useful purpose — to prune any feeling of egotism to a proper degree of insignificance, so that the new vine could then be trained up. The horse was very definitely the primary consideration, the recruit something very subsidiary indeed. One anecdote went the rounds to the effect that once when one of the men was thrown off, breaking his leg in the process and silently biting his lips in agony on the ground, the riding instructor rode over to him and bending down said, "Don't worry, Smithers, your horse is all right!" Smithers had to refrain from comment despite a violent inclination to give expression to his thoughts! While the instructor's remark became a byword, used indiscriminately with a great deal of laughter when anyone afterwards hurt himself, what the training did as the months went on was to teach us the importance of durability, and that despite hard knocks, one should not give up. If everything else had been taken away, this alone would have been worthwhile.

Time passed — occasionally men came and went, either a recruit who had joined from the eastern areas of Canada, or a man transferred to the West or to some detachment in Ontario or Quebec. Day after day the same routine continued, varied at intervals by periods of duty as night guard or stable orderly when one was excused from attending parades. Then, as night guard, one spent the hours of darkness touring the premises, on the lookout for fire and making sure that all those who were not on leave of absence were present at "Last Post" — 10:30 P.M. — and making a note of the names of defaulters. Ordinarily we all had to be in by this time, when the lights in the sleeping quarters were extinguished, but permission could be obtained provided satisfactory reasons were given to be out until 1:30 A.M., or occasionally until reveille when one had to report back in time for stable parade. If a man was late off pass he was placed under arrest and had to answer for his delinquency before the Officer Commanding when, unless he had a watertight excuse, he would be fined several days' pay or confined to barracks for a given period of time, or both. Very serious offences were punishable by imprisonment with hard labor.

Stable orderly, as the words imply, was merely a matter of looking after the stables and ensuring that they were suitable for inspection at any moment of the day. For this one was armed with a stiff broom and shovel, and spent the day getting horse manure out of sight. With the number of horses there were, this was a task that required a considerable application of energy, for if the stables were dirty when an inspecting officer or N.C.O. arrived it might bring unpleasant consequences. Surrounded by the horses all day, by evening one had quite a distinctive aroma of one's own which a good bath could remove from one's person — but not from one's clothes.

"N" Division was only one very small link in the nation-wide chain of the Force; elsewhere investigational activities went on in the various settled areas of Canada and in the far North. As at that time the Mounted Police dealt exclusively with the enforcement of the federal laws, the work related for the most part to Customs inquiries, offenses against the mails, the apprehension of narcotic peddlers and smugglers, investigation of applications for naturalization, and a variety of other duties — when called upon by departments of the Federal Government — which were either outside the jurisdiction of the local provincial police forces or required the assistance of the R.C.M.P. Included among these was the provision of guards at government buildings where funds were kept or collected; the supervision of pari-mutuel machines at racetracks as a precaution against fraud; ensuring that the requirements of the Explosives Act were properly carried out so that appropriate precautions were taken; supplying escorts on harvest trains bound for the Canadian West to maintain order and prevent misbehavior; the searching out of stills and the prosecution of offenders who, by making liquor illegally, tried to defeat the inland revenue laws; the stationing of men at Indian Reserves; and — something that was to prove of large-scale importance as the years went on — the investigation of the activities of the Communist Party of Canada, which, following the formation of the Third International at Moscow in 1917, had come into being a few years before.

In 1923 the focus of expansion of the R.C.M.P. was to the farthest areas of the North, where detachments were being established, one by one, in regions inhabited only by traders, trappers, missionaries and Indians, and on the

Arctic coast and beyond by wandering tribes of Eskimos, most of whom had seldom seen a white man and had no knowledge of any land but their own. As the Force had gained strength through its earlier years until it became the dominant factor in providing safety for the settlers and preventing bloodshed among the Indians on the Western prairies, so, during the first two decades of the twentieth century it had begun to increase its scope and to penetrate the uninhabited regions of the North, its detachments sprinkled from Ellesmere Island, a few hundred miles from the Pole, to the lands south and west that form the Arctic archipelago. Earlier it had spread through the Yukon Territory, where during the Gold Rush in 1898 it had maintained law and order among the wilder elements who had invaded the country from various parts of the globe. East of the Yukon, from the Sixtieth Parallel — the boundary of the settled areas of the provinces — it presided over a wilderness hidden in the winter by raging storms and blizzards that swept down continually, where the sun for months was seldom seen and then blazed endlessly for months when summer came.

The Mounted Police was filled with a strange assortment of characters when I first joined. Since its inception in 1873 it had drawn all sorts of persons of unusual background from near and far, who were prompted mainly by a sense of adventure and a wish to challenge life. In many cases not much was known about their origins, and all that was asked was that they fulfill their obligations. It was necessary to produce a couple of references, give the appearance of some force of character or resolution, measure up to the physical requirements of the service, and then sign on. If, after a while, it became obvious that the recruit did not possess the necessary stamina, he was speedily weeded out and discharged as unsuitable. Then, too, he could be dismissed as the result of misdemeanors he had committed after any penalties that had been imposed had been paid.

Sometimes an individual who wanted to sever his connection with the Force voluntarily was allowed to purchase his discharge, but applications were few and far between, partly, perhaps, because the small salary made it difficult to produce the money, and then most of the men were quite content to serve their three years. The turnover at the end of the period of enlistment was quite large. The fact that marriage was not allowed until a minimum of seven years had been served may have had a bearing on this. Sometimes a man would disregard the regulations and take a wife to himself without benefit of approval, but such infringements were cause for instant dismissal. It was a hard regulation for those men who had been stationed in places where they seldom saw a white woman and therefore on return to civilization were doubly susceptible, but the nature of the work in the outlying areas did not allow for the presence of women and it was necessary, in any case, to retain sufficient single men to give mobility to the Force.

There were a number of younger sons of the aristocracy of England who had chosen the hard road of policing the West for special reasons or simply because in those years there was not much excitement at home. Even in 1923 there were some of them around; a Corporal I was later stationed with inherited a baronetcy and departed when his term of service expired to manage the ancestral estates which had been left to him by his father.

"N" Division was staffed by two Inspectors — the commissioned ranks started at Inspector — a Sergeant-Major, a couple of Staff-Sergeants, two or three Sergeants and Corporals, and about thirty Constables. The commissioned officers were unapproachable except through the routine channel of the Sergeant-Major, who, in all executive matters, assumed a vast degree of importance and whose word was law. Both the Inspectors had, however, gained their promotion through the ranks, so that they were not only fully versed in all phases of the work, but also had a complete understanding of the problems of the men under their command. Despite the strict discipline, there was, therefore, a common bond of sympathy between the men — some of whom had held positions of authority themselves — and the officers, based on respect and on this understanding of the various difficulties shared. While officers could be appointed to commissioned rank from outside the Force, the large majority of the executive staff were promoted from the lesser ranks. Generally speaking those who were appointed to commissions without passing through the ranks were graduates of the Royal Military College at Kingston, or those who had some special qualifications which fitted them for the task.

The main training establishment of the Force was at Regina, Saskatchewan, nearly two thousand miles west. Ordinarily most recruits were sent there, but there were a few exceptions and I was one. I was well content to stay where I was. From what I'd heard of Regina it was no place to go, and many wild stories circulated among the men regarding the disciplinary pains suffered by recruits. It was a much larger establishment than "N" Division and until 1920, when the Force achieved nationwide jurisdiction in federal matters, had been the headquarters of the Royal Northwest Mounted Police. Now, with the name changed to Royal Canadian Mounted Police, all administrative matters were dealt with from the new headquarters at Ottawa. From there orders were dispatched to the outlying points, the Divisions, to be sent on again to Sub-Divisions and detachments lightly spotted here and there in different areas of the land.

Openings in the field were few and far between and only available when some detachment member left the Force or was transferred to other duties. Insofar as we were concerned the situation remained static, and the interminable round of grooming horses, exercising them, and doing fatigues went on day after day, to be relieved once a week when an inspection was made by the Commissioner or an Assistant Commissioner from headquarters, deputized in his place for this purpose. Then we all stood at the foot of our beds in the full dress scarlet uniform of the Force, every article of kit shined to the last possible pitch of perfection.

Occasionally diverting incidents occurred on these occasions, such as when a night guard who on any other day would have been left peacefully sleeping had been awakened just before the Commissioner arrived. Having made his bed and laid out his accouterments in the required manner, he had taken refuge in a small cubbyhole in the bathroom in which brooms and cleaning materials were kept. Closing the door and wearing only the khaki shirt he had slept in, the night guard waited in the dark until the steps of the inspection party would pass by and supply the signal which would allow him to go back to bed. Ordinarily the cubbyhole was a safe enough refuge, as when this type of high level inspection was made the Commissioner did not interest himself in the toilet facilities — which he left to the attention of others — but on this particular day for some unexplainable reason he decided to look in.

When the night guard heard the steps halt and the door to the bathroom open, he was panic-stricken and backed farther and farther into the dark enclosure he was in, hoping the black obscurity of his surroundings would hide him. It was not to be, however. In his state of anxiety he had forgotten that the main power switch for the barracks was situated on the farthest wall. As the guard retreated, his posterior connected with the open prongs. There was a howl, a smell of burning flesh and cloth and, like an arrow from a bow, the guard shot through the door, clutching his wounded seat in both hands and calling on heaven to witness his misfortune in the strongest and loudest possible terms!

At this crucial moment the Commissioner was just on the point of passing the door of the cubbyhole but halted his progress when the night guard suddenly presented himself, like an apparition before him, an uncontrollable stream of bad language issuing from his lips. The Commissioner went on and came back, passing again on his way to the door, paying no attention whatever, perhaps because he suddenly seemed to be afflicted with a bad fit of coughing. When the night guard had pulled himself together he crept out of the bathroom and made his way back to his bed, where he regaled his comrades with a frenzied account of what had occurred.

The white glistening hills of the Gatineau, rising a few miles away to the north in Quebec, were a source of unfailing delight. The cold, sharp, sub-zero air formed a pleasant and effective contrast to the tropics I had previously known. With the healthy outdoor life we were leading, there had been no recurrence of the malaria from which I had suffered in India and its weakening effects had now gone. Gradually, week by week, I had filled out physically, the fits of depression which had accompanied the disease had disappeared and now I was ready to embark on something else. There was so much of Canada to see and gain experience in that I was beginning to strain at the chains. I was beginning to forget the hard road I had traveled and the difficulties I had been up against.

Outside the barracks, winter sat ever more squarely on the buildings. The snow built its ramparts higher and higher, the trees were stark and bare — heavy only with frost — as a blizzard swept down, the wind screaming against the windows, rattling and shaking them in its rage. Except for an occasional visit to town to take in a show we were in a small, cramped world of our own. Even the horses seemed to share the sense of monotony, biting each other over the low, intervening walls of their stalls and then, on a fine day when the sun shone, prancing and sidestepping here and there when they were taken outside. Whether it was winter or not they had an unpleasant habit of trying to stand on our feet as their necks and forequarters were groomed, looking at us maliciously out of the corners of their eyes as their hooves came down armed with the sharp steel spikes of their shoes — to miss by an inch as we hastily leaped aside. Once in a while someone was unlucky, the pain and agony causing him to jump around, hugging his knee in his arms, swearing and cursing, while tears welled in his eyes.

Christmas came and went, and the New Year in all its freshness began. One day Bill, a Corporal who now occupied the next bed to me, said something that was to have far-reaching consequences for us both. We were discussing what chance there was of getting out on detachment once the summer arrived.

"It looks as though we'll be stuck here," Bill said. "It may be quite a time before any vacancy turns up. What d'you say to volunteering for the North? I hear it's pretty rough up there but maybe it's not as bad as it sounds. I'm game to have a go at it if you are — they'll be asking for names any day now."

I had heard of northern service but had not given it very serious thought — the few things I had been told about it were not encouraging, and the work called for extreme hardships in the ultimate depths of the wilderness where the temperature dropped in winter to sixty degrees below zero. I knew that once a year volunteers were called for and that no one was sent compulsorily on this type of duty because of the arduous conditions that prevailed. Besides, one had to be temperamentally suited to existing in very close association with the few companions one would have, cut off from any pleasures to be found in civilized life. One thing was certain — it would mean embarking on another adventure into the back of beyond if I went.

"You mean the Mackenzie River, I suppose?"

"Well, yes. Either that or the Western Arctic or one of those places north of Hudson Bay — there's quite a few detachments up there. Or they might send us to the Yukon. Once you apply you won't get any choice, it all depends on what openings there are."

"Let's think it over a bit. A week or so shouldn't matter much and it'll give us time to make up our minds . . ."

Actually nearly a month passed by before we heard any more about it. Then a notice came round asking if anyone wanted to volunteer for northern service. The weather was getting warmer with spring just around the corner. This and the days getting longer had been sufficient to influence me. Bill and I and three or four others applied and filled in the necessary forms.

In time the Sergeant-Major told us that we'd been accepted and that Bill was to go to the Yukon while my destination was the Mackenzie River, a pencil streak of black on the map stretching into the Arctic from a point north of Edmonton, three thousand miles away and then on for more than another thousand miles. To the west of the Mackenzie lay the Yukon, separated from it by the northern range of the Rocky Mountains; to the east, the barren lands of Keewatin and Mackenzie reached into the unknown, to Hudson Bay and beyond. And this was only half of it! From the mainland shores of the Arctic another whole world lay between them and the Pole! Somewhere along the pencil streak on the map — rather like a single hair on a bald man's head — I was to be stationed at one of the small, black pinpointed dots! All at once what I had done came home to me. This, I thought, will really be farther away than anything; even the headwaters of the Brahmaputra had some contact from time to time with Dibrugarh by river boat. On the Mackenzie there'd be nothing. The distances were tremendous — a hundred miles a mere step, five hundred little more than a long stride.

The Land of the Midnight Sun! What would I find there?

How would I make out? Would I have the mental and physical strength to measure up to what was expected of me and what I expected of myself? What happened if one got sick? There'd be no help at hand and one would be entirely cut off. The questions came flocking through the days and the nights, repetitious, a continual circling of the mind, a flame that danced and blazed as I lay awake, smoking cigarettes in the darkness as the others slept. What a great adventure it would be! I was pretty green and come what may there'd be something new to discover, something that perhaps lay hiding in that vast, forbidding country waiting only to be found.

As summer burst into flower and the ice retreated from the rivers of the North, Bill left for the Yukon and I for the Mackenzie River, following our different routes. The past year had been a pleasant interlude, but the Mounted Police had set the pattern within which I would grow up.

9

~~~~~~~~

World Without End

"WE HAVE traveled about two hundred miles on dog meat and still have about a hundred miles to go . . ." The date is February 3, 1911, the temperature is twenty-six degrees below zero, and this is an extract from the diary of the lost Fitzgerald patrol, all four members of which died of starvation and exposure. At the time it was written they had only a few more days to live.

They were close to their end in the Mackenzie Mountains and had killed most of their dogs and eaten them in order to survive. One man had frozen his fingers; all were in the last stages of exhaustion, mere walking skeletons due to lack of food. The toboggan that the dogs had pulled during the last days had been discarded, for now that the provisions were gone there was no load to carry.

The patrol had left Fort McPherson, a short distance beyond the Arctic Circle, on December 21, 1910, to make their way over the mountains to Dawson, three hundred miles away as the crow flies, in the Yukon. Inspector Fitzgerald was in charge and with him were Constables Taylor and Kinney, and Special Constable Carter. The journey had been made by others before and Fitzgerald and his party did not anticipate any trouble. It was cold when they set out from McPherson, the temperature steady at twenty-one below, with a heavy mist and light snow falling on the river up which they would travel before they reached the foothills, a short distance away.

It was much longer than three hundred miles through the snow-covered mountains, a total distance of nearly five hundred long, weary miles in all. There, the trail wound like a snake, probing here and there as it climbed higher and higher. Soon the world would be thigh deep in snow, men and dogs hauling together at the sleds as they made the ascent. Some days they made ten miles, some fifteen, occasionally twenty. It was getting colder, too. On January 8, a Sunday, it was sixty-four below, the going was heavy and nine miles was the best they could do. That night they camped on the Little Wind River, one of the channels of ice up which they would travel in the course of their journey. Somewhere, near where it rose, they would find Forrest Creek, which led over the height of land into the Yukon, and then they would be over the glacier and the Wind-Hart Divide with the back of the distance broken and on the downgrade of the frozen creeks, streams and rivers that wound into Dawson.

It was a maze of tributaries near the top of the mountains. Carter was the guide. He had come once before from Dawson over the trail and thought that he knew it, but one creek looked much like another in its mantle of snow and, when they got close to the pass, the streams led off to nowhere. Forrest Creek, the path through the wilderness that would have led them to safety, lay shrinking and hidden in the falling snow and the mist. First they tried one creek, then another, then a third but all with an equal lack of success. Then on January 14, just as they were at the worst of their predicament, a blizzard struck, holding them motionless.

Food for the men and the dogs was beginning to get very short — it soon would be gone. They searched again and, all in all, it took them a week. Then, with their last hope gone, they decided to return over the back-breaking miles they had come.

All they had left was some dried fish and tea. Very soon they'd have to start killing the dogs so that the others could be fed; then they'd have to eat them themselves. The slow journey went on. On Monday, January 30, it was fifty-one below, twelve days since they'd left the head of the Little Wind River, and they'd eaten seven of the dogs, feeding the others the little dried fish that remained. "All hands feeling sick, supposed to be from eating dog's liver. Fourteen miles," the diary says.

Then the last day. "Forty-eight below. Saturday, February 5 — Fine with strong S.E. wind. Left camp at 7:15 A.M.; nooned an hour and camped about eight miles further down. Just after noon I broke through the ice and had to make fire; found one foot slightly frozen. Killed another dog tonight; have only five dogs now and can only go a few miles a day; everybody breaking out on the body and skin peeling off. Eight miles."

And then nothing else is recorded; the diary does not show what happened in the next few days. The bodies were found the following spring by Corporal Dempster, one of the famous dog travelers of the North who had been sent in charge of a search party from Dawson. Constables Taylor and Kinney were in one place and Special Constable Carter and Inspector Fitzgerald a few miles down the river. Carter was lying about ten feet from Fitzgerald where he had been laid out with his hands crossed on his breast and a handkerchief over his face. In one of Inspector Fitzgerald's pockets was a piece of paper on which the following message had been inscribed with a piece of charred wood.

All money in despatch bag and bank, clothes, etc., I leave to my dearly beloved mother, Mrs. John Fitzgerald, Halifax. God bless all.

F. J. Fitzgerald, R.N.W.M.P.

They were less than thirty miles from McPherson.

This had happened fourteen years before my arrival in the North and in 1924, to all intents and purposes, conditions on the Mackenzie had not changed; it was still the same bleak, merciless river that since the beginning of time had speared the hidden world of the northland, in which for eight long months when the snow locked it in not a sound could be heard save the song of the wind through the trees, and where, except for the beasts of the forests and an occasional man, nothing stirred in the white, clutching grip of the frost.

The story I have told is a setting of the stage; it depicts better than anything else the unending struggle of man against the elements. But now it is necessary to explain how I had reached the edge of the Northwest Territories, where the sun sinks slowly in summer for only a few short hours before it rises again. A long way farther north, for weeks on end it would not set at all but would circle the sky like a great fiery eye. For here, at Fort Smith, we were only on the edge of the Arctic's hinterland — the "banana belt" — and we were waiting for navigation to open to take the first boat down the river. The mosquitoes were awful.

There were about half a dozen of us who had come comfortably by rail from different points to Edmonton, the stepping-off place. From there, another railway line had taken us three hundred miles through the bush to Waterways in northern Alberta. Such a railway, too! It crawled through the forest at a few miles an hour, coming to frequent stops for no reason at all when anyone who wanted to could get out and pick berries. There was no danger of being left behind if the train suddenly started, as without any major exertion one could soon overtake it. But at least it got us to our destination where the Athabaska river began.

At McMurray — next door to Waterways — we took a paddle-wheel steamer, and as it was much farther south than the Mackenzie the ice had gone out and the channel was open. Waterways, a small sheltered community of stores and log buildings, retained most of the normalities of life and yet felt the breath of the frontier. Mud roads and log shacks, a few wooden sections of pavement here and there, a stark, square hotel with paper-thin walls, and a church or so were all it consisted of then. Today it is different, still at the edge of the wilderness it is true, but a thriving community, grown from the time when I knew it.

We had to wait for a while there — a night or two — and then we were off from McMurray. The stores, equipment, and odds and ends for the settlements on the way had been loaded; the passengers, consisting of a few Hudson's Bay employees, a government official or so, a missionary and some local inhabitants, were on board; the whistle blew and the paddle wheel turned as the vessel forged out into the stream. Then, for hours on end, the banks of the river fled by as the nights passed from dark into day; past Chipewayan and Lake Athabaska; down the long, lonely stretches of the Slave — stopping every once in a while at a woodcutter's cabin so that fuel could be taken on — until after mile upon mile of a journey that threatened never to finish we rounded a bend, and there suddenly before us was Fort Fitzgerald and, cascading away in furious torrents below, a wild series of rapids which barred further progress. The whistle shrilled for the last time as the vessel pulled into the bank. It would stop here until its return cargo was loaded and then go back to McMurray.

We disembarked, looking around us. There was not much to see — log shacks and mud and an occasional frame building or two. On the crest of the bank stood a police detachment and to this we made our way. Now the pine-scented breath of the Arctic began to blow stronger; a few husky dogs roamed around, their bushy tails waving, their noses sniffing the air on the trail of any morsel of garbage. Below, the roar of the rapids seemed to mutter and thunder in warning; it was strange that this barrier was there, locking the door to the North — many people had been caught in its clutches and drowned. Here at Fitzgerald we were still in Alberta, close to where the Northwest Territories begin and then stretch out through the Barren Lands to the Pole, more than two thousand miles away. All that divided us was a portage — cross this handsbreadth from Fort Fitzgerald to Fort Smith and we would be in the Land of the Midnight Sun.

We had to wait a few days at Fort Smith — we had walked from Fitzgerald — before the *Distributor,* the paddle-wheel steamer that was to take us down the Mackenzie, was ready. As the center of government activity the settlement was regarded as the metropolis of the North, and without doubt it was larger than others I'd seen, though only an occasional church or mission building rising beyond the tops of the trees distinguished it from them.

Here, the Northwest Territories department — the administrative agency for the country beyond us — had its offices, and on the other side of the wide, muddy road was the Sub-District Headquarters of the Royal Canadian Mounted Police. Indians and half-breeds constituted a majority of the population, along with trappers, traders, government servants, missionaries and police. The hot, summer sun shone down, the dust rose, the trees at the edge of the settlement stretched on to nowhere, and the inhabitants of the community drifted by. For while it was a time of activity in the North and the people around had come in to Fort Smith now that the ice had gone out and the open water period had come, there was no need for haste — it would be cooler in the evening and, while the mosquitoes would be quite as ferocious, there was time enough then to look after what had to be done.

A day or two later, after taking in the sights at Fort Smith, we boarded the *Distributor,* the lines were cast off, and we were off on our voyage once more, each of us going to different detachments on the Mackenzie River or farther north to points on the Arctic coast. My destination was Fort Norman, about two hundred miles south of the Arctic Circle. First the *Distributor* steamed out of the Slave River into Great Slave Lake to Hay River, and then crossed westward to Fort Providence where the great Mackenzie begins. As we stood in the bow of the vessel and watched the distant approach of the land we could see where it began to funnel in, until all at once the lake was gone, and the spruce-covered banks swept by, bare, bleak and unpeopled.

We passed Providence and Fort Simpson — with a sea of trees to the east and the Mackenzie Mountains closer now to the west — and churned into Wrigley. As the steamer made its way down the river, the wail of its whistle penetrated the silence, then trailed off, getting fainter and fainter until it died in the distance.

A week after leaving Fort Smith, Fort Norman slowly emerged from the distance, curling white plumes from the chimneys crowning the squat dark houses beneath. As we rounded the point, they grew larger until as we eddied up to the bank we could see their separate shapes. There on the crest was the Hudson's Bay Company store; farther along, the sharp spike of the church and Roman Catholic mission building; a hundred yards on, the Mounted Police detachment with its flag flying in the breeze. Below on a separate level the square block of the Northern Trading Company's whitewashed houses formed a shining head to the dark sod-roofed Indian cabins that fell away, like the links of a chain, to the right.

Behind the settlement a large hill rose some hundreds of feet in the air, and at its feet a tributary of the Mackenzie, the Bear River, thrust its clear water into the Mackenzie's muddy depths. For here the mainstream of the river that had brought us to Fort Norman flowed brown and turgid, hundreds of yards wide, to where it met and rippled past the sand banks on its farther shore. Beyond, the distant land sloped gently upward to the hills, losing itself as it found refuge under their shrouded tops. Behind, the hidden mountains loomed, dark clouds cloaking them and forming great gray powder puffs against the iridescent sky. To the east, past the buildings, the pines in their carpet of green swept to the barren world within which no trees grew, but which yet ran for another thousand miles into Hudson Bay.

There was a lot of mud; that and the smell of wood smoke formed my first impression. Like everywhere else on the river a number of malemutes roamed up and down, their sharp, prick ears and bushy tails moving busily. Others slept, their noses cushioned by their feet, opening a slitted eye when occasion warranted. Mosquitoes swarmed, sticking their hungry lances into waiting flesh; later, as the eggs hatched in the pools and muskeg they would grow much worse.

It was hot too. In the sun's bright light the shadows bit the earth, running from the roofs of the houses in sharp, black triangular designs. Higher up the bank a small group of Indians with their squaws stood separate, dignified, aloof. Silent, they seemed incurious, letting the white man have his way. Close by the gangplank there was a group of three uniformed members of the Mounted Police, Inspector Eames and two Constables. They helped me with my gear and, after reporting to Inspector Eames, I climbed up the hill to the R.C.M.P. quarters.

The detachment, like the other houses in the Fort, was a log building, the crevices on the outside walls being packed with earth, a buckler against the winter wind that would otherwise blow through. Inside there were three rooms — our sleeping quarters, the kitchen where we had our meals, and a third which held the equipment — placed around a cell which was seldom used. There was a kitchen range with a quantity of split wood stacked nearby and, in the larger room, a big, square, iron stove.

Next door there was another similar log building where Inspector and Mrs. Eames lived — she was the only white woman in the settlement or for that matter for many hundred miles. There were no hospital or medical facilities; at Fort Norman we were between doctors — there was one on the Arctic coast five hundred miles north and another at Fort Resolution to the south about the same distance away. Of course, from our point of view, they served no purpose at all — there were no airplanes or radios or even outboard motors at Fort Norman in those days and before any assistance was forthcoming one would very certainly be dead.

There was a singular absence of crime in the far North. There was no theft to speak of; it was outside the pattern of behavior to lock one's cabin if it was unoccupied, for someone in need of warmth and shelter might want to get in. Occasionally, though, there was a murder, and once in a while, due to the loneliness, a trapper would become mentally deranged and shoot his partner and himself.

A good deal of our work consisted of making patrols, in the summer by boat or canoe, in the winter by dog team. On such occasions we would travel between detachments — situated about 150 and 250 miles north and south on the main river — visiting the cabins en route to satisfy ourselves that their occupants had met with no misadventure since they'd last been seen. There were many vicissitudes members of the trapping community might suffer. They might become ill, break an arm or a leg or — worst of all — go mad. Some of them lived quite alone in the woods, but now and then two men in partnership would work together on their trap lines, sharing a cabin fifty, seventy-five, or a hundred miles from the Fort. Others might make their way into the mountains and not be heard of for a year or two, but the time they would be away would be known to the police beforehand and as long as they had taken enough food not much concern was felt for their safety; they were experienced men and well able to look after themselves. One case occurred, however, up the Gravel River, which led to the mountains from the Mackenzie near Fort Norman, where two trappers who had equipped themselves with a couple of years' provisions became overdue. The police patrol sent out to learn why found them both dead from scurvy. They had each built a cabin a quarter mile from the other — possibly to avoid quarreling during the long winter period — and the disease must have hit them both simultaneously, for it was obvious from what remained at the scene that they had not been able to come to one another's help. One was dead in his bunk, the other kneeling before the stove where he had died in his last effort to keep warm.

Gradually I began to make my way with the trapping community and, as I got to know them better, to learn a lot. Once they recognized the fact that you were possessed of some fortitude and resource, they were willing to allow you entry into their brotherhood. Probably the primal necessity was to be known as "tough" and to show a capacity for endurance by not allowing the freezing weather and stark afflictions of the trail to discomfit you. If you could run thirty or thirty-five miles a day — the usual distance when the trail was good — behind dogs, camp out in the snow without a tent when the temperature dropped to thirty or forty degrees below zero, and still show no sign of disturbance, you were automatically a candidate for election to their clan. If, besides this, you could carry a couple of hundred pounds of flour up a bank on your back it made your chances much better. A good deal of pain was required before you finally got in.

Apart from the summer and winter patrols we spent a great deal of time getting fuel to keep warm. There was, of course, no gas, oil or electricity for heating purposes and it was therefore necessary to rustle wood. This we did in summer by proceeding upriver a few miles and there, cutting the branches from old dry trees that had been left stranded on the banks. Then the trees had to be floated down to the settlement and rolled up the bank, where they were stacked to await the coming of winter and the snow. Once this came and there was sufficient traction to enable the sleds to be hauled, each log had to be loaded and then dragged up the hill by the dogs to the detachment, a quarter mile distant. The winding trail was steep in places and it was possible to make only slow progress, the sled and its load sticking here and there and having to be started again by brute force. Once at the top the load was deposited at the detachment; later as the winter went on the logs would be lifted onto trestles and then cut into stove lengths by two men, one at each end of the saw. Finally split and stacked, they were ready as fuel.

About October the Mackenzie froze. One could see the freeze-up coming. First, small bits of drifting ice floated by; then, as it became colder, larger chunks, until they finally stopped and were locked tight. Below, the water rushed on, bubbling and boiling. Soon it would burst free, rending the smooth surface into great blocks of ice that would turn over and over like huge rime-covered cartwheels before the river, its last strength expended, would again settle down. Then the flat frozen surface would be gone; the level tablet abolished; the shining white plane destroyed in the last convulsive force of the struggle and turned to rough-hewn castles of ice that now stretched, rockbound, immovable, gleaming and glistening, a barrier of crystal between shore and shore.

Exhausted, the river slept. It snuggled closer to its bed, sinking lower, diminishing in volume as the ice cut off its springs and a million freshets of water ceased their flow from its banks. At its edge the first glassy level that had formed as it froze dropped down to meet it, cracking and breaking apart. The snow fell, a thick, shadowy curtain of flakes, enveloping everything. The river was now a silvery desert, its snow dunes towering, clouding the air as the frigid wind breathed and tore them in pieces. Except on a still, clear day there was a continual mist over the river, the snow falling, the wind blowing, or both. It was very cold.

Once the ice had set, we made our way on it. This was not easy, as we had to cut our path with axes, marking the trail we had made with pieces of spruce bough so that as the snow became deeper they could be easily seen. As we chipped at the ice blocks, leveling the rougher places, our snowshoes made the first trail of the winter, which later the dog teams would take to the other side. Then they would travel, finding such smooth places as they could, up or down the Mackenzie River, or would follow rambling Indian trails that had been marked out through the bush. Sometimes, when the crumpled surface of the river was impassable, the toboggans would be held up on the angled snow and ice at its edge. One false step would mean that the load and dogs would be precipitated into the ice-chaos lower down. Then the dogs would have to be straightened out, the load forced up the slope again, until perhaps after more than a mile of such traveling a smoother stretch opened up. It was hard work wrestling with one's snowshoes among the cracks and crevices, a loaded toboggan full of food and equipment on the rope, the wind and frost like a blowtorch searing one's face and always, in the event of a mishap, the prospect of a broken leg or ankle to make matters worse.

In comparison, summertime travel was more restful, for then the insect life of the land — black flies and mosquitoes in swarms — was all that caused trouble. But during the open water period we could not venture far from the river without carrying heavy loads of food and equipment on our backs, and packing with dogs — who sometimes smelt a caribou and made off — was not too dependable. For this reason, quite a few of the patrols were made in the winter when dog teams and toboggans could be put into use; given a little patience and determination one could go anywhere with these, and with experience and skill one could almost inevitably get back.

I had never worn snowshoes. True, I had seen them hanging in the trading stores or on nails in the room of the detachment where the equipment was kept. One day soon after winter had set in, I was told to get ready to go down the river to visit a trapper who lived below Fort Norman, about fifteen miles. As I was new to the business a senior member would accompany me on the patrol.

The journey being a short one, the toboggan carried very little load, and the dogs, as winter was just beginning, were feeling quite active. They barked and whined eagerly, pulling at the traces and snarling as from time to time they became entangled in a fighting, jumbled mass, sinking their teeth into whichever dog was unlucky enough to be at the bottom. They were savage animals with a strain of wolf somewhere in their background. When a fight began they had to be seized by the neck by one man while the other held the toboggan firm. The traces had to be straightened out, and once they were in line again we'd continue the journey. Finally, their exuberant spirits expended, they settled down quite amicably to their duties on the trail.

As I was the junior member my job was to run ahead so that the dogs could follow the stamped-down path my snowshoes would make. As we covered the miles with the senior member riding on the toboggan to hold the dogs back, I began to sweat, despite the cold. Soon the perspiration was pouring in streams down my face, and my legs began to feel as heavy as lead; to make matters worse, unused to snowshoes as I was, their tails kept crossing behind, hurling me into the snow. While I was in reasonably good condition, I soon found that this type of endeavor called for an entirely different set of muscles and a separate kind of stamina, far beyond anything I'd previously known. How I ever got to our destination I never knew, or for that matter how I ever returned, but somehow I made it and staggered back again into Fort Norman, completely exhausted. In later years when I hardened up, I found I could travel thirty or forty miles a day on snowshoes and occasionally fifty, but at that time the distance to and from the trapper's cabin seemed enormous.

We saw the trapping community only at intervals. When the ice went out on the river they would come in to the Fort, and at Christmas and Easter. Then, the log buildings would be filled with Indians, half-breeds and trappers, their husky dogs roaming loose by the score, baying the moon at night, the weird wail of their song echoing across the snow-covered land. Inside the stores, secure and warm, some of the white men would sit down to poker, engaging in quiet conversation, gambling the fur stake they had made in the months of their loneliness. Then they would go, richer or poorer, back to their cabins. The white trappers and Indians formed separate groups, but the Indians had been there longer and it was their way of life that in many respects we had to follow, especially in matters of travel. We saw a lot of them on the trail, sometimes sharing their tents and their food when invited.

Food in the Fort consisted solely of staples — there were no luxuries. Canned corned beef and brawn, flour, butter and bread (we made our own), bacon in the slab, tea, coffee, jam and sugar, with some ghastly dessicated potatoes and vegetables in cans to make up the remainder. If we were fortunate enough to shoot a moose late in the autumn or at the beginning of winter, a supply of fresh meat was available that would eke out our normal provisions. Occasionally we obtained a change of diet, such as canned sausages from the trading stores, but not very often; it depended on whether they had stocked up with such delicacies during the summer.

When a long trip had to be made in the winter, the patrol consisted of two men and a dog team, ten days' food and equipment being about the most that could be carried on the toboggan. Apart from the dried fish that would go to the dogs, the provisions consisted of meat, tea, sugar, beans, bacon, bannock and butter. Usually the corned beef was mixed with previously cooked rice and shaped into fist-sized balls and frozen, ready later to be thawed in the frying pan by the fire. If moose meat was handy, a frozen leg would be sawed into large steaks before the patrol set out. With a sleeping bag each, a couple of pairs of snow-shoes, a double-bitted axe or two, a rifle and some additional clothing, the load would come close to four or five hundred pounds. This was the maximum amount that five dogs could haul under any rough conditions of travel. There was no room for a tent — the space it would take and the weight of the canvas would not allow it — and in consequence our shelter for the night would be the clinging embrace of the snow.

With only enough food to make a closely estimated distance, every minute had to be put to use to cover a certain number of miles each day. Even when this was calculated with care, allowance had to be made for a small margin of time in case, due to strong head winds at thirty or forty degrees below zero, we had to take shelter in the trees and wait for the weather to improve. Ordinarily at fifty below we could travel if there was no wind, but if there was even a breeze it would cut at our faces like a knife, freezing noses, cheeks, eyelashes and chins in a matter of seconds. Sometimes when food was getting short we could not afford to stay over in the shelter of the trees but had to continue on the best way we could, breaking our frozen eyelashes apart with our fingers as our breath blew back in our faces, the moisture forming immediately into ice on any exposed surface. The only relief we could get at such times was to hold our mitts to our noses and blow into them so that the warm air from our lungs could thaw out the icicles and we could face the wind again and stumble on.

How far we could travel depended on the depth of the snow. One man — the "forerunner" — would go ahead to break trail for the dogs, being relieved from time to time by the other. There was never any opportunity for riding on the sled, as the extra weight would soon exhaust the dogs. Rather, it was necessary to help push the load through the rough places at times. When we climbed the bank of the river to secure firewood to burn so as to thaw out our food, both of us would have to heave and haul the toboggan to the top, helping the dogs. Then in the trees, safe from the wind, we would light a fire, eat our rough meal and go on. When what little daylight there was showed signs of disappearing, up the bank we would go again to make camp and rest until it was time to resume our journey next day.

Making camp at night simply meant that we dug a hole in the snow, using our snowshoes as shovels, and then felled a few trees with the double-bitted, razor-sharp axes we carried, one man obtaining old dried-out wood for the fire while the other cut down green spruce trees for the bed. Then a great fire was lit that blazed, brightening the snow and forest around us; the limbs of green spruce were chopped off and laid level in the hole we had dug in the snow; the dogs were taken out of harness and chained to nearby trees; the food and sleeping bags were unpacked from the load, and after twenty minutes work we had taken the first steps to prepare ourselves for the night. Now all that remained was for the sleeping bags to be laid out on top of the spruce bed we had made — and for us to thaw out what food we would eat, heat a metal container filled with snow for tea or coffee, give the dogs their quota of dried fish and tallow, have our dinner, crawl into the sleeping bags fully clothed, and go to sleep.

When it was really cold I don't think we ever slept much. A mere thirty degrees below zero temperature was nothing to worry about, but when it dropped to fifty or sixty it was a different matter entirely; then it was necessary to build two fires, one on each side, and take refuge in between. As the night went on the hot, leaping flames would die down, leaving ashes and embers in their place. Once, following some subconscious urge for warmth in the night, I rolled over among them and awoke to a vile, evil-smelling stench of burning feathers as I found my sleeping bag, with me in it, smoldering and throwing plumes of black smoke to the sky! If it snowed during the night one would wake up long before morning with a covering of white, two, three or four inches deep. Blowing on our hands to keep the circulation going, we would rekindle the embers again and have breakfast — a large one, for life on the trail required a great deal of food to create enough energy for the day — and set out, long before dawn, finding our way through the dark. This was the worst time of the morning, when bones and muscles ached and the fluid in our joints had not had a chance to flow freely and limber us up. The dogs had been better off. Curled in round balls in the snow with their noses, feet and tails tucked into the fur of their stomachs, they had been relatively impervious to the frost.

And so we went on. Two or three more meals through the day to keep up our strength, the never-ending white vista of the river eternally stretching before us, to be broken at times as we climbed the bank to take a cut-off or portage which would save a few miles. Then we would descend in a flurry of whirling snow, the dogs galloping down the slope as we hauled back on the toboggan to prevent its overtaking them and breaking their backs. Another thirty or thirty-five miles, then another night spent in the freezing arms of the snow.

Once in a while we would stay overnight with a trapper who lived his lonely life in the woods. This was a gala occasion, as it meant that we'd be able to relax and get warm. Really warm! We'd be able to take off our parkas and moccasins and after a hot meal and tea would be able to put our feet by the stove. No one who has not experienced it can know the pure rapture that this kind of comfort can bring!

The type of life we lived naturally toughened us. At Fort Norman, though, I was merely learning and never made any long trips — a hundred miles or so at the most. One trip especially had its unpleasant moments for a "cheechako" like myself; it was to Great Bear Lake, about ninety miles distant. One day during the early spring period a three-man police patrol arrived from a distant point up-river, its objective being to travel across the south shore of Great Bear Lake and then make its way back through Fort Rae to Fort Smith. When the patrol came up the bank to the detachment at Fort Norman its members were quite unrecognizable because of the heavy beards they wore, their faces frostbitten and eyes inflamed by the cold and the smoke of the open campfires. As soon as they said who they were I found that the most formidable-looking individual of the three was an Inspector Fraser who had been at Ottawa when I was a recruit. The others in the party consisted of Constable Logel from Fort Providence and another man who had been engaged locally in the country to accompany the patrol. They must have traveled at least five or six hundred miles by the time they arrived at Fort Norman and still had about the same distance to go through an area virtually unknown at that time. Once they left Fort Norman they would see no one at all until they had traveled all the way south to Fort Rae. To make the chances even worse Inspector Fraser had frozen the soles of his feet near Fort Simpson nearly a week before, and it could be seen by the way he was hobbling around that he was in considerable pain.

During the previous summer some caches of food had

been put in on Great Bear Lake by another patrol, and these provisions were what Inspector Fraser and his two men were depending on to get them across, for it was not possible to carry enough food for the full journey with the two teams of dogs that hauled the toboggans to Fort Norman. Inspector Fraser could not walk with any degree of comfort until the condition of his feet improved, and so after a couple of days, during which the patrol rested, I was told to get ready to drive him in a toboggan to Bear Lake.

Fraser was a heavy man, weighing about two hundred pounds, and wrapped in furs as he was, he made a considerable load. While Logel and the other man carried the provisions and equipment in their toboggans I chauffered him along. At first all went well; the Indian trail through the bush was clear-cut and smooth and the dogs made good time. Then as the route spread out onto small lakes and open places where the warmth of the sun could get at it unopposed, the first signs of trouble began.

Ordinarily a toboggan trail, due to Indians and trappers passing over it with their loads, becomes packed hard by their weight except for a surface of loose snow on the top. The depth of this depends on when the trail was last used; if a heavy fall has occurred since a toboggan made its way over it, the narrow trench may be filled with snow to the top. When this happens, as there is always a hard-packed surface somewhere beneath, the man in front of the dogs tries to find the invisible road with his feet, or sometimes by feeling for it with a stick. To bypass it makes much harder pulling for the dogs in the deeper snow on each side, as they then have to wallow belly deep, devoid of secure footing. With the beginning of warmer weather in the spring, however, the reverse is the case, for then the loose snow at the sides melts in the sun and gradually sinks down, leaving the hard-packed trail level and solid up above.

This was the condition of the trail for a large part of

the journey between Fort Norman and Bear Lake. As Logel and the other man had passed over the path with their loads, the toboggans had from time to time slipped off. As a result when I followed with Inspector Fraser in the sled, every few yards the toboggan head would go down and more often than not the whole load would land in the deeper snow on its side. Then there would be an interval of heaving and tugging with all my strength until the toboggan was back on the trail and the dogs could make headway again. This is hard work and very wearying indeed — quite different from the usual imaginary picture of a dog team, in which it lightly skims over the snow, the driver comfortably ensconced on the back of a sleigh, shouting encouragement to the dogs to speed up!

At all events, due to the extra amount of labor involved, I soon found myself becoming worn out. The first day was bearable although it was extremely frustrating, and by applying every effort of will and ounce of energy I possessed I was able to keep up. The next two days were agony, however, heightened probably by the fact that I'd been eating frozen bannock, and I developed cramps in the stomach as I went along. Although the pain was so severe that I could not walk upright, I still had to force the toboggan back on the trail every time it upset. Naturally I could not eat anything, and when night came we all crammed ourselves into the very small tent the patrol carried. The tent was necessary, as the south shore of Great Bear Lake where we were bound had only small scrub trees which gave no protection from wind. My condition suffered a turn for the worse when I saw what my companions were preparing for supper — pemmican, bacon fat, broken-up hardtack biscuits, melted cheese, and a few strips of bacon on top! With my insides in the condition they were, this greasy mess was enough to remove any trace of appetite I otherwise might have had. So in addition to my other difficulties, I had to go hungry through most of the trip.

Finally, after three days of such travel, we reached our destination and there the great expanse of the lake lay before us — an inland sea more than twelve thousand square miles in area — frozen in the flat, unbroken white of the land. Inspector Fraser's feet were still badly blistered, but despite this he apparently had no thought of turning back — a few hundred miles more seemed to mean nothing to him — and the patrol again prepared to set out the next morning. As soon as they were gone I would return to Fort Norman, this time, thank God, without any load except a sleeping bag and just enough food for myself.

I shook Logel's hand. "Good-bye," I said. "I'll see you sometime, I hope — maybe at Providence when my turn comes to go back outside . . ."

"So long," he replied. He was bending down, straightening one of the traces on his dogs. "I guess this may be good-bye for good." He looked out over the great frozen lake where the wind was blowing the snow in a thick curtain of drift. "I wonder if we'll ever get through . . ."

The patrol arrived at Fort Rae, but when they got there at first no one knew who they were, due to the hardships they'd suffered and the amount of weight they'd lost. After leaving the west end of Bear Lake, and several days' travel, they reached the main cache of food — only to find that it had been broken into by bears. They were stranded without enough food either to go back or go on. After discussing the matter between them, it was decided that Logel would take half the small quantity of provisions that remained and set out by himself in the hope of finding an Indian camp. The chances of his being successful — bearing in mind the size of the country and the few people in it — were not more than one in ten thousand, but amazingly enough when he was at the very end of his resources he arrived where a few wandering Indians were encamped. As a result the patrol was able to secure some additional provisions and made its way for approximately another hundred and fifty miles into Fort Rae.

As the weeks followed each other the sun rose higher in the sky; the streams began to run from the side-hills, limpid and cold; patches of earth appeared here and there and the ice on the river slowly rotted. With the advent of warmer weather, patrolling with dogs became a thing of the night when the temperature sank and the melting snow hardened. We rested by day, and as evening came on made our way by starlight when the sky was unclouded. The moon shining on the snow-heavy trees formed patterns of indescribable beauty, their heavy black shadows carving the sparkling snow in long raven columns. Now for the first time since winter set in we could cast some of our winter clothing aside. The dogs pulled their loads at a fast trot, the slippery surface glided away under the toboggan as the miles unrolled and we ran light-footed behind them. There was a lifting of pressure as the door of winter eased back, letting in the first faint traces of summer. A flower burgeoned here and there; a bush or two loosened tips for the green that would later burst forth; great arrowheads of ducks and wild geese made their way northward, clamoring and honking; and over everything, hills, valleys and forests, there seemed to be a curtain of waiting. Soon, any moment now, the Mackenzie River would go out, and we looked forward each day for the first sign of its breaking.

During the winter there had been no communication with the outside world and in a sense it had been as though we were buried in the ultimate depths of a prison; when the ice went out it would be like a suddenly opening door. We wondered what had been happening far to the south in the civilized places. During the winter there had been one dog team mail which came down the river carrying only letters. When its arrival had begun to seem likely, the inhabitants of the Fort had each day strained their eyes toward the point round which the team would come, eagerly scanning the distance. At the first welcoming shout those who were not already watching the point ran from their cabins to meet it. The load was unpacked, the small bag of mail distributed, and then after a rest overnight the dog team and its driver continued to the next Fort on the way down the river.

This had happened four or five months before, and now with the passing of spring and the coming of summer the ice had gone from the river, leaving it clear. Slowly, as the sun circled the sky — there was hardly any night — the wide plateau of ice had begun to move, churning and grinding, and turning over here and there as its path was blocked by some sandbar or shallow point that impeded its progress, only to shift again as the irresistible pressure behind forced the blocks over and under the mass of the inexorable stream. Then, in a day or two it had vanished, following the snow on its banks which had long since disappeared, and another cycle had started. Winter had passed and in place of the ice that had locked us in, the brown, muddy river flowed past to the sea.

Confined as we had been with each other for so long a time, it was with a sense of relief that I heard that I was to make another general patrol to Bear Lake, this time by open water. To get there it would be necessary to travel by canoe, accompanying a band of Indians who were returning to their camp on the lake by way of Bear River, a fast-flowing body of water split halfway about forty miles up by a turbulent, cascading series of rapids. The Indians were using a long, narrow scow which they dragged up the river with the help of an assembled variety of dogs. When the water became too turbulent to make progress with my canoe possible, I loaded it on the scow and helped the Indians hauling the lines to which the larger vessel was attached. Then, after pulling and tugging the scow through the rapids — at times waist deep in the roaring maelstrom — we emerged in a week's time on the shores of the great lake which I'd seen for the first time the previous winter. After staying with the Indians for a further two or three days, I prepared to return.

Looking over the sweep of Great Bear Lake's green, heaving expanse with nothing in the world around one except sky, water and land, I felt as though I were standing virtually on the brink of nothingness, perhaps as a result of the complete emptiness, the silence, and the terrible feeling of space around one. Looking to the north there was only the Soviet Union, nearly three thousand miles away; to the south the cities of Canada another thousand or so; to the east a few pinpoints of habitation until one reached Europe; and to the west the uncharted Mackenzie Mountains with the Yukon on their farther side. Somewhere in between was a handful of men who lived at Fort Norman. Here, on the shores of Great Bear Lake, one was not even as large as a fly speck in the realms of the wilderness.

There was not a sound save the wash of the water as I picked up my paddle and pushed off. I wondered how I'd manage when I came to the rapids — I'd be on my own in a sixteen-foot canoe.

The river was very fast. It swept round a bend in a right and left turn at a speed that I judged to be ten or twelve miles an hour. Just as I was in the full grip of the current, a large rock raised a formidable head. Paddling as hard as I could, I still found myself being forced down upon it, gradually being swept broadside to where white water was billowing over and descending in a deep series of troughs on its further side. There was only one way to save myself — if I could straighten out quickly, I could ride down on their crest. In a flash I was over, the rock a dim blur of gray in the water beneath me, the waves breaking and falling away as they lashed at the speeding craft raised above on their tops. It had been a near escape and I breathed with relief. If the canoe had been forced sideways over the rock it would have turned over and over and I would certainly have been drowned. It would have been virtually impossible to make my way to the shore, to the shallow places where every stone could be seen in the crystal-clear water, for in the middle the river boiled in a swirling mass of dark green.

In the open stretches, there was nothing to do but drift with the current, with an occasional touch of the paddle to keep the bow straight. The banks slid by, slower now where the river had widened out and the speed of the current had decreased. In a few hours at most I'd have to concern myself with the rapids, a prospect I viewed with some trepidation as in those early years only a very few people had traversed them before.

Soon the roar of the rapids could be heard a mile or so downstream! I had left Bear Lake in the evening and the light was still bright in the sky when I reached them. They made a nasty sight with the wild water tossing as the river fell away, gaining speed. I pulled into the bank, tied the canoe, and stepped ashore to look them over and decide which channel, if any, offered the most safety. But there did not seem to be much difference between them, and a flashing, cascading torrent of waves formed a white, dancing bridge — a dazzling barrier of movement — that stretched to the middle from each shore. Every time I looked, trying to decide which avenue to follow, the water seemed to get wilder and rougher until I was sure there was no safe and sound way to get through; all that could be done was to launch the canoe at the center and pray with all my might that it would not be upset and sucked down. After having made sure that the heavy rock I had placed in the bow of the canoe to weigh it down was secure and in place, I pushed my light craft into the current and set out.

Quicker than it takes to tell, I was in the maelstrom. The white water plucked at me, turning the bow sideways no matter how hard I pulled at the paddle, the wild surge of the waves breaking to right and to left and below, the rocks fleeting past as I missed them by hairsbreadths. There was no time to think of anything but the fight with the river, the exact place into which the paddle should plunge to make a deep hole in the water, the degree of heave that must be applied to avoid the boulders. It was wildly exhilarating — the canoe jumped and lurched as at one moment it sank to the bottom of a trough only to be smacked round from behind by a following wave and raised the next instant to its crest. Clouds of hissing, sparkling diamonds filled the air as the spray beat back in my face. There was a sound like thunder as the rapids bellowed and roared — and then, all at once, I was through to where the green of the depths filled out the river in a wide, semicircular fan and quickly flowed on.

Behind me, the noise of the rapids, now reduced to a threatening growl, told where their long, clutching fingers stretched out. There was a good deal of water in the bottom of the canoe but the passage had not been so bad as it had seemed from above, and once I had bailed it out I could go on; from here, by comparison, the river moved slowly to Fort Norman, half asleep. It had taken seven days to go up the river and seventeen hours to come down.

That year I was moved to Fort Smith.

While serious crime had passed us by at Fort Norman, in 1924 there was a history of murders that had been committed in the Northwest Territories over long intervals of time. Approximately ten years before, two priests, Fathers Rouvier and Le Roux, had been killed by Eskimos near Bloody Falls on the Coppermine River, northeast of Bear Lake, and the culprits had been arrested following a two-year investigation of the crime. A year or so later, a couple of explorers named Radford and Street had met their deaths at the hands of another branch of this tribe at Bathurst Inlet. In 1920, far to the east, a trader named Robert Janes had been killed at Cape Crawford. In 1921, there had been a massacre among the natives of Kent Peninsula because of rivalries induced by a shortage of women, and far to the south in the same year the murder of an Indian woman near Fort Providence had occurred. More recently, Corporal Doak of the R.C.M.P. had been murdered by an Eskimo at Tree River on the Arctic coast during April 1922. All these investigations — which required many extensive patrols over great distances that had to be covered for the most part in the freezing blizzards of winter — were successful. Due to the difficulty of the patrols finding their way on the empty, uncharted lands of the Arctic, however, some investigations took a great many months to conclude before the men who had committed the crimes were brought to trial. Farther south again, the work of the Force went on undiminished across Canada, but on the Mackenzie River, at Fort Norman, things were comparatively quiet. Patrols came and went, their duties merely of a preventive nature — effective, however, against any upsurge of crime.

One of the most difficult tasks of the R.C.M.P. was the escorting of lunatics over the winter trail to some place where they could be given care. While I was fortunate in never having had to make such a patrol, I could very well appreciate what it meant — with axes and rifles close at hand there would be little chance to sleep. Perhaps the worst of these trips had been made many years before when on two occasions violent madmen had to be taken over great distances, in one case close to a thousand miles. In the first instance, a Corporal Field and an Indian guide delivered their charge after a six-week journey under almost unendurable conditions. In the second, the Constable who had to take the maniac out subsequently went temporarily insane due to the terrible circumstances he encountered with his charge. After staying six months in an asylum in the south, he recovered sufficiently to be transferred to other duties in the Force.

10

North to the Yukon

I HAD a different perspective when I returned to civilization. In two years I had become used to the quiet and stillness of the North and, now in their place, I found myself breasting the current again, a unit in the hurrying stream of life. It reminded me of the days when I had come out of the jungle — the same feeling of emerging from a cavern, yawning, stretching, half asleep. Things had changed. My feet hurt — I'd become so used to wearing moccasins that shoes caused blisters, and whenever I could I put on bedroom slippers to walk the city streets.

It was difficult to talk to anyone at first or to find interest in anything they said. I was out of touch — conversation seemed inconsequential, matters of little moment assuming degrees of importance far beyond their worth. This was the same old world but garbed in unremembered colors now; here other things took charge and those to which I'd grown accustomed — the basic elements of life and death — had little part. But of one thing I was certain — that here, as in the forests, the struggle still went on. It was only the environment that had changed, to crowds and buildings instead of lonely lakes and trees.

For a few days I was at a loss. Then, as I began to familiarize myself with this new setting, I slipped back into the groove, the idioms and modes of speech returning and echoing through the senses where they had lain dormant through the last two years. During the first week, even to cross a road had taken quite a bit of thought — how could one tell unless one waited, watching, that one wouldn't be knocked down? A road was filled with noise and tumult and the sound of all things rushing on!

If, in the beginning, I felt at variance with my fellow men, the lessons of the wilderness now proved of inestimable worth. For the first time, the things I'd pictured in the campfire places took on solid life and form. Now, even taps and running water seemed like bounties from the gods! It had been different in the North — there you'd had to carry pails of snow or ice and melt them on a stove. This took time. Now it was a matter of seconds — you turned a tap and all at once, like a miracle, there was water, crystal-clear! Why had I never thought of this? And what about silver knives and forks and tablecloths of purest white and tall, clean glasses, through which the sunbeams shone? A rose! It was a new thing — I'd never really looked at one before. Now it was the essence of beauty, the birth of life as its petals opened out. You could watch it. Before, it had been a blob of color that you glimpsed in passing, or gave — again in passing — to some girl. Not so much because it was lovely but because it would make an impression — she would pin it on her dress or stick it in a vase or something and, never knowing, say how nice it was. Nice! What a remark! There was nothing nice about it — glorious, yes — as all things are that come as gifts from God.

I don't say that the North did this to everyone, and that was just as well — it was a heady wine which required a steady head. One did not speak of it to one's friends; they might not have understood. It would have made sense only to a man who had suddenly regained his vision, or to a prisoner released from long confinement in a cell. Or to the man who was found singing on a raft in a shark-infested sea. "Why are you so happy?" somebody asked. "Why wouldn't I be?" he replied, "when for three days I've been swimming alongside in the water, hanging on!" All of them extremes, I know, but nevertheless ones that seem to have a common touch.

We had come back to Edmonton but we were not to remain there for long. Once we'd found our feet and, in a manner of speaking, had become acclimatized again, we were sent to different areas where our services could be used. I don't know where the others went but I was transferred to British Columbia, first to Vancouver — a reservoir of manpower similar to the one at Ottawa — and then to Penticton, a small detachment in the fruit belt of the interior.

During the time I'd been away on nothern service, the responsibilities of the R.C.M.P. had not changed to any marked degree and, in the provinces, enforcing the federal statutes comprised the full extent of the work. At Penticton it was certainly a change from the Mackenzie. We occupied our time in making raids on certain elements among the Chinese population trafficking in drugs in nearby towns, and in looking after the interests of the Indians on their Reserve, a mile or two away; every so often, some of the Reserve's inhabitants would be found drinking or gambling, which was against the law. Once, with two others on the detachment, I found myself involved in a fight with about a dozen Indians when making some arrests and came back with a number of them, our uniforms bloody and torn and our charges and ourselves almost equally the worse for wear, but beyond this and one or two other incidents of a less exciting nature, nothing much occurred. It was a kind of paradise after the strenuous days of the North. The surroundings were glorious. There were orchards filled with apple, peach, and cherry blossoms in the spring, and warm, blue lakes that spread like giant sapphires north and south, mirroring the soft, sail-set clouds that slowly floated by. We had a horse there — a patient, tranquil beast — and when I was not otherwise engaged I had to groom it and take it out for exercise. Mostly, we used the horse to ride on the Indian Reserve where, in certain areas, more modern transport could not go. It was a peaceful spot — a complete antithesis to the cold harshness of the Mackenzie — but unfortunately my stay in this Elysium was not to last long, for after a year I was suddenly promoted to Corporal and transferred to the Training Depot to act as assistant to the Sergeant-Major.

This was a job that one had to approach with the cold-heartedness of a Scrooge. It had to do with the whipping into shape of newly joined recruits and this, of course, had never previously come within the range of my experience. However, having received my orders, there was nothing to do but go and discover what was expected of me; and so, with a singular lack of enthusiasm at the thought of leaving Penticton, I set out for Regina.

In comparison with the establishments at Ottawa and Vancouver, "Depot" Division was a huge place, serving on a much larger scale the same general purpose, a proving ground from which men were sent into the field when fully trained. Here, everyone stood at attention when spoken to by their seniors and did everything at the half-run. Drill formations marched about, orders were shouted here and there, and officers moved to and fro punctiliously returning salutes. The Depot was steeped in the traditions of the Force, for through its doors almost every recruit had walked for more than forty years. It was a bleak place, the frozen wind sweeping across the flat prairie lands with nothing to obstruct it, at extremes of temperature which sometimes dropped to forty and fifty degrees below. As spring came the snow disappeared, and soon the young wheat forcing itself through the soil formed a table of green that stretched everywhere like some gigantic lawn interspersed with little ponds. Then as the year advanced, in place of the green the land would be golden, the long, waving stalks of the wheat

174

forming a sea that stretched everywhere as the breeze caressing them made slow, lazy waves on their surface. Flat though it was, all through the summer it was beautiful, the unending plain spreading, rippling and sparkling in the sun to the distant horizon.

There were few trees. Round the barrack square, some raised their heads in the air, neatly spaced at intervals, but these had been there for a long time and had been carefully planted by hand before the turn of the century. Now, fully grown, they provided the only shade apart from the wedges of shadow cast by the buildings. On one side were the barracks and the administrative offices; on another the officers' quarters, on the third some more officers' houses and the officers' mess, and on the fourth a further barrack building and the chapel. Beyond the administration building was a line of stables, where the horses were kept. The whole was under the command of an Assistant Commissioner with a staff of officers and various non-commissioned officers who were employed either as riding instructors, drill sergeants, or in other capacities. As they had all been stationed at the training "Depot" for years, they not only had the demeanor necessary to instill respect in the recruits but were also exceedingly well versed in their work. What I had been told at "N" Division four years before was entirely true — the discipline was very strict.

It was also very effective. As the standards of deportment, smartness, and conformity with the rules were set at an exceedingly high level, in my new capacity of Division Orderly I found myself fully occupied in seeing that the requirements of my seniors were carried out. A commissioned officer was almost a creature of another world — quite unapproachable! So the Sergeant-Major was the main person to instill discipline and as his assistant some of the aura that surrounded him was reflected on myself. My task was to assist the Sergeant-Major generally, call the roll on parades, take the names of offenders — even the slightest deviation such as a dirty button or not enough shine on some article of equipment or uniform was sufficient to bring down condemnation — and, in the absence of anyone senior, to make a nuisance of myself in carrying out the Sergeant-Major's wishes to the pain and detriment of those who did not measure up. It was not a vocation in which one could be popular, but at least it gave me an opportunity to see the tremendous changes that took place in the appearance and personalities of men during six months' time. There was a vast transformation for the better between the unfledged individuals who entered "Depot" Division as recruits and the same men who marched out as trained and qualified component units of the Force.

I managed to avoid the condemnation of those who were in command, but it was trying work that did not lead to much. I could see that if I gave satisfaction in the job I might be retained in it indefinitely, and this, with the continual picking and fault-finding that were necessary, might result in undesirable fixed channels of thought. After all, I thought, there should be other pursuits that did not hold this possibility, and accordingly, after about a year, I began to cast around for something else to do.

Many persons have heard of the "Call of the North" but few have been able to define it. It is an essential fact, though, that anyone who has known the great, empty spaces of the land has for some queer, inexplicable reason a compelling feeling to return. Perhaps it is the challenge of the wilderness; perhaps merely a seeking for the larger things of life which cannot be found readily in the cities; perhaps only that one has gained an affinity for those things of nature which, in the woods and forests, one has come to know — the voices of the silent places which once heard never are forgotten. Or it might have been, in my case, some kind of deep-down wanderlust — the same old idea I'd had in India that by going on I might find something out! It was only the faintest shadow of a question mark, but the things

I'd seen — the dancers at Raipura, the great empty spaces of the sea, the Barren Lands, the struggle that I'd known and the sense of awareness I'd had when I returned from the North — might these not all be signposts on the path? Lying awake on successive nights with the first light of dawn creeping through the windows, I thought about it; there was no doubt, it was like a finger beckoning, compelling me to go.

On June 1, 1928, the Province of Saskatchewan contracted with the Government of Canada to have the R.C.M.P. instead of the Provincial Police. Immediately, in addition to its federal responsibilities, the Force was again assigned the duty of enforcing the Criminal Code and provincial laws as it had done until ten years before. This was the first step, for in 1932 many of the other Provinces were to follow suit and disband their local bodies in favor of the Royal Canadian Mounted Police. Now, in Saskatchewan, a period of much greater activity began. Instead of concerning themselves only with breaches of the federal laws, the members of the R.C.M.P. had to deal with cases of murder, theft, assault, and the hundred and one other types of crime which had been under the control of the Provincial Police. I was not, however, to have anything to do with this interesting change, as I had made up my mind and put in an application to go North again and, by now, was under orders to leave, this time for the Yukon. On a fine summer morning I boarded a train for my new destination.

After the spit and polish of Regina, it was very enjoyable traveling across the western prairies with the unknown before me once more. Under the wheels, the flat land rolled by, the telegraph poles beside the track forming a blur of movement as they passed for hour after hour. Then, in the distance, the foothills of the Rockies came in sight, and soon we were winding through the snow-crested peaks of the mountains. Finally, as we emerged, the blue waters of the

Pacific appeared, and there at Vancouver the vessel was waiting on which I was to embark for Skagway in Alaska, and the Yukon.

After four or five days the ship reached Skagway and then I was on another train that puffed up toward the height of land where the first detachments had been established by the Northwest Mounted Police in 1898. It was here in that year, with the arrival of tens of thousands of adventurers at Skagway and Dyea, that these frontier outposts had been installed to ensure that, come what may, the law would be upheld. It had been different at Skagway, the headquarters of the notorious "Soapy" Smith — who with his gang had terrorized the area in 1898, levying toll on those who passed by on their way to the gold fields — but once the boundary line was reached an entirely different situation existed, and all those who crossed it were required to conform with the hard and fast rules laid down for their safety. Finally the train pulled into Whitehorse, the Sub-District headquarters of the Force in the southern Yukon area.

After crossing the Coast Range, the land had opened up. This was different country from the Mackenzie. Here, in place of the flat, level areas of that other part of the North I had known, the land disappeared around one in low undulating hills. At Whitehorse, it was much more civilized too, as there were stores and buildings and a general air of activity such as might be found in any small town farther south. Even in 1928 you could buy almost anything you wanted within reason, but beer cost a dollar a bottle and other commodities were priced on a corresponding scale. In the Mackenzie District at Fort Smith we had been much less up to date. The Yukon, however, had felt the Gold Rush of thirty years before which had brought in a modified form of civilization. It was still the North, though, retaining all the characteristics described by Robert Service in his ballads of the country, but wearing a coat now instead of standing naked, grim and stark. As the train came to a stop in the station, I could hear the roar of the rapids where, after surging through Miles Canyon a mile or two above the town, the river widened out.

At the dockside close to the terminus a paddle-wheel steamer was waiting, and I went aboard. We passed Lake Laberge — just an oversized pond compared with the mighty inland sea that was Great Bear Lake — and for hour after hour swept downstream toward Dawson. After a couple of weeks — I'd had to stop off at a waypoint to look into a complaint about bootleggers to which I'd been detailed before I left Regina, and then took another boat on — I was there.

Dawson in 1928 showed clearly what it once had been. Fronting the river, the main street stretched, straight, muddy and broad, toward the farther end of town, the old hotels and buildings rising high on each side, most of them broken down and deserted but retaining by their size, shape, and furnishings some of the elegance they'd known thirty years before. Then it had been a boisterous place filled with gold-seeking adventurers, but now only an occasional movement showed that life still went on. It was very quiet on the street, the only sound being the noise of the wind as it whined round some cornice. Here and there, branching off on the side roads, were old wooden sidewalks, their planks broken and rotten.

Away from the main street there was a good deal more action. Men walked about greeting each other as they went about their business or sat conversing in small groups on the thresholds of the buildings. Some were old-timers who had taken part in the stirring events of the past; others were a new crop who had either been born in the area since the days of the Klondike or had arrived in the country during the intervening years. Part of the city was quite up to date, with churches and a hospital and even a movie theater where sometimes a pianist accompanied the silent films, and a number of stores displayed merchandise of all kinds in their windows. Nothing — not even a chocolate bar — cost less than twenty-five cents, as no coins of smaller value were circulated. Many of the houses that were occupied had carefully tended gardens with flowers in profusion, and probably the most prominent structures in the town were the government buildings which lay well back from the river, and the Mounted Police barracks, which at one end of the main street looked out over the water. On the farther side, the Klondike — small in comparison — flowed into the Yukon, which now for more than a thousand miles would stream northward through Alaska until it reached the Bering Sea. Away from the city and on the farther side of the river, the banks rose sharply into the hills, and behind the town a small mountain known as the "Dome" towered high in the air as though to protect with its bulk the buildings below.

I don't think that the population of Dawson could have numbered more than about four hundred people in 1928. Included in that number were twenty or so police, who did not look after the interests of the town exclusively — there were three or four men detailed specially for that — but who traveled the outlying districts and formed a pool from which the strength of the detachments all over the Yukon could be replenished. For here, as elsewhere, Division headquarters was the administrative center and it served as a base from which instructions could be sent to our men throughout the country. There were detachments everywhere, one or two men being stationed either at strategic points on the river or in communities elsewhere, where the population level made it necessary.

Sprinkled around in the outlying districts were a number of prospectors who had survived the years since the Gold Rush and lived in log cabins by themselves. Mostly, they spent their time panning for gold, hoping either to make ends meet or, if fortune was with them, to strike some rich vein in their sink holes, and part of our work was to visit them occasionally and make sure that they had not suffered some form of misadventure since they'd last been seen. They lived very solitary lives on the creeks and hillsides, and those who had been around during the boom days of the Klondike were getting on in years.

Around Dawson, the mountains and hills rose in every direction. In contrast to the Mackenzie, which had been a trapping and fur trading region without any mining, here was a prospecting and mining area with fur as a side issue. But the character of the men of the creeks and woods on both sides of the mountains remained almost identical, a curious mixture of toughness and kindness. There were many cases which showed the generosity of the inhabitants. One that I heard of had to do with a man who suffered from cataracts in both eyes. When this became known, all his friends passed the hat and sent him to Vancouver for an operation, and on his return he found a store completely furnished with goods which had been provided by his companions to secure his future.

And yet, it did not do to cross these men, for an occasional one would stop at nothing if he thought he was justified in taking action according to the particular code of behavior they followed. One such involved a resident of the country who lived by himself close to Hootalinqua. When two newcomers encroached on what he considered his territory he warned them to leave, but not understanding the danger, they laughed at what he said and went on with what they were doing. A week or so later he came up through the snow from behind a hill and opened fire with a rifle, killing one of the men and, notwithstanding a rattle of bullets, missing the other. When the police came to arrest him, he was lying on his bunk in his cabin, his rifle neatly oiled and hung on two pegs on the wall of the building. He made no remonstrance when taken away, merely asserting that he had told the two men what would happen if they did not fall in with his wishes. Now having fulfilled his purpose, he was content to abide by the consequences. Fortunately such incidents were rare.

Due to my experience with dogs on the Mackenzie, as soon as winter came I was given the task of making most of the patrols out of Dawson. Sometimes I would go to Forty Mile — it was closer to fifty miles than forty — in the direction of the United States border, sometimes to Stewart two or three days' journey south. It all depended on where there was an investigation to be made or how long a time had elapsed since an area had been visited. During my first winter, after I had made a trip or two to Forty Mile and to a number of other places up and down the river, orders came through that I was to patrol to the vicinity of Glacier, about a hundred miles away, and there arrest an individual whom I will call Harry Stravich, who had failed to pay a large debt he had incurred at one of the Dawson stores. In the Yukon in 1928 there was a statute — long since repealed — that required debts to be paid, and if one defaulted one could be imprisoned. All that was necessary was for the person who had extended the credit to make complaint and express himself as being willing to pay a certain amount toward the prisoner's upkeep, and the debtor would remain behind bars for the period ordered or until the obligation was liquidated. In Harry Stravich's case, I was sent out to get him armed with a warrant that stated that unless the sum of $1000 was paid he would be committed to jail for six months.

Harry Stravich lived in a very inaccessible area on the farther side of the mountains and, to make matters more difficult, his cabin was almost next door to the United States border. One or two attempts had been made in the past to take him in custody, but every time a patrol went out he could not be located — either by chance or otherwise, he'd gone beyond the jurisdiction of the Canadian authorities. As the patrol could not go over the border or wait around indefinitely for him to come back, so far he'd managed to escape the clutches of the law.

Traveling the mountains was a new experience. Two of us set out one morning and climbed through the forest to where, at the summit, the trail leveled out and soon came to open windswept spaces. Here on the hard-packed snow there was no path to follow, but an occasional marker showed the general direction. When we came to one of the mountainsides that we had to cross, away in the distance below we could see the faint marks where the trail cut though the softer snow again in the valleys. Actually, underneath the snow there was some kind of wagon road that was used in the summer. Now for the most part this had been blown in and iced over by storms. It was tricky work traversing these slopes at a forty-five-degree angle. We had to cut in the crust with our axes, one man holding the dogs and loaded toboggan from above while the other pushed from below. Sometimes, in an unusually bad place, we'd have to let the dogs loose and lead them in their traces over the face of the mountain; then we'd have to come back and wrestle the load across, leaving only the toboggan. Once again we'd return and, on the third trip, take the toboggan across; lighter now, it was less likely to sweep us down the long slopes to the bottom. At really difficult places, the only thing that prevented this from happening was the thin parallel strips of iron on its underside which bit into the crust while we hung on grimly and placed our feet in the steps we'd made when we 'took the dogs over. It was trying work and by the end of the second day both of us were feeling quite exhausted. To make matters worse, my partner, who was new to the business, had strained a muscle in his hip from the continual exertion. This, for the time being, put him effectively out of commission, but we were fortunate in being able to spend the night at a trapper's cabin and, as the owner was home, I was able to leave him there to recover.

I'd pick him up on the way back when I'd found Harry Stravich.

Next morning, the dogs and I set out by ourselves, and that evening I was considerably relieved when I saw a faint pinprick of light appear in the distance, a single glimmer of gold that shone in the darkness. This, as I got nearer, proved to come from the window of a log cabin belonging to a miner named Jack Spratley who lived by himself in the wilderness. It had been a very hard trip crossing the mountains, with temperatures ranging well below zero, and I was exceedingly glad when I found myself, at last, in shelter and warmth. Two rough bunks, an old cook stove, a chair and a rickety table made up the furnishings, and light was provided by a candle stuck on the end of a stick in the floor. It was the light of this small flame shining through the window that I'd seen from higher up in the valley.

Jack was about sixty years old, slight, with gray hair and a long drooping moustache that fell away on each side of a sharp, bristly chin. His shoulders were hunched after many years of crouching over a pan washing mud and silt in his continual search, and there was nothing in his appearance to distinguish him from any other old prospector who grubbed for a living in the country. One would have thought that he did not possess a nickel in the world and would have considered him to be in the poorest of circumstances. He had finished supper, so I unpacked my food from the toboggan, made the dogs comfortable for the night, and while I was eating inquired in a roundabout way regarding Harry Stravich's whereabouts. I told Jack that I was looking for Harry, but gave him no details.

"He's up the trail a bit," the old man said. "You can't miss his cabin. Just follow the track through the woods. It's well marked because he's been down here once or twice lately. The two of them live together, his brother and him . . . haven't seen the brother, though, this winter. Harry says he's hurt his leg or something . . ."

This was the first I'd heard of the existence of a brother and the news wasn't good. The warrant was emphatic that I produce Harry at Dawson, and I wondered if the brother would be capable of looking after himself with an injured leg if he were left alone. On the other hand it would be impossible to take him over the rough trail through the mountains. I tried to find out from Jack how badly injured he was, but as he'd not seen him he could add nothing to what had already been said. Well, there was no point in meeting trouble halfway — it would be time enough to worry when I found out the exact situation. After some desultory conversation, I lay down on the top bunk and went to sleep, my last thoughts being of what I might find when I got to my destination.

Early next morning, the dogs, fresh after their night's rest, took off at a run in a flurry of snow down the clearly marked trail. Soon, however, they slackened down to their usual pace with their tails up and their eager noses smelling the air, searching for caribou. In the frost-laden air, their heavy breathing seemed magnified out of all proportion.

The trail wound through the trees until, rounding a bend, the team suddenly picked up speed as they sighted a snow-covered cabin. A small man dressed in the usual clothes of a trapper stood by the door. He carried a pair of snowshoes in his hand and evidently was just on the point of going somewhere, for a team of dogs stood, already harnessed, behind him.

For a moment neither of us said anything. Then, "Who are you?" he asked. "Ain't seen you before to my knowledge..." He had a soft, modulated voice and sounded as though he might be a Pole or Ukrainian.

"Mounted Police from Dawson," I replied. "I'm looking for Harry Stravich."

"Well, that's easy," the other said. "My name's Stravich." I'd walked up past my dogs and now we were face to face with each other. There was an expression of concern in his eyes. "What would you be wanting me for?"

Now that he was closer, I could see that he was another old man, perhaps a year or two younger than Jack Spratley. A pair of faded blue eyes peered out from gray, bushy eyebrows. I did not enjoy what I had to do, but it was best to get it over with as soon as possible.

"I guess I've got some bad news for you," I said. "I've a warrant for your arrest. It'll mean your coming with me to Dawson."

He was shocked and for a minute or so could say nothing; then he gathered himself together.

"That's *really* bad — what's it I'm supposed to have been doing?"

"Nonpayment of debt — a thousand dollars. I've got orders to take you in unless you can settle up the amount."

While we'd been talking, notwithstanding the apprehension in his voice, he had shown no antagonism, only anxiety. He stood looking down at his snowshoes.

"Well, I'll need to get some stuff together if we're going all that distance," he said. "Come inside and we'll have something to eat. Only thing is, my brother's hurt himself — doubt if he can look after himself all alone . . ." The words trailed off as the full magnitude of his difficulty struck him.

I could see that the subject of his brother being left on his own was bothering him deeply. I tried to think of something useful to say but it was difficult, for here was tragedy.

"What's wrong with your brother?" I asked. The forebodings of the previous evening came back to me — it looked as though there were going to be complications on this trip.

"Hurt his leg — ain't properly well yet. Can't leave him long by himself. Mostly he's all right, but he ain't strong enough yet to move much around. If he falls it would make it that much worse . . ."

Just then Harry's brother came to the door. He was supporting himself with a stick and moved with a limp. It turned out that he'd sprained his knee hauling wood.

"This is my brother," Harry said. He turned to make my identity known. "He's a Mountie from Dawson . . ."

"Come in, come in," the brother said. "I was just putting coffee on the stove — sure am glad to see you!" He hadn't heard the conversation outside, and I went in thinking that he might not be so pleased when he knew the reason for my presence. The cabin had much the same appearance as Jack Spratley's and it was plain to see that Harry and his brother were not blessed with much. It was fortunate that they had a big woodpile outside — I'd noticed it on my way up the hill — as this would mean that the brother could keep warm without too much difficulty while Harry was away; at the same time it would not be too easy for him to do all the chores alone. It was safe enough to leave him on his own for a day or so, but a period of months was a long time indeed and no one could tell what might happen. While the coffee was being passed around, Harry explained the reason for my presence, saying that he would have to accompany me to Dawson but skirting around the subject of the length of time he'd be gone.

"Think you'll be able to manage on your own for a while?" he asked his brother. Immediately, the same worried look appeared in his brother's eyes that I'd seen in Harry's when I'd first told him who I was.

The brother said nothing for a moment. "Sure, I guess so." There had been a slight pause while he busied himself reaching for a container of sugar that lay on the other side of the table. "How long d'you think it'll be for?"

Harry seemed to be having some difficulty in replying. The moments rolled by as I slowly lit a cigarette.

"He doesn't know for sure," I finally said. "May be for quite a while . . . he'll be back as soon as he can." It seemed a lame remark, but I could not tell him that Harry might be away for six months unless the $1000 was paid.

"We'd better be on our way," I said, when we'd finished the coffee. "If we go now, we'll be able to spend the night at Jack Spratley's place and then go on from there in the morning. I'll see if he won't drop in here once in a while, at least until your brother's leg is better. I guess he'll be glad to . . ." I wasn't too sure; Jack Spratley was long past the time when this would be easy.

By late afternoon we were back at Jack's cabin. Nothing was said about Harry's predicament and Jack didn't ask any questions. The morning would be as good a time as any, I thought, to discuss what to do about Harry's brother.

As Harry and I had a long way to go the next day, we all turned in early, Harry taking the upper bunk and Jack Spratley the other, while I spread my sleeping bag on the floor close to the door in case Harry, in desperation, tried to get away in the darkness. The Alaska border was not far away, and once I lost sight of him he'd be gone and I'd be held responsible. Letting a prisoner escape, in the eyes of the Force, was a grave offense.

When the candle had been extinguished, it was pitch black in the cabin. Jack Spratley was awake and I had a good idea, too, that Harry wasn't sleeping. An hour or so went by and, all at once, Harry started crying. It was a terrible sound, an old man sobbing in the darkness. I lay there, thinking what a bad trip it was going to be on the way back to Dawson.

Jack Spratley suddenly spoke. "What you're making all that bloody row for, Harry?"

Harry's voice was half strangled. "I've got to go to jail for six months if I don't pay a debt . . . I'm worried sick about my brother . . ."

"How much is the debt?"

"A thousand dollars."

"Well, cut out that racket and let's get some sleep. I'll give you a thousand dollars in the morning!"

Nothing more was said. After a while, Harry stopped blubbering and I went to sleep. I could do this safely now, for if

Jack Spratley was going to pay Harry's debt there'd be no point in his trying to get away. He knew as well as I did that when one of these old men of the hills said that he'd do a thing, inevitably he did it.

In the morning, true to his word, Jack gave me a check.

"I'll have to take Harry in with me to get this cashed," I said. "I still have to produce him in answer to the warrant, but as soon as he pays what he owes he can come back. It'll take about a week. It might help out quite a bit if you looked his brother up while he's gone."

"Sure, I'll do that — I'll tell Harry. I'll go over there just as soon as I can. If his leg'll stand up to the trip maybe I can fetch him over — he can bunk with me until Harry's through with his business."

He held out his hand. It felt gnarled and hard, a mere bag of bones, but firm. For some reason I was surprised that it was not larger.

"It's been quite an experience meeting you," I said. "I don't think I'll ever forget it. Just for the sake of asking, do you think you'll ever get the money back?"

"I don't know," he replied, "Doesn't matter much, I guess — just couldn't bear to hear the old man cry! Anyway, the check's good — maybe I'll have a few cents left over —" Smiling, he turned to say good-bye to Harry.

On the return, I picked up my partner where I had left him and we made the journey back to Dawson in another two days. Crossing the mountains again, Harry and I seemed to have some bond of sympathy. Now he didn't seem like someone who was being taken in on a warrant — he was more like a friend. For the first time I'd seen something tremendous in the sense of humanity. I kept thinking about it, helping Harry over the rough spots as best I could. Perhaps there were other things more worthwhile in life than just being tough — besides making better time than the next man on the trail, besides chewing tobacco and spitting out the juice, besides striking matches on one's teeth when the spirit moved

189

one. Perhaps there were things which, once seen, transcended all things material; perhaps this had been another marker on the road I was following; perhaps it was just that Jack Spratley's compassion had made an impression.

Before a week had gone by, Harry rejoined his brother. The next December, a parcel addressed to me in nearly illegible scrawl arrived at the R.C.M.P. barracks at Dawson. In it was a piece of brown paper, torn from some wrapper. "With best wishes for Christmas — from Harry," it said, and in the box was a set of colored woolen decorations for the five dogs I drove, which had made the trip with us from Glacier to Dawson. They were not the kind of things one could buy. He'd made them himself, with infinite care, during the long, dark evenings of autumn!

11

White River Patrol

AN R.C.M.P. diary never tells the whole story. It is like a diamond, a concentrated essence lacking in dimension, the very soul of brevity, and requires a lot of filling in between the lines.

This is an account of a patrol which Constable Sidney May and I made in 1930 and from which we were lucky to return. It was the winter after my trip to Glacier, and due to the conditions we encountered we were so long overdue that we had been given up as lost. Here is the first entry in the record.

January 28. Left Dawson 1 p.m. Camped Ryder's cabin 4:30 p.m. Miles traveled 14. Good trail. 30 below.

The orders we had received were clear. We were to proceed up the Yukon River as far as Coffee Creek and then go overland to Wellesley Lake and on to Snag on the White River. From there we were to head down the White to its junction with the Yukon and then down the Yukon back to Dawson. The route would be in the form of a triangle, and along it we were to visit all the Indians and other inhabitants of the country. Besides this we were to look into conditions generally, and take action when law violations, including those of the game laws, came to our notice. In all a distance of nearly seven hundred miles was involved, and it took us nearly two months. The patrol consisted of May and myself and a team of five dogs, and three weeks after starting we had reached the White River.

February 19. Left Wellesley Lake 8:30 a.m. Traveled to Snag arriving 5:00 p.m. Jacob Doland in residence. Good trail. Miles traveled 25. 20 below.

So far it had been a hard, rough trip for four hundred miles but still pretty much routine. We had visited the few camps and cabins we'd come across on the way, and had looked into one or two complaints, but there is nothing of interest in the diary except on February 15 when it refers to the condition of the dogs.

Breaking trail all day. Dogs all in. 350 lbs. on toboggan. 15 miles. 20 below.

This was probably where our troubles started, and they were to develop as we went along. Four days later the dogs were even more exhausted and we were tired too.

It was evening as we stood on the bank of the White River, looking down its length. On each side the forest stretched interminably, the trees dead and abandoned in the solitude of the land. We had stopped for a breather after coming out of the bush, and before us on the farther side of the river we could see the cabin where we would stay for the night. The snow, sloping to the roof, made it a small, white hill in the limitless expanse of the valley as it stood silhouetted against the wall of the forest. In front, a toboggan trail fled, nebulous and ghostly, into the gathering dusk. It was Jacob Doland's cabin, the only white trapper for forty miles around.

"Hope he's at home," May said, spitting reflectively at the tips of his snowshoes. "Be nice to get some good hot grub." He bent down to look at the lead dog's paws and

192

pulled a piece of frozen snow away from where it had stuck to the hair between its toes. "Not so good," he continued. "Feet getting raw. Soon the whole lot will be lame." He was a big man, nearly six feet in height, with a face lined by the storms and blizzards we had faced and a stubble of beard-framed lips cracked by the frost.

I nodded agreement. "Hope so, too. Maybe he's out on his trapline. Anyhow we'll have to stay over a few days to rest up the dogs..." I looked at them where they lay curled in their traces at the edge of the bank; they were skin and bone only, but Doland kept a wilderness trading post to outfit the Indians and we had been told that we would be able to purchase some food from him. It was important, for now very little remained and we still had a long journey down the White. Calling to the dogs, we went down the bank to find shelter before darkness set in.

Just as we climbed the trail to his shack, Doland came out, having heard the noise of the team. He stopped, surprised. He was a short, dark man, with hair in greasy locks to his shoulders. At some time in his youth he had injured his back and, while his frame was powerful, the upper part of his body was emphatically stooped.

"Evening, boys," he said as the team drew up by the door of the cabin and came to a stop. "Glad to see you — wasn't expecting anyone around these parts for a while. Come in as soon as you've fixed up your dogs. Guess you'll be wanting some grub."

He was in his shirtsleeves and in no condition to be kept outside talking. Shivering, he rubbed his hands together and hurriedly went back inside.

We unhitched the dogs, tied them up for the night and, taking our bedrolls with us, followed Doland into his cabin. It was the usual type of log shack, a little larger than most and divided into two parts, one forming the sleeping quarters and the other the store in which his trade goods were kept. After the open camps we'd been used to, the heat from the stove was like a furnace blast, but to Doland it was normal; he'd not been out on his trapline for a week or so and was accustomed to the thick, dense air, in which we could hardly breathe.

In the half dark of sundown he had not recognized who we were.

"Mounties, eh?" he exclaimed when I told him, his eyes showing his astonishment. "Well, you're a long way from home. Look as though you'd been through a hard time, too. What with all the snow, never expected to see a patrol through here this winter — no one's been round for months save the Indians."

He put supper on the table, and after we had eaten I asked him if there had been any new arrivals in the district during the summer when the river had been open. He thought for a moment.

"Not last summer," he replied. "But old Solomon Albert passed here about eighteen months ago. I hear he's got a shack somewhere up by the canyon and he had lots of grub when I saw him, but I've heard no word from him since. Guess he's all right though. Knows his business — he's been moving around by himself for years. Another one's a young fellow up around Frying Pan Creek — think he came in during the fall, maybe over the mountains. Just heard tell of him, though, from the Indians; haven't been that way myself."

Frying Pan Creek was about sixty miles away, close to the Alaskan border and in the same general direction as the lower canyon of the White where Solomon Albert had gone, and I wondered who this young man was. If he'd come up the White it would have come to Doland's attention, as this was the main watercourse that led to the area, but if he had come over the pass in the mountains from Alaska he'd be in the country illegally and trapping without the license required by the game laws. It meant extending the patrol for another hundred miles or so and for another week or ten days, but that was what we were there for — who he was and what he was doing would have to be looked into. Besides, Solomon Albert was supposedly in the same general area and, if we could, we should find out his whereabouts; it was strange that nothing had been heard of him for a year and a half and it was possible that he might be lying dead in his cabin or have met with some accident. If we could stock up with food from Doland we had no choice but to go. I asked him what spare provisions he had and he said we could take what we liked as long as we paid for it. He had not done much trading that winter and his store had all the flour and staples we needed. Flour was $35 for a hundred-pound sack and a pound of sugar would cost us a dollar, with everything else on much the same scale.

May and I talked it over that night and decided that, after the dogs had been rested and fed all they could eat for the next few days, we'd head for the mountains and the upper reaches of the White and visit the mysterious stranger Doland had mentioned. When the light had been put out and we had crawled into our sleeping bags, one of the dogs howled and was answered by a wolf in the distance. It was a mournful sound full of the presentiment of evil and what with the distance to be covered and the difficulties to be faced, it kept me thinking for a long time before I finally slept.

After a couple of days' rest, during which Doland told us of the Indian camps in the vicinity and one or two minor troubles they'd had, we thought that we had better go out and visit them and see how things were. The situation turned out to be ordinary — a lot of talk about shortage of food brought about mainly by poor trapping conditions, with only one complaint of any significance, a case of the alleged seduction of a teen-age girl who had given birth to a child a month or two previously. There was nothing that could be done about that; if any action was possible it would have to be left until the river opened up in the summer, for it was impossible to take a woman down the White under winter conditions to where she could give legal evidence. It would be too tough a trip and it was quite possible that she might die on the way. In another two or three months the river would open up and then the journey could be made quite easily by canoe without any of the hazards a winter trip would entail. The matter was allowed to rest there and May and I began our return journey to Snag.

Traveling through the woods took up time and it was not until five or six days afterwards that we got back to Doland's. Now, for a change, a pleasant surprise awaited us. We found that the stranger for whom we intended to search had come in to the trading store, having snowshoed the sixty odd miles from his cabin to see if Doland would supply him with food. Jim was about the same age as I, with a sharp, angular face on which there were a few freckles, a pointed nose, and a shock of reddish hair which by its look had not been cut since the fall. He was very thin. Doland told him who we were, and as soon as the preliminaries had been looked after I asked him how he had entered the country and what he was doing at his camp.

There was a moment's hesitation. Then, "Might as well tell you the truth," he said. "Came in over the mountains before the snow came last year — thought the trapping might be good with no one around. Didn't turn out that way though. Found an old broken-down cabin on Frying Pan Creek and holed up there for a while. Pretty soon I was nearly starving to death so I came in to find out what the chances were of getting some food . . ."

He had known of the penalties attached to crossing the border and trapping without a license but had decided that the risk was worth it. He could go through the pass, live off the country with his rifle, and once he had gathered sufficient pelts to show a fair profit, return by the way he had come. But he had failed to allow for the snow. When it came he found himself trapped.

"Never knew it could snow like that," he said. "Once it started it never let up. Things looked kind of bad, but luckily I shot a deer and snared a few rabbits or I would have been dead!"

As soon as he'd finished speaking, I knew we'd have to take him to Dawson. Quite apart from his having broken the law, he could not be left by himself in the desolate area that was Frying Pan Creek; he'd either starve or go out of his mind. As I looked at him now and at the fixed stare in his eyes, he already seemed on the verge; if his condition got worse he might shoot himself or some passing Indian and then we'd have a real tragedy on our hands. In a sense it might be doing him a good turn to take him with us to Dawson, I thought, and once we got him there it was only a comparatively short distance to the border and he could make his way to one of the small settlements on the other side. If he was left where he was, he'd not be able to cross the pass back to Alaska; it would be a long time before the snow disappeared in the mountains and until it did his retreat would be entirely cut off. When I told him that he'd have to go with us down the White he raised no objection and seemed in a way to be glad. Perhaps he felt it to be the lesser of the two evils he faced — at least he'd be fed and looked after on the way.

"What about my gear up at the cabin?" he asked. "I've a bit of stuff — one or two odds and ends ... bunch of traps, too, spread out through the woods."

"We'll have to go there and pick them up," I replied. "Then we can cross to the White and come back to Snag. Anyway, we've got another small job to do ..."

I told him about Solomon Albert and asked him if he'd seen him. The answer was no.

"Haven't any dogs so I've only been able to go a few miles from the cabin to set out my traps." He pointed to a small sack of fur he'd brought with him in exchange for which he'd hoped to get food. "That's about all I've been able to get all winter. Can't get very far when one only has snow-shoes."

I looked at the fur. It was worth very little and, with food the price it was at Snag, it wouldn't fetch much. It must have been quite a trip coming in all that way from Frying Pan Creek and I was surprised that in his weakened condition he'd made it, but he'd been desperate and in no position to go counting the odds. Now that he was in our custody, the fur would have to be confiscated, to be produced in court in due course. It was late in the evening by the time we'd finished talking, so laying our sleeping bags out, we got undressed and turned in.

The diary is very terse about what happened next but it was bad while it lasted.

February 27. Doland's shack caught fire 4:30 a.m. owing to dirty stove pipe. Helped put fire out. Stayed Snag all day.

Coming back from the Indian camp and running behind the dogs had soaked us in perspiration, and we had hung our underwear beside the stove before getting naked into bed on the cabin's hard floor. Doland had crammed the stove with logs to make up a good hot fire, but the danger of the extra heat setting fire to the soot in the pipe had not been considered.

In the early hours of the morning, a dull red glow filled the cabin, and the walls were hidden in billowing smoke. Lying sleep-bemused on the planking, I could see something in front of me jumping up and down and gibbering. Just as I was on the point of getting up to inspect the apparition more closely I became fully awake — it was Doland in a high state of excitement, shouting that the roof was on fire.

There was not a moment to be lost! If the fire took complete hold, all our equipment and the provisions would be lost. They were the only supplies available in the country and there would be no hope of obtaining anything more.

While these thoughts were running through my mind I was on my feet and on my way to the door. There was only one bucket of drinking water in the cabin, but it was impossible to find it with the smoke surging round and any delay might be fatal. The only hope was to climb on the roof and loosen the burning logs, which would help put the fire out, and the melting snow running down the cracks would assist in quenching the blaze.

I grabbed a snowshoe to use as a shovel in the three-foot-deep snow. On the roof it was twenty below and torture without any clothes on, but by working furiously I managed to clear some snow away at the seat of the fire close to where the stove pipe came through. Just as I began my attack on the logs, there was a shout from below and the flames were gone with an accompanying hiss of steam. Doland had found the bucket and with a lucky shot had hurled its contents at the center, finishing the job I had started outside. I got down in a hurry. Now, the fire defeated, I suddenly realized how cold I'd become. Diving through the thigh-deep snow I raced for the door of the cabin. The soles of my feet were numb and I had lost all feeling in my hands, fingers and toes, but once inside again, by jumping around vigorously and flapping my arms in a whirlwind of action, I brought the circulation gradually back as the blood forced its way through my veins.

As soon as the fire was out, Doland lit the stove in the other room — the trading store — which had not been touched by the flames and, after I'd swallowed several cups of coffee to stop my teeth chattering, we all eventually went back to sleep and slept soundly again until late in the morning.

We spent most of the following day helping Doland straighten things out. Then on March 2 the three of us, left for the mountains. The diary says:

Traveled 15 miles and made open camp. No trail. 400 lbs. on toboggan. 10 above.

Now that spring was somewhere around the corner it was getting warmer, but this was no guarantee that the temperature would remain constant; one day it would rise unpredictably — only to sink again by nightfall to well below zero. There was no trail ahead as all Jim's tracks of a day or two earlier had been blown in by the wind, and we were faced with nothing but a thick, powdery mass of deep snow. Not knowing how long it would be before we reached Frying Pan Creek and then returned to Doland's cabin at Snag, it was necessary to take a heavy load of food and equipment on the toboggan for ourselves and the dogs. They lay curled in the snow, each with its nose covered by its tail and the pads of its feet warm against its belly, watching with distaste our preparations to leave. Finally, caught by the scruff of the neck, they were dragged protesting from the snug beds the heat of their bodies had made to their places in line, and the collars slipped over their heads.

Doland had been viewing the proceedings with amusement. "They're all the same." he said, smiling. "Just like humans — never want to get up in the morning. Stay there all day if you'd let 'em."

"That's why they call it a dog's life," I replied. "Just like ourselves — give them a square meal and a place to sleep and they're as happy as can be!"

He became serious. "You'd better watch your step when you come down the White from the canyon. Ice is pretty bad up there, so the Indians say, what with the fast water. Keeps cutting away underneath — hard to tell just how thick it is under the snow. Here and there just a skim, maybe, but at points the river's broken through. Wouldn't want you to fall through some place where it's weak — wouldn't have any more chance than a snowball in hell!"

I thanked him for the warning, but I didn't see how we

could avoid traveling the White since we had to go there to look for Solomon Albert.

At first May went ahead on his snowshoes to break the trail down while I stayed behind to handle the load. At each step he sank twelve inches or more into the soft, fluffy mass, stamping it down so that the dogs could find footing. I urged the team onward, pushing and straining. Sometimes we'd travel a mile in an hour, sometimes two. We could travel only while it was light; to go on after dark would be asking for trouble — it would mean swinging razor-sharp, double-bitted axes in the darkness of night to make camp, and one glancing blow off a tree could bite through a moccasin deep into the foot. Then there would be no effective remedy, so notwithstanding the difficulties it was up to us to keep plowing along, hour after hour, with very little rest.

That evening we made camp in a grove of trees, fifteen miles on our way. Soon the trees came thundering down at the bite of our axes, showering us with clouds of snow as their thickly blanketed branches surrendered their load. In a few minutes the logs were blazing cheerily, their roar and crackle echoing through the dead-still calmness of the night. It was refreshing to listen to the tumult of the dancing flames, for we had been deprived of all sound during the day except when we shouted to the dogs, exhorting them to greater effort as we came to some particularly difficult place on the trail. Now, in the warmth of the fire, the trees were sharply etched in black and flickering red, giving us protection from the wind and seeming almost friendly. Listening to the meat sizzling in the frying pan we were, for the moment at least, at peace. When it was cooked we would eat, the dogs would be fed, and once the fire died down we would sleep.

Gazing into the burning logs I wondered why we did it. Certainly there could be few more uncomfortable ways of earning a living, fighting the elements step by step when one false move could bring disaster and a cold, unpleasant death.

Even a wrenched ankle or — worse — a broken leg, as we slid down some slope holding back the toboggan so that it would not overrun the dogs, could bring this about; then we could travel no farther until help, which might be long in coming, finally arrived. We must be crazy, I thought, to take these risks for the small salary we earned each day. But it was something deeper, really, that kept us going. It was the battle that counted, the continual day by day fight against the land, the hardships and the cold, and more important still, the knockdown and drag-out struggle with oneself when one's feet refused to move another step and yet went on.

It had taken us longer than we expected to reach the mountains, and it was late in the afternoon four days later when we came to Frying Pan Creek and the cabin which Jim had put in order for himself. Here, unlike the small hills and valleys through which we had passed, the heights surrounded us, cloaked in heavy snow, seemingly insurmountable. The great trees rose like giants, reaching their white crowns into the leaden sky, looming malignantly at us, the trespassers, as we pushed our way along the creek bed in their quiet demesne. Another half hour and we were at a small group of broken-down shacks which once had been a thriving community, built at the time of the Chisana gold strike some fifteen years before. It was now a ghost settlement, for the most part in ruins and knowing no human habitation except for Jim since it had been abandoned a decade or more ago. One cabin had been repaired sufficiently to make it livable, although like the others it was still much the worse for wear. A few blown-in snowshoe tracks round its door signaled the fact of Jim's previous presence. Except for a small piece of frozen meat, a half-filled sack of rice, and a few odds and ends of personal belongings there was nothing. I could see what had forced Jim to go to Doland's — he'd been in the last extremity of hunger, close to starvation. If he'd waited longer he would not have had the strength to do it, and the frost, waiting its chance, would have trapped him. No wonder Jim looked thin — it was amazing, considering his condition, that he'd survived at all.

May and I exchanged glances. "This all you got?" I asked. Jim nodded, dumbly. He had been eating our food on the trip from Doland's and, while he was still weak, he was feeling better. We had picked up his traps, spread here and there through the woods, as we went along, and once he had collected his meager effects there was no reason for us to stay longer. I was anxious to get on. In view of what Doland had said about the condition of the ice, there was no knowing what we would find when we got back to the river.

The cabin where Jim had been staying was twenty or twenty-five miles from the White. We had spent the previous night in an old abandoned shack, some fifteen miles closer. Although the accommodation was very poor, it was a good deal better than the tumbledown structure on Frying Pan Creek that Jim had been using. As the days were getting longer and it was still light enough to travel, we decided to return there. Picking up Jim's few possessions, we left, reaching the cabin at ten o'clock at night, having traveled thirty miles in fourteen hours on the trail that day. Next day, cutting through the woods, there was no trail at all and we were only able to make eleven miles before we camped early in the evening, in the open. The following morning we came out on the White River, thirty miles from Snag where we'd left it.

March 7. Reached White River 11 a.m. Found Solomon Albert's tracks. Started down White. Bad going, no trail, three feet of snow, heavy load, open water and dogs tired.

The river made a broad ribbon of snow, untouched, unsullied and pure, except where a double line of tracks skirted the edge and vanished in the direction of the lower canyon, a few miles beyond. They could belong to no one but Solomon Albert, we knew, for we'd been told he had suffered some accident to his feet a few years previously and this was clearly revealed by the marks in the snow. We bent down to examine them closely.

"Made a day or so ago," May said. "Probably yesterday afternoon — it snowed a bit in the morning so he must have passed here since it fell."

The tracks were sharp and clear, the impressions quite plain — if they'd been made earlier they would have been full of drifted snow. They formed a straight line along the edge of the river and seemed to point up the solitary existence of the person who had made them a few short hours before — at least they showed that he was still alive. If he was walking around, under the circumstances there was no point in following the tracks upriver. The dogs were too tired and we had more than a hundred miles to go in the other direction down the White. We'd be lucky if we made it. I looked at Jim. He was squatting on his heels; as it was we'd have quite a job to get him to Dawson, for his muscles weren't in the same condition ours were and he was weak from the restricted diet he'd been eating. The dogs were no better — why, there was nothing there at all! They swept in a flat slope from their chests to their haunches, the rounded part that should have been their bellies making a direct line from half-way down their forelegs to their tails.

"Well, we can't go after him," I said to May. "We don't know how far up the river he lives. It might mean an extra two or three days. Probably be a wasted effort, anyway. If he can travel around the way he's doing, by the look of it there can't be much wrong with him."

As we'd been talking, I'd been taking a careful look at the river. What Doland had said was true enough — the ice was very bad. In the dull morning light small diaphanous patches of mist could be seen rising from the open spaces where the water escaped momentarily from its prison and, with a rustle of silk, fled green, dark and menacing under the deep blanket of snow on its farther side. Although we would be on top of three feet of snow there'd be no way of knowing whether or not underneath there was only a thin shell of ice. If one fell through, the icy cold water would do the rest and that would be the finish — next summer one's body might be found far down the river. Jim would be better off; he could come along behind and be safe, following on the firmer ground over which we and the toboggan had passed.

"Looks like a dirty business," I said. "We'll both have to go ahead of the dogs if they're going to get traction. Otherwise, snow's so deep they'll just wallow. Perhaps with both of us out in front we can pack the trail down so that they can keep moving. Jim can try and get them going from behind."

I led the way downriver, with May eight or ten yards behind, then the dogs and toboggan with Jim bringing up the rear — it was easier there as the trail was packed down by the weight of the load as it passed. I was testing the ice at every step with an axe and wearing moose-hunting snowshoes nearly five feet in length which would hold me up for that critical extra moment of time if the ice gave way. I'd be able to feel the thick snow subside and, if I was quick enough, by exerting every ounce of strength I possessed I might be able to jump to something more solid. But it was an unpleasant feeling, especially when one came near the dark, cavernous holes and could see the rushing torrent speeding by. It was tiring work, too, lifting one's knees as high as one's thighs every time a step forward was made, and every half hour we changed over, May going ahead while I followed behind. Once the ice gave way beneath him and once under the heavy weight of the toboggan, but it was surprising how much energy could be produced when one was faced with an immediate prospect of drowning. Each time by a violent effort he and the dogs escaped, leaving a deep, gaping hole where a moment before there had been a clean, flat surface of white. I too was fortunate. Once I felt the ice begin to go, gently subsiding, but by running as fast as I could in a long convulsive series of leaps I was able to get to where the ice was firmer.

Notwithstanding the heavy snow and our difficulties in breaking trail in front of the dogs, Jim's poor condition prevented him from keeping up, and by the time he overtook us at the campsites we would have the fire going and the food cooked. I watched him carefully through the lifting smoke, knowing that if he could make the first few days, his strength would have improved before we began the hardest part of the patrol, the journey from Doland's cabin down the White River to where it entered the Yukon, a hundred miles away.

March 8. Broke camp 7 a.m. Same going as yesterday. Traveled 13 miles. Made open camp 4:30 p.m. Blowing hard this p.m. Had to backtrack several times to cross open water.

In the afternoon it was still about zero and a minor blizzard started to rage up the river, freezing our faces as we forced our way on. The holes were getting bigger, too; sometimes they stretched right across, the snow coming to an end under the lee of a bank. There was no way of going up through the bush — it was so dense that we would not have been able to make headway — so then we would have to backtrack, crossing where the ice was firmer and breaking trail again down the other side. This was the day both of us were so exhausted that, when my turn came to take the lead, I put the axe away on the toboggan feeling that if I fell through the river it might be a welcome relief. What was the sense of testing the ice at each step? The clutch of the current would mean only a few moments struggling, then the agony would be ended and there would be peace!

March 9. Broke camp 9 a.m. Reached Snag 2 p.m. Snow not so deep near Snag. Miles traveled 7. About 10 above.

We had managed to make our average mile and a bit an hour despite the conditions, and it was a relief when for some reason the snow began to thin out as we got closer to Snag. Not that this made conditions much better — the thinner the crust became the more chance there was of going through. Instead of the heavy snow subsiding slowly now it might give way underneath without even a moment's warning. I didn't care much. Anything, I thought, would be better than going on living under such conditions — and God how tired we were, how very tired. And yet, when you felt the snow gradually thinning out as it led to some open stretch of water until ten or fifteen yards away you could see the dark, swirling millrace almost beneath you, it was curious how quickly your mind changed and how hastily you turned back to find some safer channel; for fear confronting one is the strongest deterrent I've found against letting go the short strings of life. Whatever the odds are, one always hangs on.

This was the time, too, when my training on the Mackenzie River helped me immeasurably. I was in better condition than May — it was his first trip — and as all that Jim could do was to follow the toboggan and dogs, lagging a long way behind as we made the trail through the snow, I had found myself taking the lead more and more as the hours of the last two days had gone by. Besides, as the senior member of the patrol, I had a moral duty now that conditions were getting worse to stay out in front. It was with more than a feeling of thankfulness, therefore, that on rounding a bend in the early afternoon I saw Doland's cabin standing, a virtual paradise of safety, on the bank. Like a lumbering bear and forgetting all exhaustion, I ran the last hundred yards or so, caring for one thing only — to get to firm ground and be away from the river. For nearly twenty-four hours while we'd been on its surface it had waited for us to go through like some animal biding its time for attack. I sat down in the snow with solid ground under me and waited for the others, who now slowly came plodding down the length of track I'd made with my snowshoes, the dogs coming to life again as they saw the cabin before them and the prospect of rest.

But it could not be for long. We were long overdue; they would be getting anxious about us at Dawson and, if we were to avoid a search party being sent out, we would have to get on. March 10 we spent outfitting at Doland's drying out our moccasins and our gear, and then the next day with our supplies replenished we set out again on our journey down the White.

Below Snag the conditions were much the same as up-river:

The traveling down the White is very bad. Open water abounds on all sides and in many places there is no ice under the snow.

We had a heavy load again as, with no trail at all, there was considerable doubt when we would reach the Yukon. It might take us a week or considerably more — it depended on what we might meet with each day. As it was, a number of unforeseeable contingencies arose.

Doland, with the good nature that was always an ingredient of character in the North, had offered to go three days' journey with us to help break a trail with his dogs, and I had accepted this proposal with enthusiasm. It meant that May and I could go ahead, with Doland and his toboggan following after and Jim and our team bringing up the rear on easier going. There were six hundred pounds on our toboggan and the arrangement made the traction much better for our dogs.

March 11. Left Snag 9 a.m. with Doland and prisoner. Traveled 16 miles and camped in cabin. Deep snow for 6 miles, then glare ice and overflow. About 10 below.

208

It had soon become obvious that we'd not be able to make much distance each day. Instead of the twenty miles we had hoped for, the best we could so was eight, ten, or fifteen — and in a hundred-mile journey this might make a difference of as much as three, four, or five days. It narrowed our margin of safety and threatened our food supply.

It was early afternoon and we had gone six miles when another tribulation beset us. Somewhere ahead a tributary was entering the White, the force of the current pushing the water over the snow. The river before us was suddenly a sheet of glare ice, and in those places where the water had not frozen we would have to wade through it halfway to our knees. A great cloud of fog hung over the river caused by the free-flowing flood of the tributary meeting the sting of the sub-zero air.

When we reached the first ice the dogs' feet scrambled frenziedly. We made it across until we came to the water and there the lot of us waded in. The water would extend for fifty or a hundred yards, then there would be an interval of glare ice, and then water again. Each time we were free of the water we would have to change our socks and moccasins or our feet would freeze; sometimes, if the stretch of ice was not too long, we would run as fast as we could over the glassy strip with our snowshoes in our hands and into the water on the other side. It was always a race against the clutch of the frost at our flying feet until we found refuge and warmth in the grasp of the water round our legs again. For while it was ten degrees below zero in the open air, the temperature of the water stayed close to thirty-two degrees above until it froze into ice on the surface and then hardened all through. That night we camped in an old, abandoned cabin, sixteen miles on. Writing up the diary, I remember thinking that it had not been a good beginning, that day.

March 12. Left cabin 8 a.m. Traveled 16 miles. Good traveling on glare ice but lots of water necessitating changes of footwear. Made camp in cabin at mouth of O'Brien Creek. About zero.

Once the dogs had become accustomed to the glare ice they made better time than when they were pulling the toboggan through three feet of snow. Except for their feet slipping it was like hauling a sled over a skating rink, but they had trouble when they came to the open stretches of water and had to wade through. Running over the glare ice, May and I outdistanced them, waiting from time to time for the toboggan to arrive. At last they reached us, their sides coated with ice. The dogs lay down, licking the icicles from their bellies and paws.

March 13. Left cabin 8 a.m. Overflow and glare ice ended. No trail. 550 lbs. on toboggan. Reached Tom Gwynn's cabin 5 p.m. Distance traveled 8 miles. Dogs tired. Deep snow and open water. Searching for passage across for two hours today.

Eight miles! It wasn't very much, but try as we would, until we reached the mouth of the White this was going to be close to the best we could do each day. Perhaps March 13 was an unlucky day; it started out well, the open water and glare ice ending an hour or two after we had left the old, deserted shack at the mouth of O'Brien Creek. Not for long, though. Soon we were in deep snow again and then there was open water extending without a break from bank to bank across the White! I could hardly believe my eyes! Was it safe to wade through it as we'd done in the other shorter stretches over which we'd passed? This was something different — previously the strength and texture of ice frozen solid in the in-between stretches had helped us to judge whether it would be firm under water. Here the water was deeper — below there might be nothing but a treacherous succession of broken holes. We'd taken enough chances already; this might just be one gamble too many. Using our axes, we cut a short portage over a point of dry land, hauling and heaving on the toboggans to help the dogs as they strained and tugged their way through the bush, coming to frequent stops when their harness and the load caught on deadheads and stumps. Two hours later we were back on the river a few hundred yards below, the snow firm and deep again, the open water left behind at least for the time being.

March 14. Left Gwynn's 7 a.m., Doland returning to Snag. Made open camp 4 p.m. Distance traveled 10 miles. Same going. About zero.

Tom Gwynn was the only person we would see for the full distance between Snag and the mouth of the White. Our stay with him had lasted a few short hours only, but it had been a pleasant change. The sight of his cabin meant that we'd be saved the exertion of making camp and cutting wood. It made a big difference to pull into a shack that was occupied for a change instead of having to dig the snow away from the door of some old cabin or camp out in the bush. Tired as we were, it had been a godsend to find a place where we could enjoy some comfort overnight — even though four of us extra in the small space available meant sleeping, packed like sardines, on the floor.

In the early morning Doland made his preparations for the return trip to Snag.

"You'll know you're close to the mouth of the river when you come to the bluffs," he said. "They're on the right-hand side, about fifty miles down — can't mistake 'em, they stand right out. Becker's got a cabin there and then it's only half a day's travel to Stewart. You'll be able to get some more grub there if you run short."

Once we reached Stewart I knew that our troubles would

be over. I'd been there before. It was a fair-sized community close to where the White joined the Yukon River, and from it a well-used trail would take us the last seventy miles into Dawson. It was a much more inhabited area than the White and all down the Yukon there'd be cabins to stop at. However, the next several days on the White would be very difficult, since with Doland's departure only May and I would be left to break trail for the dogs.

Although the snow was as deep as ever, the patches of open water now decreased. The river was broadening as well, and we were able to travel on the snow-covered sandbars, avoiding the main current except when, for some reason, we had to cross. That evening, nine hours from our time of departure and ten miles farther on, we made camp in the bush.

March 15. Broke camp 7 a.m. Traveled 10 miles, made open camp 4:30 p.m. Same traveling conditions. About 10 below. Blowing hard this evening, dogs tired and fear they will play out.

Things were beginning to look bad enough, but the White River now chose to spring another surprise. We had stopped to eat our lunch at noon on that day when I noticed the scarlet mark on May's foot.

"Spot of blood," I said. "Snowshoe strings must be cutting in."

He took off his snowshoe and felt the lampwick binding. It was iron stiff.

"Frozen!" He inspected it glumly. "Guess they never dried out last night — must have hung them too far from the fire or maybe got 'em wet again this morning."

I squatted down to take a closer look. The binding had rubbed the skin away from his toes and the wound would gradually grow deeper until his moccasin would be a mass of blood. He must already have been suffering some pain during the morning but had said nothing about it. It was characteristic of him — he had plenty of guts.

Now there was only one thing to do. I'd have to go on and break trail by myself while May and Jim stayed behind the toboggan. There, the strain on his foot would not be so great, for on the level surface over which the toboggan had passed he would not have to pump his legs up and down every step. May didn't like the idea much but Jim was all for it.

"You know what I've been thinking?" he said.

May questioned him with his eyes.

"Why, just that if you two fell through the ice they'd think I'd murdered you — wouldn't have much chance at all even if I did get to Dawson."

I smiled. There was macabre amusement in what Jim had said. It would not have been so awkward from his point of view if Doland had been along as a witness. Although the danger was less now, there was still a chance that such a thing could happen.

"Guess I'd better stay behind with you then." May took up his place on the trail behind the toboggan. "Can't have anything like that happen — think of the tough time you'd have explaining!"

The situation was growing worse. Now I had to go on alone to make a path for the dogs, but with only the weight of one man on the snow the team had no traction and every mile or so I would have to stop and return to where the others were waiting. Then I'd turn round again and go on ahead while the dogs, urged on by May and Jim, would flounder along in the thrice-trodden trail I'd stamped out with my feet.

Even behind the toboggan, May's foot grew steadily worse, the blood congealing and freezing. When the long hours of the day came to an end and we made camp on the river's edge for the night, we had to soak it in the frying pan before his moccasin — which could not be cut off because there weren't enough spares — could be removed. Although he knew that his pain would be repeated with even harsher intensity the next day, he brushed it off lightly and made no complaint.

March 16. Snow in night and March blizzard blowing. Broke camp 7 a.m. and traveled 4 miles. Snowing and blowing so hard could not see 50 yards. Dogs played out so pulled into timber and cached everything except provisions, and made packs for ourselves to lighten the load. Storm abated in p.m. so traveled another 3 miles. Distance traveled 7 miles. Made open camp 5 p.m. 10 above.

This was the worst day of all. What with the roar of the wind and the thick, drifting snow, there'd not been much sleep for us in the night as we huddled together to keep warm. When morning came there was nothing to be gained by staying where we were. We were running short of food, and in the final analysis every mile we could make and every hour on the trail would count — as we very well knew. The weather was bad, but it was not yet a full-scale blizzard and we could see far enough ahead to keep stumbling on. Shaking the snow off our bodies, we set out again in the order we'd followed the previous afternoon with myself breaking trail in the lead.

It must have been about noon, when we had traveled four miles, that the full force of the storm hit us without warning. Before, the air had been full of drift that fled past, a thin curtain of white that hemmed us in on all sides but through which for some distance ahead we could see. Now a great mass of boiling white forced onward by the screaming wind came down the river, the snow darkening and almost blotting out our sight as the gale rushed on, lashing the dunes into a thousand million fragments that cut, bit and spat in our faces as the blizzard gathered strength. The dogs lay whimpering and whining, refusing to get up. They were deaf to all urging and we could not stay exposed any longer to the hurricane force of the wind. While May and Jim tore the sleeping bags, the rifle and axe, and Jim's furs from the toboggan, I unhitched the team, let the dogs loose and, followed by the others, ran for the shelter of a nearby island and the refuge of the trees. The dogs, now that they were free, shook themselves and came after us a few steps behind.

Once within the forest wall we brushed the snow and ice from our faces and built a windbreak of spruce to sit out the storm. It was warmer here than on the river's face where no one could survive. Would we ever be able to get up and go on? That was the question!

Listening to the raging wail of the storm and watching the nearby trees bending in abject surrender, we rose to our feet from time to time to free ourselves of the snow that climbed on our shoulders. On the river and beyond, the storm plunged past, a seething torrent of white, sweeping the branches bare. We crouched in our shelter, our backs to the wind, the drifts climbing slowly about us, eddying around our bodies and legs. And then, after an hour, the volcano of sound slowly grew less, the hurricane shriek subsided and, as the last sparse ranks of the blizzard's battalions fled by, a cold, frost-ringed sun peered out for the first time that day. By its light we made a small fire to loosen the frost in our bones, and retrieved the sled from the river, fastening the rifle to a fork in a tree. Next summer, when the river was navigable, we or someone else would have to return and find them. We tied a rag to a branch to mark the place. Then, wading into the thigh-deep drifts of the river, we left, carrying everything we had on our backs. The dogs, relieved of the dragging weight of the toboggan, accompanied us cheerfully, their tails curled stiffly.

It was the middle of March and the days were lengthening. As each hour dragged itself out in laggard succession we were able to stagger on. Three miles farther on we pulled into the timber again and made camp for the night. It had been a hard seven miles.

*March 17. Stayed in open camp to rest dogs. Blowing.
30 below at night.*

Despite the diary, it was no doubt we who most needed the rest. The brief break in the weather of the previous afternoon had given way to wind and it was getting cold. The idea of facing the blast that headed down the river was more than we could take after the happenings of the previous day. Besides, I thought we had made it. Some distance down the river we could see the bluffs which Doland had described, and from there it could not be far to Becker's cabin at the mouth of the White. We still had enough food for a day or so and could afford to take a short holiday from the never-ending trudge down the trail. It would be time enough to go on in the morning now that at last the bluffs were in sight.

The next day broke clear and cold, and early in the morning we went on our way. Soon we came to the bluffs and passed them, searching for some kind of habitation to come into sight. But there was nothing and the river still wound on and on!

Now we were close to disaster. Where we had expected to see the Yukon before us we were confronted instead by the same old winding ribbon of the White. Perhaps we still had another twenty or thirty miles to go? It was a dismal thought. In our condition, short of food as we were, another two or three days might make all the difference. I stopped and waited for the others to come up. At first none of us said anything. Then . . .

"Must be some other bluffs farther on." May spoke through lips badly cracked by the frost.

"Trouble is we don't know how far they are. Might be ten miles — might be twenty — might be more."

I stood up, scanning the distance for some sign of high land, but the landscape was as flat as a plate. Behind us, the bluffs we had passed two or three hours before stood clear on the horizon, mocking us, laughing at this last grim joke the White River had held up its sleeve. For the first time a real doubt entered my mind — were we going to make it? Could we travel for another day, perhaps two, maybe three? We were all in bad shape. Another night, a few additional hours, and then what? The prospect looked very grim, but there was nothing to do but go on.

About five o'clock that afternoon when searching for some place in which to make open camp, we rounded a bend in the river and suddenly saw the cabin! I shouted to the others. They lengthened their steps, the dogs running around, looking forward and back. I made my way up the bank and opened the door, but there was no one inside. Whom did it belong to, I wondered; it wasn't Becker's shack — that should have been at the mouth of the White but this was stuck away at the edge of the woods with the river still stretching on out of sight. I could tell that the cabin had been recently used; there were some dirty plates stacked up and wood chopped ready for use and all the snow cleared away from in front of the door. The owner must be away on his trapline, but there was no way of knowing just when he'd be back. But these were lesser considerations — the main thing was that now we'd have shelter for the night. Grimy and squalid as the cabin was, to us it was nothing less than a palace and we sat down on the bed and the two chairs at the table with a feeling of inexpressible relief. Using a pan he found in a corner, May was able to give his blood-covered foot a good wash for the first time.

Becker's cabin couldn't be very far now, we knew. I went outside and walked a few steps down the river where there was some sign of an old toboggan trail, drifted over with snow. I felt it with my feet. It led in the direction we were going and it had a hard surface underneath. Probably it was the trail used by the owner of the cabin when he visited Becker; if this was so, the next day would be much easier traveling, for our snowshoes wouldn't sink in quite so deep. After a good meal we went to sleep, convinced that our troubles were over.

The next day we pushed on. The knowledge that the cabin was there to come back to if necessary had lightened our spirits, and with the hard trail under our feet and a couple of good meals inside us we all felt much better. May's foot was the only cause for worry. With the continual drag of the snowshoes on his toes, after a mile or two his moccasin, as usual, was soggy with blood. He grinned cheerfully, however, when I asked him about it, knowing as we all did that we were nearly out of the clutches of the White. Even the dogs seemed more alert, sensing the end of the trip was in sight.

It was getting close to evening on March 19 when we saw the second set of bluffs rising out of the frigid world ahead. On the better trail we had managed to cover eighteen miles, and just beyond the bluffs we found Becker's cabin where Doland had said it would be, with the broad expanse of the Yukon River beyond it. As we came closer, Becker's dogs began barking, one or two letting off their usual timber-wolf wail, and our team, hearing the noise, began to run ahead eagerly. I waited for May and Jim to go past to the cabin while I turned round for a last, long, loathing look at the White. I shook my fist at the river, and taking my snowshoes off, climbed the last few steps up the bank.

From here it was easy. The trail between the river's forks and Stewart was packed down and hard, and after a night's rest at Becker's we covered ten miles, arriving at noon the next day. There we telephoned Dawson to let our headquarters know where we were — and after two days' rest, with a borrowed toboggan we set off on the last seventy miles of the trip. The dogs, knowing that they were on the home stretch, made time at a steady run, pulling willingly at the traces, as anxious as we were to get home. At one o'clock in the afternoon on March 26 we pulled up the slope from the Yukon River into the barrack square. Since we'd started out fifty-eight days ago we had traveled six hundred and eighty-four miles. The White River patrol was over — we had won!

We all showed signs of what we'd been through. Our faces, covered with scabs from the frost and burned black by the wind and the sun and the smoke of a hundred camp-fires, were scarcely recognizable as the team came to a stop and the men came out to meet us. After a few minutes' conversation I left May and Jim and went to report.

The Commanding Officer looked me up and down from behind his desk as I stood at attention and saluted.

"What happened?" he asked. "You're nearly three weeks overdue. We'd given you up as lost and were going to send out a search party tomorrow!"

"Had to go to the head of the White to pick up a prisoner, sir — took us longer than we thought."

I described the traveling conditions on the White River briefly and told him about Jim.

"Must have been quite a trip?"

"Yes, sir, a little rough in places — had to leave a rifle and toboggan behind."

He nodded. "Well, we can pick them up easily enough in the summer," he said. "I suppose you marked the place?"

"Yes, sir — tied a rag to a tree at the edge of an island. Shouldn't be difficult to find."

I saluted and turned about, glad that the interview was over and I could go and change the clothes I'd worn for two months. Apart from their being filthy, warming myself at the campfires had burned most of the seat from my pants!

After a few days' rest Jim was fined a nominal sum —

12

~~~~~~~~

The Quiet Place

EVERY man in his lifetime has a number of challenges to face. Call them what you will — dragons or ogres on the path — they are there and, come what may, unless you overcome them, you yourself are lost. Sometimes they are there in profusion, sometimes they raise their heads singly — regular giants — barring the road on which you wish to go. For me, the White River patrol had been the last one — quite a monster! — and now it was time for something else, not so formidable perhaps but taxing on the senses just the same. Different.

Spring had come and gone and with early summer the ice on the Yukon River had slipped slowly downstream, leaving the water clear. At Dawson, the snow had vanished from the streets and sidewalks, bringing in its wake a sea of viscous mud. The leaves spread themselves on the trees like quiet hands that stretched to meet the sun, and flowers bloomed beside the rills and freshets that, boisterous and chattering, spoke to each other on the hillside slopes. Trees swayed in the breeze, fresh and green, the wind in their tops singing its own soft melody of sound. It was a fresh wind, too — light, pure, and cool — that breathed ever so gently from distant snowtopped summits which hemmed in the northland. Soon the sun — rising higher day by day — blazed upon the city until it sank and slept the few short hours of dark away. The mud hardened, the lilting voices of the creeks sank to a murmur as their violence lessened, and the great river streamed past, serene and peaceful, bearing the sternwheel steamers that now intruded from the outside world. Full summer had come and, slowly like a young girl waking, the land had risen from its winter sleep.

As usual, it was a time of activity in the northern world. During the spring, as the ice loosened its grip, there had been no traveling, and in the barracks, to all intents and purposes, we had been very much shut in. Now, with the arrival of the open water period, men could be moved on transfer here and there, and before long I found myself under orders to go to Carmacks, a single detachment on the Yukon River between Dawson and Whitehorse. This time I was to be stationed by myself — Carmacks wasn't important enough to justify a second man.

When the steamer dropped me at this backwoods place I quite welcomed the idea. It had become monotonous living in the barracks at Dawson — there had been the usual tensions and quarrels between men closed in by themselves — and to be quite by oneself would, I thought, be a pleasant change.

The settlement ran along the river's edge, most of the houses separated by several hundred yards. At one end was Howard McMillan — the telegraph operator — and his wife; then a small chapel at which services were held in the summer by visiting student missionaries; a trading store run by an old bachelor; the police detachment; a cabin occupied by a trapper and his wife; a few Indian shacks grouped together, standing much on their own; and lastly, at the farthest end of the trail, an old married couple who looked after a roadhouse. After winter closed in this trail would form part of the route the caterpillar tractors took when, infrequently, they carried passengers and mail between Whitehorse, more than a hundred miles south, and Dawson, nearly twice as far in the opposite direction. Looking about me, it seemed much like the settlements I'd seen on the Mackenzie River two or three years previously but a good deal smaller, and the houses were more spread out. Except for the telegraph line between Whitehorse and Dawson, the river steamers in summer and the occasional tractor in winter, there was no communication with the outside world and once the river froze the settlement was sealed in.

About fifty yards back from the river was the police detachment, a frame building painted white with one large room to serve as an office and bedroom, a kitchen with a wood stove, and another small room adjoining the bedroom. Outside and to the rear of the detachment was a pile of wood, fuel for the winter, and, at the far end of the police lot, a small log shack which was used as a store house and in which, when not in use, a canoe and various essentials — dog toboggans, dog harness, dog food, etc.— were kept. Chained to their kennels to one side of the detachment were five dogs which, when I went close, sniffed at me curiously. They were a good-looking team, big and strong, and one in particular — a ginger-colored dog — showed by its face and figure more than the usual ancestry of wolf. Out in the district there were a few miners and trappers, and in the hills on the other side of the river some roving Indian families who lived off the country and came to Carmacks from time to time to trade their furs.

Although it was the summer of 1930, there were no facilities in the detachment such as people now enjoy — no radio, no outboard motor for the canoe, not even a typewriter to use in making out reports. There were a few books — I had brought some with me from Dawson — but of course mail, newspapers and periodicals were available only at very long intervals. In summer it was a reasonably busy place. There was quite a lot of traffic on the river and when a steamer came I could load the canoe on board and embark on the vessel, getting off fifty miles or so upstream, then slowly floating down, stopping here and there and visiting the inhabitants who lived along the banks. There was no crime to speak of, the presence of the detachment in the area being an effective deterrent, but one weak point existed which was hard to get around — there was no magistrate closer than Whitehorse, and to get there and back required up to ten days' journey in winter. The Indians, well aware of this, knew also that some crime of consequence would have to be committed before anyone was taken in. As a result they felt free to indulge in minor misdemeanors — getting into fights, making intoxicating liquor, and beating up their squaws. On such occasions my job was that of counselor rather than policeman and, because there was no court nearby, a warning — often disregarded — had to take the place of more drastic action.

It was soon after the ice on the Yukon River had gone out when I arrived at Carmacks, and during the summer I had much to do; with the long daylight hours, the task of patrolling the area and looking after the requirements of the settlement fully occupied my time. In a sense it was an ideal existence; I had no one to tell me what to do — very different from the barracks at Dawson where orders from a variety of persons had issued fast and free. In a few short months, I thought, the snow would come and I would be able to continue my excursions all by myself, to see what was going on in the mountains when I could get there by dog team. It was a pleasant prospect, but like other shining objects one comes across in life, it was to prove only an illusion; as winter settled on the land, it faded, vanished — and in its place, silent, grim and waiting, there was a very different phantom. A lurking, stealthy beast, which when I was not traveling the district to visit the infrequent inhabitants was to prove quite formidable. Isolation.

Early in October the first flakes fell, at first a handful, though as morning turned to afternoon they grew thicker and thicker until they blotted out the river. The sun now peered for shorter intervals each day and in the evening the flakes came cascading, buffeted by the rising breeze until, in the reflected glare of the gasoline lantern hanging from the ceiling, they seemed a sweeping horde of tiny moths, silvery-gray, that fluttered against the glass. Soon, where the light of the lamp cut the outside blackness, there was a thick blanket of white covering everything. Not long after, the river froze, the ice creeping along, noiseless, until it was solid. That was the difference one felt most of all — there was no sound whatever.

Sometimes, one saw a bird — a raven or crow — that hopped about, picking at the snow with its beak like some disciple of doom trying to pluck the dead eyes from corpses. As the days went on, I grew to hate them; they were always there, following along, jumping a few steps away if one shouted, always watchful, hoping and waiting. It was so quiet that in the detachment even a sneeze or a cough was a cataclysm, roaring off the walls and then losing itself, a stone dropped into the dark, bottomless well of the stillness. But one can no more describe utter silence than one can a vacuum. There's nothing there, nothing that has form or shape of any kind, but as the clock ticks over each second, each minute and hour following interminably on the other, the quiet that surrounds you turns to a heavy hydra that presses on the senses. Thoughts run at random, purposeless and blank, having no cohesion. Let no one question the savagery of the creature. It has killed many men as it wrapped itself round their minds and fulfilled its grim purpose!

As soon as winter had come and the snow had settled on the ground, I'd hitched the dogs up for a trial run. They sat there, one behind another in their traces, looking back at me with an expression of wise interest in their eyes in which was mixed some doubt. I knew what they were thinking. Was it a nice pleasant winter before them or would they have to work? Dogs are curious animals and know everything that goes on; in an instant, as soon as they hear a voice raised in command, they make up their minds whether you or they are going to be in control. I think that something, imperceptible to human senses but conveying an immediate message to a dog, enables it to decide at once whether it will accept you as the leader of the group. At all events, I've seen it time and again — some men can never drive dogs, others can handle them just as they wish to, at will. I don't know what it is — perhaps some cadence or timbre in the voice that makes them decide, without hesitation, just what they'll do. I had no trouble with the other four dogs — only with Rusty, the quarter wolf.

Rusty was a long, slinking beast, close to eighty pounds in weight, and had all the characteristics of the hereditary makeup of his clan; one could see it in his cunning face, running as it did to a sharp, pointed nose, with light-gray savage eyes, set back. There was nothing friendly to be found there, only hate, suspicion, fear and stealth. Even the manner in which he ran along in the traces, slinking, pushing his head from side to side, trying all the time to catch a glimpse of what was behind him, showed that this was some creature of the wild which, unlike the others, had never quite been tamed. He was dangerous, too, for as one passed along the side of the team to straighten out the traces — the dogs were continually getting their feet over them when they stopped for a moment and the leather went slack — he would snarl, crouch down, and show his teeth. If one took one's eyes off him on such occasions, as soon as he thought he was out of reach as quick as a flash he'd cut the traces with his razor-edged fangs, as though to show his defiance and emphasize the fact that under no conditions would he be compelled to work.

Nothing I could do that first day would change his opinion. While the other dogs ran happily along, tugging at their traces, Rusty held back, firmly refusing to do his share. This could not go on. Soon, unless I mastered Rusty, the remaining dogs would be influenced by his behavior and, instead of a hard-working team of willing animals, I'd have a bunch of dogs that gave continual trouble, and in a tight spot this might be very dangerous indeed. One or the other, either Rusty or I, would have to submit. It was a known fact that if one dog attacked, the others on the team might well join in and, if I was away on patrol and at some distance in the woods, I might be hard put to defend myself. In the Mackenzie district, as I knew, Indian children had been killed by dogs running loose in a pack; somewhere, a long way back, in most of them was this ancestry of wolf, liable to flare ferociously when their natural savagery asserted itself.

The second morning Rusty decided to make a stand, refusing to leave his kennel, and try as I would I could not pull him out. Although he had a chain round his neck, he simply placed his front feet against the woodwork on the other side of the opening that served as a door, hunched his massive shoulders up, and however hard I pulled, remained fixed, solid and immovable inside, snarling and showing his teeth at every move I made to try to force him out. The other dogs looked on with interest. Obviously they were wondering what I was going to do — which of the two protagonists was going to come out on top. On my part, I knew a lot depended on the answer. This was the climax of the battle which had gone on between us ever since the previous morning when I'd first hitched him up.

There was only one way to remove him from the kennel and that was to go in and drag him out. Kneeling down in the snow, I crawled a step or two forward. I'd had to let go of the chain as I needed both hands for what I had to do. A foot or so away Rusty crouched, baring his fangs, his head filling half the kennel door.

As I approached, Rusty backed away, snarling still but drawing in his head. He could not go far though — any retreat he might make would be blocked by the farther wall. My head and arms were through the door, Rusty's nose and mine an inch apart, his lips curling upward, ready to go for my throat if he could just summon up the courage to sink his teeth in. Now I had to push my hands round to the back of his head, catch him on each side by the scruff of his neck, and slowly haul him out. This was the dangerous time, while my arms circled the air, leaving my face and neck open. I found myself snarling, matching his ferocity. The whole thing had to be done with infinite care as any sudden move might precipitate the attack, but I was banking on what I thought would be the natural cowardice of the wolf; and after what seemed an eternity of time as we stared at each other, my fingers found the fur and closed. Now I was snarling harder, showing my teeth, no doubt as evil-looking as he was, just as much an animal, I suppose. But it worked, and when I had a firm grip on both sides of his neck, I could move away, hauling. Rusty still held back, as fierce as ever, but I knew I'd won. If he hadn't dared to go for me when my head was in the kennel he would not do so now, and once I'd got his shoulders out through the door the rest was easy. Picking up the chain and dragging on it with one hand while I held on to his neck with the other, I pulled his long form out. But it was only a temporary victory, I knew; he crouched at full length on the ground, eyeing me malevolently, not quite daring to spring. The other dogs were quite excited — they ran from one side of their kennels to the other at the full length of their chains, barking and howling to the full extent of their lungs.

I dragged Rusty to the traces and hitched him up to

see if he was willing to work. But still Rusty slunk along, always looking back. I had to go through the performance three mornings running before he finally admitted defeat and decided to accept me as the leader of the pack. Having done so, he agreed to work with the team and do his fair share in hauling the toboggan along. But even then it was not quite a victory. Every time I passed him to straighten a trace or help a dog whose feet had balled up with snow, he'd lift his lips and take a slash at the heels of my moccasins — never quite daring to sink his teeth in — as much as to say that he'd given way because he had to, but that in his opinion there was something wrong with me — I wasn't quite a wolf. In time I got to like Rusty. I admired him — there was always challenge in his eyes. After the third morning of snarling at each other like a couple of wild animals, he came out of the kennel quite willingly and I never had any further trouble with him or, for that matter, with any of the other dogs. But as I've suggested before, dogs are funny and rather like people in some ways — there are good and bad and you have to know how to handle them if you're going to achieve anything worthwhile.

Each day in the settlement, when I was not traveling the district by dog team, I'd wander down to the Indian community to remind the inhabitants that I was still about. There's been trouble caused by their potent home-brewed beer, and this had led to dissension and arguments and sometimes black eyes and bruises for their wives. As warnings served no purpose, something had to be done to bring them in line, for otherwise in the heat of an argument someone might get himself badly injured; and so one afternoon I arrested the Chief's son for celebrating not wisely but too well and told him that he'd have to come with me to Whitehorse. He didn't believe me at first — no one had done this before — and argued that he'd be away from his trapline for an unconscionable period of time, during which the wolverines would destroy all his fur. But I knew that if I made one example — and especially one applied to so important a person as the son of the Chief — it might serve to give weight to any future warnings I issued, and that the Indians might then be more punctilious about what they should do. Next day we set out to cover the hundred-mile distance to where court could be held, with the temperature hovering around the fifty-below mark, and after four or five days' hard travel reached our objective where my prisoner was dealt with by being fined $10, the minimum sum for being drunk. The mere fact of having had to make the long journey, however, had served its purpose. After that I had no further trouble with the Indians. Paradoxically, this proved a mixed blessing, for now, with the Indians behaving themselves, in the dark days of winter it was quieter still, and apart from the small daily chores there was less and less to do.

Christmas had gone and the year had come to its end, and now the snow reached well up to the windows, a flat plane that grew deeper as day followed day. It had been different in the jungle when I'd been alone, I thought as I stared through the glass. I'd lived with the mahouts, speaking their language, being almost one with them my-self. There had always been someone to talk to, either going about one's business when the elephants were working or in the warm evenings when they were fed and the men sat around the small fires in the camp, cooking their meals or chatting. Everywhere in the forest there had been a variety of sounds as animals called to each other. A buffalo or bison moved, breaking the jungle down. There, one could get around. Here, where light melted away quickly, the silence clamped down in my small box-like room to be broken only once in a while as a husky dog howled or shook itself, rattling its chain like some restless ghost trying to break out of its tomb, while the windows revealed only the black dark outside with the cloudy white light of the snow drifting down. All the work had been done, all the books read from cover to cover, the detachment swept and cleaned to a degree far beyond that required for inspection, and still the long weary hours followed each other bereft of achievement or of any kind of stimulus with which the mind could be filled. It was like living in a void. When, after its brief appearance, the sun slid down over the western horizon and everything had been done which could be given even the slightest attention, I would stretch out on my bed, staring at the ceiling, trying to remember what the outside world was like by looking at the pictures in a thick, commercial catalogue that someone some time before had left behind. By following the pages, one after the other, I could embark on a series of fantasies — a dangerous procedure — to fill in the gaps which, like a runaway movie film, ran down my brain. Now I could understand why trappers sometimes suffered delusions when winter set in. But my situation was, of course, much better than theirs, as every so often I could visit one of the others in the settlement and, by hearing a human voice, steady myself again in the sense of companionship. There were, however, a great number of afternoons and evenings and solitary days and nights to get through.

Under such conditions, one has to find something to cut down this hydra, a type of claustrophobia that tries to wrap itself round and strangle any sane thought in one's head. I suppose that if crossword puzzles had been available, or if I'd had the vision to bring a box of paints or some musical instrument to study at Carmacks, any of these would have helped immeasurably in such a struggle, for as long as one had something to occupy one's mind the beast that besieged it could be held there at arm's length, quite harmless — one might never even see it.

A radio or television set — anything to distract one — is of course a very fine aid in such circumstances, but failing such modern accessories one has to fall back on whatever other weapons one can find. A pencil? There were two or three in the detachment and one day I picked one up. Perhaps with this, in the dark of winter when black night descended, I could untangle the arms of the thing that wrapped itself round me, and fashion in my mind still sharper instruments with which to drive it back. Some people painted; others played musical instruments; quite a number wrote stories; a few even tried to catch dreams from the air and reduce them to verse. Why shouldn't I? Which was the hardest? Poetry! Turning out a sonnet would be a difficult thing, requiring full concentration and every effort of mind, but I'd done it before in the jungles and other places when I'd been quite by myself.

This was a strange weapon, perhaps, with which to subdue such an adversary, but it was all I needed to fill in the seconds, minutes, and hours of the evenings when the only sound breaking the stillness was the faint, hissing splutter made by the gasoline lantern that hung overhead. Not surprisingly, I wrote about the things which I saw around me or experiences which impressed me deeply.

SNOWBLIND!

Almost out of sight we saw him, leaden-footed in the ice,
Just a tiny fly, slow moving, on a tablecloth of white,
Staggering, falling, rising, calling, trapped within the Arctic
*   vise,*
With the frozen sun above him, blinding in its spear-tipped
*   light.*

Fate had crept upon him quietly through the timeless winter
*   days,*
All unseen the ghosts had dogged him, talon-fingered,
*   crooked to seize,*

Day by day they'd followed after, watched the sun's expanding rays,
Rising slowly through the seasons from the far antipodes.

Round and round the space-hung heavens moved the Archer on his quest,
Hungry-eyed for something moving on the snow plain far below,
Never resting, never sleeping, in the east or in the west,
Circumambient, ever watchful, scanning all the ice plateau!

Many months had gone before him since he passed below the rim,
Left the jeweled world aglitter in the silver of the moon;
Taking shafts and bow and quiver, climbing down the crimson brim
Of the frost-draped Arctic Ocean where it forms its vast lagoon.

Now again he'd come ahunting as the Spring was given birth,
And the winter night departed on her velvet-cushioned feet;
And he lay not quite in hiding, past the limits of the earth
With the dawn mist wrapped about him like a blossom-painted sheet.

Soon he peered above the world lip, catching at his fiery bowstring,
Raised his shoulders gently . . . gently . . . as a hunter stalks his prey,
Fitted arrow to his longbow, sailing on a lifted gold-wing . . .
Raider of the northern heavens, now embarked on his foray!

Now the time had come for action! Now the Archer flexed his bow,
Kneeled and aimed, and drew the bowstring . . . drew it flaming to the chin;

Loosed — and watched the arrow set the nether-world aglow
As it sped toward its target . . . and blinding entered in!

He was dead when we came near him, lying starkly on his
*   back,*
And his tortured eyes stared bloodshot at the skies' cold
*   biting light;*
But the tale of what had happened lay, in script, upon his
*   track . . .*
Where he'd staggered, blind, in circles, when the sun blacked
*   out his sight!*

Now that I had mental exercise, I began to feel better as the winter went on, but there was still not much to do and I began to ponder my future. Promotion was very slow in those days and try as I would, I could see nothing before me but a vista of driving dogs in the North. Or, if I was transferred later on, of winding up somewhere where there'd not be much scope.

Then an amazing thing happened, for suddenly I was able to take a tremendous step upward and find myself standing on the outer rim of the chasm with the road ahead clear. Howard McMillan brought me a telegram after plowing his way to the door in his fur cap and old heavy winter clothes. I took it, looking at the prefix with surprise. *Inspector!* Obviously someone at headquarters was getting careless, making such stupid mistakes. I opened it with McMillan, a twinkle in his eye, looking on. I had been promoted to commissioned rank! It conveyed the congratulations of the Commissioner and said that I was to go to Regina for training as soon as possible. I sat down on the bed, stunned. Some fool among my friends at Dawson was pulling my leg! There could be no other answer to it. I said so to Howard.

"No," he said, "it's quite genuine and official — I've checked back."

I was so dazed that I could only sit on the edge of my bed, swearing, the telegram in my hand! The news, arriving with all its implications after the solitary months of the winter, had startled me out of my senses, for the escape toward which I had in actuality and subconsciously been striving was now close at hand. The barriers were lifted and the road ahead free.

Soon I recovered and sent a telegram of thanks, asking for further instructions. When the reply came I found that I could make my departure as soon as convenient, leaving the detachment vacant after making provision for the dogs. My replacement would arrive later when necessary arrangements had been made. Looking after the dogs proved to be no problem. Howard McMillan would see that they were fed, and it would not be long, in any case, before the new man arrived. I said good-bye to them. They had been my companions on the trail when I'd been away on patrol and I thought a lot of them. They moved their tails slowly from one side to the other, fawning and seeming to know what was going on. Only Rusty remained aloof, hinting the same old challenge with his eyes. I patted him, running my hand along his back, but he would have none of it. He moved away, looking into the distance, yearning perhaps for all the other wolves! Then he turned his head and regarded me steadily for a moment. I could almost tell what he was thinking — now, at least until some other competition came along, he'd be leader of the pack. As I walked back to the detachment he was still watching me. I felt sorry for him — he was a wild thing, solitary, alone as all such creatures are in their inward thoughts. Looking at the other dogs I saw them scratching themselves, lying down and half asleep.

When the caterpillar tractor came, I got on board bound for Whitehorse; it was a new experience listening to its engine's roar drive silence back into the woods as we plowed southward in comparative comfort through huge drifts of melting snow. Spring was here again; soon the Yukon would be behind me. Here was another great adventure; the old life was cast away again and, in its place, only the future stood, mysterious, demanding and unseen.

When I reached Whitehorse I learned that another young man, Corporal Belcher of the western Arctic — later to become Deputy Commissioner — had been promoted at the same time as myself. It was all very unusual; no one seemed to know why — bearing in mind our age — we two had been singled out. Ordinarily such recognition was withheld for men who'd proved themselves in the more settled areas farther south and who had a great deal more service. It was only when I arrived at Regina that I learned the reason. I received a letter from the Commissioner saying that it had been decided to promote two young men who'd had experience in the North so that they could return there in administrative charge. This was understandable — it was a very tough country for anyone who was past his first youth.

A day or two at Whitehorse and I was on my way to Skagway, on the Yukon and White Pass railway, to take the boat from there to Vancouver. The next morning I boarded the steamer and in less than a week's travel reached Regina, the city I'd left almost three years before. As I had no proper uniform after the Yukon's wear and tear, I bought myself a suit of clothes and some odds and ends to make myself presentable and reported at the barracks, presenting myself for the first time in my new capacity, at the Officers' Mess. I could hardly believe it; I was still a Corporal in my own mind and seemed to have no business there!

One thing I'd discovered at Vancouver was that, quite unknown to myself, I'd been a Sergeant for a month. Due to a delay in mailing and the distance involved, the letter simply hadn't reached Carmacks before I'd left the North!

Part III

13

The Road Ahead

I FELT like a fledgling, a new boy at school, someone who enters a strange world not knowing what is in store. It was the same impression I'd had when I first came to Canada. And yet, not quite the same; then I'd been part of a long procession of immigrants, each and every one distinct and individual, knowing no ties which would bind them together. Here, by some inexplicable paradox, in some way or other unrelated, undefined, it almost seemed as though I was coming home. Yes, it was like coming home, but in a different capacity. I was an officer.

It was a fine, bright morning in spring when I arrived at Regina from the West, and a car was at the station to meet me. After a twenty-minute ride, the familiar surroundings of the training division came in sight and, entering its gates, I was deposited with my single suitcase in hand at the Officers' Mess, a large, massive building which stood next to Assistant Commissioner G. S. Worsley's house at one corner of the square. I got out, filled with trepidation. Three years before when I'd been a Corporal, the only access I'd had to it was when I was sent with some message to deliver and had to wait for the Mess waiter to open the door — never with enough temerity to stick my nose in. I wondered what it looked like, this sanctum sanctorum, where as the only unmarried officer in barracks I would be expected to live. For the seventh time in my thirty-year existence this was a different world I was entering, another environment in which I'd shoved up my head. Standing on the sidewalk and looking at the building, it seemed just at that moment that I was forever jumping from one kind of life to another, beginning all over again at every turn of the trail. Faintly now, somewhere deep down I had the faintest shadow of an understanding of the thing I pursued, but it was one that was so nebulous and ephemeral that it was past the possibility of words — something to do with an appreciation of values, a rounded perspective which one could obtain only by a search of far places, some type of knowledge in depth which could be achieved by experiencing hardship and suffering to gain a true realization of the value of the material pleasures of the world. This was no place, though, to consider the abstractions of life or indulge in metaphysical musings — the bare, brick walls of the Mess beckoned, and I had to go in.

I looked at the bell which, three years before, I'd rung on various occasions, but this time decided that signaling my presence would be too emphatic. The situation had changed; the last time I'd done it had been as a junior N.C.O., having no weight, will, or presence of my own. Now I was a separate entity, responsible only to myself, an acolyte who approached the threshold of the temple with diffident footsteps, wondering what mysteries would unfold as soon as he entered. No, as a novitiate I could not go about ringing bells. Far better that I should slide in gradually, mastering the situation moment by moment without awakening the gods! Perhaps the Mess would be filled with officers. In the apprehension I felt, I hadn't stopped to think that at that time of day they would have all gone to work.

There was no one there! In a moment or so, though, I heard the sound of movement. It was the Mess waiter and

I greeted him with respect as the familiar of these new surroundings.

"Good morning, sir," he said. "You must be the new officer I've been told to expect."

I gave him my name and he took my suitcase and led the way upstairs, showing me into a fine large room which looked out on the barrack square.

"May as well have the big room, sir," he remarked, "seeing as how you'll be the only one living in. All the rest are married and only come in once in a while. Lunch will be a little after twelve. In the meantime there are some magazines if you'd care to look at them downstairs."

I thanked him and began to unpack my belongings. It didn't take long — I had no uniform yet, only the few shirts and socks and other necessities I'd bought in Vancouver. The uniform would have to wait. I knew that I'd have to be measured by the tailor and would have to buy it. It was quite different from the type worn in the ranks which was issued free of charge. As lunch would not be ready for an hour or two, I washed off the dirt of the train journey, went downstairs, and left the Mess to find someone to whom I could report.

It was quite a long walk to the administration building on the other side of the square, and I knew that when I reached it I would meet my first hurdle. I hadn't been looking forward to it as I didn't know just what the reaction would be. But I needn't have worried; I came across the Sergeant-Major as he was coming out of the door.

We both stopped. There was a moment's hesitation.

"Good morning," he said. I stood there, the only thought flogging my mind being the fact that when I'd last seen him, I'd had to stand at attention and wait until he condescended to tell me what to do. Now I felt my heels dragging together — this would never do! Probably he had some idea as to what I was thinking, for an expression of what might have been amusement crossed his face. I agreed that it was a nice day or something, reciprocating his greeting in kind.

He hadn't changed at all — in his uniform he looked just as awe-inspiring. However, something I would never have believed — there were very human depths in his cold, blue eyes, after all.

"Well, I daresay you're glad to be back!"

"Why, yes, I am, Sergeant-Major — and I must say, a good deal surprised!"

"Well, you're not the only one, but we'll not talk about that . . ." Obviously, he was trying to think of me as an officer but the idea had not fully penetrated his mind; half of it held on to what had gone before, to when I'd been his assistant, the Division Orderly Corporal responsible at all times to his wishes. As in my own case, it would take him a little while to adjust.

"Perhaps you'll be wanting to see the Officer Commanding?"

"Yes, I suppose I'd better report and let him know that I'm here."

He turned and led the way down the passage, passing the open door to the Adjutant's office, which was unoccupied. I remembered it well — this was where I'd had to muster the defaulters, waiting, then marshaling them in. Faces I knew swam by, one by one, people I'd worked with, separated now by some indistinguishable wall, floating by gently like so many disembodied ghosts from the old days, whom I would have given much to hold out my hand to stop. But I was in the grip of officialdom, my eyes glued to the Sergeant-Major's back as he strode down the passage and, after a score of yards, knocked at the Assistant Commissioner's door.

"If you wouldn't mind waiting a moment, sir, I'll see if he's free."

I looked at him with respect, hardly believing my ears

— the Sergeant-Major was actually *requesting* me to do something.

"Why, yes, of course."

He went inside and returned after a short absence, leaving the way free to go in. "The Officer Commanding will see you now, sir, if you'll be good enough to step inside." Saluting, he turned about and returned the way he had come down the passage while, composing myself, I entered.

It was a big office with a desk in the middle and, situated as it was on a corner of the building, the windows jutted out on two sides, one facing the chapel and the other the square. Standing at attention and looking over the Assistant Commissioner's head, I could see a drill troop marching up and down, turning about, its members swinging their arms stiff from the shoulders while their legs shot before them in a series of synchronized movements all together, as one. Farther off in the distance, the trees bordering the officers' quarters raised their heads like so many Gorgons, their branches in the early spring season standing out in a massed, pointed jumble, their tips naked and twisted. In between, the great flagpole stretched its way upward to heaven, the Union Jack a mere postage stamp in the sky, blowing free. A murmur of voices floated through one window crevice which was open, interspersed with sharp barks of command as the drill sergeant made his wishes known and the phalanx of men turned about, a single automaton bent to one purpose, striding backwards and forwards, lifting their feet. Well, they might be recruits, I thought, but no more than I was as I stood rigid and motionless before the Assistant Commissioner, waiting for him to speak.

There was a gleam of recognition in his eyes.

"I remember you," he said. "You used to be a Corporal round here some time ago. How long was that?"

"Yes, sir, three years ago. Division Orderly, sir."

He stared at me for some moments, sizing me up. He

was a big man, tall and heavy, a gentleman of the old school with a white pointed moustache. When he was satisfied, the pale blue eyes turned to look at some paper on the desk, then focused on me again, pinning me down as though I was some queer specimen which perhaps he should stick a pin through, a beetle which if preserved for future study might have facets that would be rewarding to explore.

"Well, you'll have to get yourself some uniform and we'll see what we'll do with you after that. Let me see . . ." He looked down at the paper again, studying the paragraph or so it contained. "Mackenzie River, Yukon, Regina . . . you'll have a lot to learn as an officer. I'll get you a room where you can study and then I'll set some examinations for you later on."

"Yes, sir."

"Got in this morning? I suppose you're all fixed up at the Mess? Quite comfortable?"

I felt most encouraged that this dweller on the heights should condescend to inquire about the welfare of the new disciple who now stood before him. The last time I'd seen him I could only look at him from a distance or jump energetically to attention, saluting as he approached majestically and made his way on.

He nodded. "You can go now," he said. "I'll get in touch with you later."

"Very good, sir."

When I got back to the Mess there were one or two officers there drinking coffee. It was still early, an hour to go to lunchtime, and they'd come in to make themselves known and with some curiosity no doubt in regard to the new arrival who had joined their circle. They were at least twice my age with much longer records of service, but they made me quite welcome, accepting me as one of their own. Later, during the course of the next two days, I met the other officers — there were about ten of them — and renewed my acquaintance with some of the senior N.C.O.'s, who outwardly seemed to regard the situation as nothing unusual although inwardly they must have had mixed feelings of their own. One Staff-Sergeant, old and wise in the ways of the Force, who had been in Regina when I was there before, went so far as to pay me a compliment. "We don't mind you being given a commission and being jumped over our heads," he said, "but if it had been anyone else . . ." Here, he left the words to trail off to limbo, leaving me to form any conclusion I liked; it made a difference though, and as the days went by I found no one who was other than helpful and disposed to regard my interests as his own. It was the organization that counted, and provided that I could hold up my end, they were prepared to do their share.

The weeks went on and I began to learn gradually. First a period of training in regard to police matters in general and the responsibilities of an officer and what he should be expected to know. The requirements of courtesy in the Mess. How to take a parade. The intricacies of sword drill. The Criminal Code and the mass of information it contained. The necessity of adopting a proper attitude — one of regard for their knowledge and an understanding of their problems without encroaching upon the limits set by their dignity — toward those to whom I was responsible in this new position I'd assumed. To hit exactly the right note between being friendly and familiar and to try to maintain their respect. It was not easy, requiring a great deal of tact and politeness and a sense of balance, and each evening when the day's work was done, I wondered whether I'd quite made the grade.

Six months passed and, the examinations over, I was judged competent to assume some kind of command. First a term in an administrative capacity dealing with work in the criminal field; then, the Adjutant being due for transfer,

I was elevated to the position he held. In a sense this was familiar ground, as it had not been so long ago when I'd had to accompany him on his travels, making notes of what he required me to do. Now when I made my rounds — sometimes accompanied by the Sergeant-Major — there was another Division Orderly who in his turn had taken my place. Every time I looked at him it was with a sense of astonishment. I could see myself, alert, tensed for any edict which would fall from the Adjutant's mouth, standing stiffly at attention, waiting there. I don't know what I felt on such occasions — perhaps a sense of amusement at the whims of the fates which had placed me in this unusual position, mixed with some idea of humility that in some unaccountable manner I'd managed to get there.

It was a time of change. Apart from my own reversed position in affairs everything was different, even the country. In 1928, the wheat crops had flourished, the green stalks sprouting in the spring and turning golden as summer led onward to autumn. Now, in 1931, the years succeeding to the great depression of 1929 had started and were to be followed by a period which was to be known as the "Dirty Thirties," a long time of drought in Saskatchewan. The prairie dried to a desert of dust which blew everywhere, rising high against the walls of the farms and creeping, day after day, in long, slow-moving banks to the windows. Year after year the wind swept the west where nothing now grew, picking up everything, even the grain sown in the spring in the hope that the rain would come at last. But the dust went on. Cars traveled the highways with lights on in the daytime when a strong wind was blowing, making their way through the brown, swirling fog.

It was a bad time. Unemployment was rife and there was no money. A large part of the population was on relief and without means to obtain food or clothing. Naturally, under such conditions there was an increase in crime, and robberies, thefts and assaults took place in profusion adding to the work of the Mounted Police.

Under the tutelage of a new Commissioner, Major-General J. H. MacBrien, the Force itself was expanding and changing. On April 1, 1932, the provincial police force of Nova Scotia and Manitoba were dissolved and their duties assigned to the Royal Canadian Mounted Police. At the same time the Preventive Service of the Department of National Revenue, with its fleet of thirty-two vessels and approximately two hundred and fifty officers and men, was taken over and was to prove a most effective weapon in the hands of the Force in controlling the incursions of rumrunners and smugglers wherever they were found in Canadian waters breaking the revenue laws. Two months later the provinces of New Brunswick, Prince Edward Island, and Alberta followed suit. Now the strength of the Force numbered nearly 2500 men with more than 450 detachments, an increase of approximately one thousand members in a year.

All this, of course, had a great effect on the organization as a whole, including the training program. More and more men were coming in as recruits and, charged as I was with the first stage of their education as Adjutant, I noticed that most of them were a different type from those who had been my companions at Ottawa when I'd first been taken on in the Force. The old variety — the ex-soldiers, the adventurers, the men from far places — was disappearing, and in its place a new breed was joining, some of whom had already made their mark in some other vocation but who, owing to the depression, had not been able to continue at their jobs. They were good men, too, up-to-date and keen, the products of the new and more mechanized era which the last ten years had brought.

Although the training remained basically the same with a good deal of drill both on horseback and on foot, a large number of new subjects were introduced. For the first time the syllabus of instruction was divided into two parts, the first of which — comprising a four-month period — dealt with riding, physical training, foot drill, rifle drill, musketry and revolver practice, lectures on the history of the Mounted Police, first aid to the injured, minor essentials in police work, and tact and politeness with the public. Provided that the recruit had passed his examinations and obtained the 60 per cent mark, he was then moved on to the second period, in which he was taught the theory and practice of handling automobiles, advanced physical training and jujitsu, the more intricate aspects of those laws he would have to deal with and — something entirely new in the police field — the touch system on the typewriter. Then after final examinations, he was sent where he was needed. Today, many more subjects have been added and I touch upon this initial change as something with which I was concerned, marking a turning point in the development of the R.C.M.P.

It was a time of large-scale activity in the training division and, with the many other changes resulting from our expansion, I found myself taking on additional duties. Besides my usual work of looking after the disciplinary requirements of the barracks, taking parades, etc., I had to give lectures on various subjects whenever an instructor was required for either refresher classes or recruits. Sometimes I felt I could never keep up. On the one hand I was increasing my knowledge as to what was required as an officer, and on the other imparting such information as I had gained from books and in the course of my service in the ranks to those who now followed in my steps. It was another challenge, though, and I did the best I could, watching my seniors, picking up such scraps of information as we were offered, trying to fit myself for this new and important task.

And so the days passed quickly, almost at a run. Squads of men marched by in formation or assembled in classrooms, being told what to do by the instructor in charge. Parades were formed up and inspected, then moved off. On

Sundays, at three-week intervals, every man on the strength and all the officers were mustered early in the morning on the parade square in the full dress scarlet tunics and ceremonial uniform of the Force instead of the brown jackets and blue breeches worn for ordinary duty occasions in the course of work, line by line, rank by rank, with the Assistant Commissioner in command. Then, after the roll had been called and the men inspected they were separated into groups, according to denominations, some making their way to another church in Regina while the remainder filed off to the R.C.M.P. chapel on the square. It was an impressive place, diminutive beside one of the great barrack's buildings, filled with plaques emblazoned with the names of the dead.

Sometimes when there was no one around, I used to visit the chapel. Somehow in its sanctuary there was a feeling of quietness and peace, a place in which, away from the world, one could let one's mind range. There was some outer presence, I thought, that seemed to fill all the universe, far beyond everything, and that in the narrow confines of the chapel with its bare wooden benches was close at hand. I'd had this feeling in other places, too; in the woods, on Great Bear Lake, when the sun was coming up in a blaze of glory in any place where it was quiet, or sinking slowly to rest, crimson-hued and lovely as evening came on, its great circle of fire fading moment by moment until it vanished over the horizon and only a few, last pink rays were left. But you had to be by yourself — it was no time for other people. It was only when you were alone that you could achieve this impression, an idea that you were in some way part of the firmament — an atom only — belonging to, a complement, however humble, of all things that Nature in her bounty bestows. And yet, there was no way of explaining it. Yet it *was* there — the thing that one searched for as the years went on, far out of reach, beyond human finding, and by some peculiar paradox, invisible but still a part of oneself. All you had to do, like all men from time's beginning, was to try

"What were you doing there?"

It was a dangerous question which I shied away from immediately. Like the Ancient Mariner I could have held them for hours. But it wouldn't have been understandable — it was a different world — and if I figuratively clutched them by their collars, naturally enough they'd begin to edge away. Any reply I made must be within the pattern.

"I was on detachment . . . a place called Carmacks."

"Oh!" Anything away from the usual orbit was fishing in unfamiliar waters. "Well, you must find it quite a change. Hope we'll see you around . . ."

"Thank you very much."

And so they'd passed on and I must say that I couldn't blame them much.

And yet strangely enough it was at this gathering that I met the girl I was to marry. Looking around and trying to find someone who might have some common ground of understanding and to whom I could talk, I saw her — one of the very few young people in the room — over in the distance by the other wall. I recognized her immediately, for I had known her briefly and in a passing fashion when I'd been in Regina three years previously as a Corporal. She had come down the steps of a building one day when I was in the city during my off-duty hours, tall, slim, fair-haired and blue-eyed, and somehow to someone who had been as much encircled by men as I had, giving the impression that here was a creature one might expect to meet at dawn in a glade, a trim, long-legged fawn in a wood. It had been a fleeting fancy only, but she had made a pretty picture in that moment of time when she'd passed on her way, leaving me watching as she went down the street and turned a corner and was gone. Then, on some later occasion, I'd met her, and before I went back to the Yukon we had come to know each other, going out in the evenings together once in a while when I could get away from the barracks.

Now I walked across the room and stood close beside her. Things were different now — the seven years of service required as a bachelor was no longer an obstacle — but there was still one formidable difficulty in the way; I knew that before long I would have to go north again. It was no country for a woman and I wondered how I could ask any town girl to put up with such hardships. She would need a lot of courage.

But notwithstanding the difficulty — difficulties are only very small hurdles in this kind of thing — a year and a half later Mary Dillon Ware, daughter of Colonel and Mrs. Francis B. Ware of London, Ontario, and I were married on November 16, 1932. It was something to rejoice about and get light-headed over, for now I knew at last that I would have a companion and the solitary years of the past would be gone.

Five months later, when we were comfortably settled in an apartment in Regina, word came through that I was to be transferred again, this time to the Western Arctic, the farthermost rim of the world. I told Mary, who was expecting a baby.

"How do you feel about it?" I asked, wondering, knowing the conditions, thinking that so soon after we'd been married I might have to leave her again at least for a year until the rivers opened up the next summer and she could join me after our child had been born. Or it might be three years — there was no knowing what food there might be or how an infant could be raised in an outpost on the fringe of the Beaufort Sea. I did my best to explain this other world while she listened, but I might as well have saved my breath, for when I had finished she looked up and smiled.

"Why, of course I want to go!" she said. "It will be the biggest adventure — we'll both have the greatest fun."

And so the die was cast. It would be an adventure all right — nobody could doubt that — for just then I was seeing the Mackenzie River again, the land where the blizzards raged down. The stakes would be very high. It would be the dark days in November when the baby arrived, the sun would be gone and there'd be little light at all, but she had no hesitation.

We had a month in which to get ready and then, on a morning in May when the snow had disappeared and a bright sun was shining, we were off. The wheels turned and we leaned out of the window of the train, waving to our friends on the platform as they disappeared from sight, and then settled down to the two-thousand-mile journey which would take us first to Edmonton and then on to Aklavik — "The Place of the Bear" — where the Mackenzie River breaks apart into the separate channels of its delta and, a short distance beyond, enters the Arctic Sea.

14

~~~~~~

Western Arctic

"WHAT a terrible place to bring a young girl."
I did not hear the remark — it was passed on to
me later — but if I had, I would probably have agreed
with Mr. Bibby, as much the same thought was running
through my mind when I first saw Aklavik. Mr. Bibby was
the only tourist on board the *Distributor*, which had
brought us from Fort Smith to the Western Arctic, and he
was concerned about the welfare of my wife.

Mr. Bibby's perspective was a bit different from mine,
as this was the first time he had visited the North and
he had been looking forward all through the trip to seeing the Eskimos. They were there on the bank watching
the vessel come in, but Mr. Bibby didn't seem too impressed, and this was natural enough as the weather was
bad and it was a dark, depressing day. Besides, there was
a cold wind blowing from the ice-pack in the ocean and
this did not lend to the comfort or appearance — everyone
seemed to be shrinking into their clothes — of those in
the settlement who had come down to meet the boat. Mr.
Bibby would have liked it better if he could have seen
the sun going round and round in the sky as it usually
did in July, but on this particular day the clouds rolled
over the world as if to veil the overabundance of space

on all sides of us. Thinking this over, I felt it to be just as well; otherwise the impact of nothingness might have been too much for Mary to take in.

The land was still the same old Mackenzie country which I remembered so well from Fort Norman, but here it had flattened out even more where the delta had split into separate channels like a great open hand laid on the wilderness, with dirty, brown fingers pointing to the sea. The houses seemed to huddle on the brink of the barren lands which stretched to the east for a thousand miles on. Only to the west, in the distance, the mountains thrust themselves upward, their flanks dim and nebulous, their crests lost in the mist and the clinging gray shroud of the sky. To the north the trees grew, stunted and dwarfed, for a short distance down the river, and then faded away into the heavy, dark overcast which curtained them in. Beyond, I knew, the world would spin itself out — no trees ever grew there — until it came to its end in the ice-coated sea. Mr. Bibby was quite right — it *was* a terrible place to bring a young girl, and now that Mary was seeing it for the first time I wondered what her reaction would be.

There were the usual log shacks on the river and one small, frame building with a flagpole before it a bit away from the shore. Situated at the edge of an open space and surrounded by other buildings which formed a rough square, it might, I thought, be the house which Mary and I would occupy for the next couple of years and the others the offices and quarters of the R.C.M.P. Western Arctic command which I was to be in charge of, now that we had come to the end of a journey which had taken us two months to make since we'd had to wait for the ice on the rivers and lakes to go out. Looking farther along the bank I saw a sign that confirmed this; it bore the words ROYAL CANADIAN MOUNTED POLICE over a make-shift archway that opened on the square.

We had been watching what was happening on shore.

As usual there was a great deal of mud, beyond which a low bank rose sharply where the people of the settlement were standing while some of the crew splashed around nearer the vessel, fixing the gangplank and tying the ship's lines to some hammered-in wooden stanchions to hold it secure. I stole a look at my wife, wondering about the mud, thinking that unless I carried her she'd go in well over her ankles once we disembarked from the boat. She hadn't said anything for some time and neither had I, and I'd been waiting for her to make some remark about this new world and its vastness. Finally, I asked her, trying to find out what was going on in her mind.

But still there was silence — either she hadn't heard me or she was preoccupied by something which took precedence. She was staring at the group of men on the shore. Perhaps she was looking at the Eskimos in their sealskin boots and fur-trimmed clothing and with the characteristic upturned slant to their eyes. As the moments dragged on I repeated my question, apprehensively.

"What do you think of it?"

It sounded stupid, inane, rather like asking a child to explain about God, but I had to make some beginning.

"I don't know . . . it's all so new . . ." She looked at me, the words trailing away, losing themselves in the shadows of an incomprehension which, I saw, would persist until she had focused her thoughts on something in this immensity. I waited.

Soon she did focus on something and it wasn't the Eskimos or the buildings or the bare, barren scenery, or anything unimportant like that. When it came, it was a woman's question.

"Which one do you think is the doctor . . . ?"

So *that* was what was worrying her. I could understand it, for it was one of the main things bothering me too. We had been told that there was a doctor at Aklavik — someone who in addition to his medical duties doubled

256

as Government Agent — but beyond that hadn't been informed of much else. Naturally, this was the first thing she'd want — to see the person who, in this desolate spot in the months to come, would be of such crucial significance. Over the years there had been only two or three white children born in the Arctic, and there was no way of knowing just what the conditions were or what the hazards might be.

It was hard to answer her question. Except for the Eskimos, nearly everyone on shore was dressed either in windbreakers or mackinaw shirts, the usual clothes people wore to break the icy, cold wind from the sea. There were about fifteen or twenty people on the bank, including two or three women, and among them a large, heavy man who stood a bit apart from the others and wore, under some kind of top coat, a white open-necked shirt and a baggy, blue suit. There seemed to be an indefinable air of authority about him — possibly he'd be our Government Agent, who also looked after the health of Indians, Eskimos and whites. I said so to Mary, pointing him out, but apart from looking at him briefly she paid no more attention and soon turned away.

We were on the upper deck of the *Distributor* and the time had come for us to leave. The gangplank was now secure, and there was a lot of coming and going. At the bottom of the companionway someone who must have had my wife's interests in mind handed her a pair of long, rubber boots, removing the problem of how to get her past the mud in her thin silk stockings and light summer shoes. She put them on and then followed me ashore, wading through the sludge underfoot. There, at the top of the bank, we were met by Inspector and Mrs. Eames, with whom I'd been stationed at Fort Norman nine years before and whom I was relieving at the end of his second term of northern service. He would be returning to the south when the boat left the next day. He introduced us to the others — one or two people from the local missions and Hudson's Bay and Northern Trading Company stores, and to Doctor Urquhart, who turned out to be the heavyset man I'd picked out; and after a short exchange of conversation we made our way — accompanied by Inspector and Mrs. Eames — to the R.C.M.P. quarters to meet the men and to see our new house.

The R.C.M.P. establishment at Aklavik at that time consisted of an Inspector in charge, a Corporal, four Constables and three special Constables — a French Canadian, an Indian, and a Dane, who were employed in their various capacities of handyman, guide and interpreter, and cook. Except for the French Canadian and the Indian, who lived in the settlement, the Constables and the cook occupied a small log cabin about twelve feet wide by twenty feet long, while the Corporal had another smaller cabin to himself on the other side of the square. A couple of warehouses and two other log buildings in addition to our house made up the remainder of the premises. At the back, farther away from the river, were the dog lines where ten or twelve dogs were kept chained during the summer — the regulations required this as a safeguard against anyone being attacked. They would not have to work until winter arrived.

Besides the police buildings, Aklavik had three trading stores which carried very little except the basic essentials of life for the use of the trappers who lived in the district and the local inhabitants; two missions (one Roman Catholic and one Anglican); a Royal Canadian Corps of Signals station, equipped with wireless for communication with the outside world; a number of cabins occupied mostly by Indians or half-breeds; and not much else. All told, the population varied from thirty to forty people, since the staff, trappers and Indians came and went, this being increased only when the trappers and Eskimos came in to the settlement at Christmas and Easter and at one or two other times in the year. Ordinarily the Eskimos did not live at Aklavik but — depending on the season — in skin tents, igloos or driftwood houses which were spread out in groups of a few families to east and west on the coast.

After some conversation about official business and the affairs of the country at large, Inspector and Mrs. Eames returned to the *Distributor,* on which they were to stay overnight, and left us at the house. It was a frame building painted white and at first glance seemed as empty as the country around it. Except for a couple of iron beds and two sleeping bags in the bedroom there was nothing. In the kitchen, though, there was an old wood stove, a large water barrel made from a forty-five-gallon gasoline drum, and a small pile of fuel stacked in a corner. These and a couple of kitchen chairs and a table comprised all the furnishings. Next day when our effects were unloaded from the boat it would look a lot better, I thought, but in the meantime its appearance was very stark and not much to offer my wife. There were, however, three rooms in addition to the kitchen, and a lean-to tacked onto the back, so that from my more case-hardened point of view it was quite commodious.

I don't know what Mary had been thinking as we made our way round the house, as she had merely looked the rooms over without making any remark. It was only when we got back to the main room — the living room where there was a large, mushroom-shaped stove — that she asked a question. Something especially incongruous had caught her eye.

"What are all the lamps for? Why do we need so many?"

As it was never dark in the summer I could understand her curiosity. There were eight coal-oil lamps hanging on nails in the living room and others in the kitchen, and they looked very redundant.

"They're for the winter — the dark days. Then, except for what light there is from the moon and the stars, it'll be dark for quite a bit of the time and they'll have to be kept burning all day."

The dark days! It was bad enough now in the summer to try to explain this new environment, but her question about the lamps had made me think of the winter when things would be worse. I knew what it would mean as the days grew progressively shorter. The sun would vanish under the edge of the earth. From early in December until the beginning of January, night would close in. And only then would the sun peer again over the world's rim, just a few moments the first day — only a pale pink blur on the horizon — and then becoming a round, red ball slowly ascending higher and higher every twenty-four hours as spring passed to summer and the seasons revolved. As winter came on the temperature would drop far past the zero mark, the wind would howl across the wide sweep of the Arctic, the blizzards would rage as if all hell was blowing, the stovepipes would rattle and shake and it would sound as though the whole house was coming down, falling apart. That would be the time when we'd have to have ropes stretched between the buildings to hang on to, for if one strayed off the path for a moment there was always the chance that one might never return. No, I didn't want to think of the dark days!

Mary had noticed my hesitation and perhaps guessed the reason, as she had gone back to the kitchen without saying anything more. I found her looking out of the window at something she'd seen but not remarked on before. It was a small, wooden outhouse, about thirty yards back near a group of low spruce — a very primitive contrivance.

"Pretty cold in the winter?"

Well, yes, it would be cold all right, I agreed, but there was no alternative; it was a thing one got used to, after all.

"What about a bath? What do we do about that?"

I opened the kitchen door and went outside. I hadn't seen it in the house, but from past experience I knew it must be somewhere around. Sure enough, it was there leaning against the wall — a large galvanized iron washtub, big enough to hold one's frame in a cramped position if one bent one's knees. Beside it was a flat scrubbing board made of wood and metal with corrugated sides.

"That's the bath," I said. "It's no job in the summer when there's lots of water from the river we can use. Becomes a bit more difficult in winter though — then you have to gather snow and melt it. Takes quite a time — you only get about an inch of water for every bucketful of snow."

Mary picked up the scrubbing board and looked at it thoughtfully.

"For the washing, I suppose?"

"Well, yes, for the time being we'll have to do the best we can. I'll try and get something better to help later on."

She bent down and tapped the bottom of the washtub with her knuckles and got a loud, booming note in response.

"Well, it's in good voice anyway," she said. She stood looking about her, taking everything in. Then she turned and faced me. She was amused — she was smiling. "Imagine a real galvanized iron washtub to have a bath in and a house with ice-cold refrigerated plumbing laid on — why, it's all too exciting for words!"

I began to feel better. Up to now I'd been worried as to how she would react — now I knew. As she stood there, her eyes full of laughter, I thought of the time when I'd have to be away on long dog-team trips in the winter when anything could happen of which I'd have no knowledge at all. It would be difficult for Mary. Apart from the cold and the blizzards there'd be the danger of fire — the soot catching alight in the pipes when she and the child were asleep, the house burning down. It would be lonely, too, for no one got around much in the settlement at sub-zero temperatures when it meant stumbling around in the cold and the dark and the snow. There would be very few visitors, and as she could not take an infant out of doors unless the weather was suitable — and it seldom was — there'd be little opportunity for her to get around.

"Come on," I said. "It's time to get back to the boat. We can have our meals on board until it leaves tomorrow, but we'll have to sleep here tonight."

"In the sleeping bags?"

"Why, yes, of course! It'll only be for one night though. Tomorrow we'll get our own things unpacked."

She laughed. "Well, it'll be a new experience, anyway. They look rather awful and scratchy but I might as well find out what they're like."

We walked through the door. Outside it was still gusty and blowing, and somehow it seemed that the wind had grown colder and carried a much sharper chill. Perhaps it was the dull, gray panorama that stretched all around us, perhaps the black clouds in procession above us, perhaps something else. For now that at last we were here all at once the full significance of Mary's presence began to hit me, leaving me filled with a great deal of doubt. Two months ago before we'd left Regina it had been a very different thing. Then it had only been the beginning of another adventure; one to be thought over carefully before we embarked on it, it is true, but nevertheless something which was a long way off. Now the situation was right at our doorstep and I wondered if we hadn't both taken on something which, however much we tried, we couldn't possibly do.

But it is the approach to such things that makes the big difference. As we walked down the path Mary stopped and looked back. In the last few minutes the clouds must have crept lower; now they seemed to be all around us and a light sprinkle of rain was beginning to fall. She clutched her coat tighter and then took my arm.

"I think it's just fine," she said. "Once we get it fixed up with a few pictures and tables and things it'll be lovely to live in. I'm ever so glad that I came!"

It was the kind of remark to which just then I could think of nothing to say in reply. It was a good beginning, I thought, if one regarded the deeper things, for now I knew that with such strength and such spirit to help her, the North could do its worst but would never defeat her, never win! We looked at each other for a moment and then climbed down the bank of the river through the sticky, black mud to the boat.

In the great expanse of the Western Arctic the Mackenzie forms the one single line that is dimly discernible, like a vein of brown silk which fades into nothingness. The green of the trees and the grayish shades of the barren lands come to an end as the river — the great northern lifeline — meets the white, frozen ocean, loses even the small identity it had, and just disappears. The river means nothing, merely a mark on the mind, on the memory, as shading your eyes with your hand you turn them north to the Pole. It gives you a curious feeling even to think of it — the land and the river, both so important, winding and spreading south to the cities and yet as they vanish having no meaning here.

In all that area of the Arctic coast very little habitation existed in 1933 — a few trading posts, some missions, half a dozen police detachments, a few groups of wandering Eskimos, that is all. Farther south on the Mackenzie River it was much the same, with a settlement at intervals of one or two hundred miles, and a few trappers and Indians in between. Northward, the R.C.M.P. had some of its detachments, six in all, which covered a distance of almost a thousand miles as far east as Cambridge Bay. Even now, thirty years later, there has been little change; some airfields, the Dewline, a network of radio stations, and a slightly larger trickle of white men and women — like motes of dust floating down from some other world.

Aklavik was the administrative center of the region (there is a new one now at Inuvik on another channel of the delta) and from it instructions, when conditions allowed, were sent out to the coast and river detachments. This was not often, though, for in those days communications consisted of one mail in summer which was brought from Cambridge Bay by schooner, touching at intervening points such as Coppermine farther west until it reached Herschel Island near the Alaska border in the Beaufort Sea. From there the mail was carried — again by schooner — across Mackenzie Bay southeast to the Sub-Division headquarters, at Aklavik. There was no definite arrangement; the mail arrived by whatever means it could on a very loose schedule during the summer months when the sea ice receded sufficiently offshore to give passage to vessels moving east and west. Similarly, from Aklavik, mail was distributed along the coast by whatever method was available before the ice closed in. In winter there was one mail also, which was relayed by dog team between detachments on the Arctic coast and after a journey of several weeks reached Aklavik in the spring. The only other method of obtaining information about what was going on on the coast was through the Royal Canadian Corps of Signals station, which could communicate by wireless with either Coppermine or with the R.C.M.P. vessel *St. Roch*,* a floating detachment of eight men which plied the coast in summer until it was frozen in.

At Aklavik, therefore, for most of the year we were cut off from the coast unless something really momentous occurred such as a murder, and even then a considerable time would elapse before in some form or other — perhaps

* The *St. Roch*, an 80-ton vessel, was sheathed in Australian ironbark, the only wood which could withstand the pressure of the ice floes. Under the command of Sergeant Henry Larsen (later Superintendent) it made history by traversing the Northwest Passage in 1941-42 from west to east, the first time that this had ever been done. The next year it made the return journey over the roof of the world again from the Atlantic to the Pacific. In 1954, after again gaining recognition as the first ship ever to circumnavigate the North American Continent, it was installed as a Maritime Museum at Vancouver, British Columbia, where it had been built.

2 6 4

by the *St. Roch* or perhaps through Coppermine — word could reach us.

Along the Mackenzie River much the same situation existed but to lesser degree, for there, with the recently inaugurated mail plane service operated by the bush pilots of Western Canada Airways, word could be brought to Aklavik from our detachments on the river and from the outside world six times a year. As a result we were able to keep in better touch with this area of the Sub-Division, which extended as far as Fort Norman, about 450 miles away.

No one should think that due to the lack of communication we were not busy. Month after month on the coast and the river there were frequent patrols to be made both in summer and winter, and besides concerning themselves with their main task of policing the country our men had many other duties as well. These included the collection of fur tax, acting as Game Guardians, collecting customs dues and income tax, looking after the interests of Indians and Eskimos when, due to poor fishing and hunting conditions, they found themselves in destitute circumstances — to mention only a few. The R.C.M.P. was the chief instrument of government in the North and as such when anything had to be done, whatever it was, it invariably fell to our lot. The unpredictable element was danger.

In July 1931 a trapper who gave his name as Albert Johnson arrived at Fort McPherson, a small trading settlement about eighty miles south of Aklavik, from somewhere in the forests to the west. A stranger to the area, morose and taciturn, he refused to answer any questions as to where he had come from or to speak of his background. After obtaining some supplies, he left Fort McPherson by canoe down the Peel River with the professed intention of trapping in the Rat River country near where the mountains begin.

Nothing more was heard of Johnson until the following

Christmas, when some Indians who were visiting Fort Mc-Pherson complained of a strange white man who was interfering with their traps. There was no police detachment at Fort McPherson at the time and consequently a patrol consisting of two men — Constable A. W. King and an Indian Special Constable named Bernard — was sent immediately from Arctic Red River by dog team to find out what the difficulty was. After a couple of days' travel they came to the Rat River and the solitary cabin which Johnson had built on its bank. Square, squat, and half covered with snow it stood, grim and forbidding, on a small open space on a bend.

When King asked permission to enter, Johnson refused to reply, although King could see him through one of the windows. In the face of this refusal to open the door, King and Bernard trekked all the way to Aklavik — about eighty miles — to get a search warrant. However, they had no greater success on their return. On the approach of the patrol Johnson shot King without warning from inside the cabin, wounding him seriously and leaving him stretched on the ground until under the covering fire of another member — Constable R. G. McDowell, who had been sent with him from Aklavik — he was able to crawl away. McDowell now had a gravely injured man on his hands who had to be given medical attention as soon as possible if there was to be any chance at all of saving his life. As there was no possibility of routing Johnson from his cabin, which was built like a fortress with loopholes covering any approach to the door, McDowell set out for Aklavik with the wounded man in the dog sled, making the distance in a night and a day — a tremendous feat considering the conditions and sub-zero temperatures — with the result that King finally recovered.

A posse consisting of police and volunteers was now formed and left for the Rat River to arrest Johnson, but notwithstanding the assaults on the door — including the use of dynamite — by Inspector Eames and his men, a barrage of bullets fired by Johnson made it impossible for them to force their way in. Food for the men and dogs was running short — they had not been able to carry much under the conditions they faced — and as it was obvious by this time that a protracted siege was involved, there was nothing to do but to call a temporary halt to the battle until they could return to their base and replenish supplies. When the posse returned some days later, its strength now increased by additional numbers, they found the cabin empty. Johnson had made his escape in its absence, his tracks hidden by the driving wind and the snow.

Searching about the creeks and the hillsides a few days later, the pursuing party came upon Johnson lying in ambush in a thick grove of trees and, in the gun battle that followed, Constable Millen of Arctic Red River detachment was killed, while Johnson again disappeared in the darkness, keeping to the snow blown hard by the wind on the sidehills and leaving no signs again as to where he had gone. Finally, after some weeks of hard searching, the fugitive was encountered again on the Eagle River, and in the exchange of rifle fire which ensued, Staff-Sergeant Hersey of the Signals station at Aklavik (who had joined the posse as a volunteer) was seriously wounded and Johnson was killed. There was nothing on the trapper's person to give any clue to his identity, and although widespread inquiries were made over a long period of time, no one ever found out who he was or has to this day discovered from where he originally came.

I've often wondered about Albert Johnson and what caused him to do what he did. There were many expressions of opinion — some thought that he was a criminal who may have murdered a partner either in the Yukon or perhaps in Alaska and that, thinking he would be arrested, he had reacted accordingly when the R.C.M.P. first came to his door. But this, I think, is doubtful, despite the fact that his cabin had been built to withstand some kind of siege.

I'd had a good deal of experience in the North by this time and knew what strange things it could do to people who lived alone in the woods. One man I'd heard of in the Yukon had been afraid of an enemy who he thought had feet like a caribou and, whenever the tracks of these animals were found in his vicinity, he would run around shooting at anything he saw. When there were no tracks, to all outward appearances he was entirely normal. There were others, too, whom I'd met who had obviously been just on the verge; and from there on it was just a matter of time and a question of how much resistance they had before they went mad. I don't know about Johnson. He may have been a criminal, but on the other hand it would seem just as possible that he might have been completely insane. Whatever the reason — no one will ever know — it had cost the life of one of our members and two other men had been seriously hurt. He was properly named the "Mad Trapper of Rat River" and, whether criminal or lunatic, the North with its silence had claimed him for its own.

Soon after we arrived at Aklavik, two emergencies arose which, although of considerably lesser significance than the Johnson case, may serve to illustrate the conditions under which we lived.

The first was the failure of the Hudson's Bay vessel, which carried the year's supply of provisions for the coast, to arrive at her destination. This ship, which usually made the trip each year from Vancouver through the northern Pacific and Bering Straits to Herschel Island, damaged her hull on an ice floe and had to turn back, which meant that all the settlements along the coast would be short of supplies with, in some areas at least, consequent risk of starvation.

This was a serious matter and we heard the news with dismay. Would there be time in the short summer season to duplicate the stores and send them in by some other way? It would not be possible by the coastal route, for that would take too long and before the ship could return winter would have set in. It was a difficult and dangerous journey and other mishaps had occurred in the past when vessels had either been lost or abandoned in the ice. One ghost ship, it was said, still sailed the sea to the north without crew or captain, held fast in the ice where the floes locked it tight; there would have to be some faster and more certain way, and the only other route by which provisions could be brought in was the Mackenzie.

No one had used the river before to ship supplies to points farther along the coast, for there was no riverboat of sufficient strength or size to make its way on the ocean. The *Distributor,* a paddle-wheel vessel, would break up and sink if it met with bad storms or very rough water. The new stores would have to be brought as far as Aklavik and transshipped to smaller craft, which could then take them on to their Arctic coast destinations.

Time was the essential factor, and on hearing of the disaster the Hudson's Bay Company immediately went into action, arranging for another consignment of supplies to be sent in on the *Distributor* while a fleet of small craft was marshaled at Aklavik to meet the vessel on arrival. At first no one was sure whether during the short period of summer this could be done, but eventually the stores arrived and were transshipped to the schooners, some of which made their way east along the coast while others traveled west to Herschel Island where the *St. Roch* was waiting. There, the R.C.M.P. vessel was loaded to her utmost capacity and I watched her make her departure for the east with some anxiety, for if a heavy gale struck before she had discharged at least a part of her cargo no one could be sure just what might happen. But fortunately the schooners from Aklavik and the *St. Roch* all arrived at their destinations in safety, and the emergency came to an end without any hardship or suffering being imposed.

No sooner had this emergency been dealt with than another arose. Herschel Island is about 150 miles northwest of Aklavik and lies close to the international boundary, a short distance from shore, where the Yukon comes to an end at the edge of the Beaufort Sea. This tiny dot in the ocean was the main community center, the focal point to which the trappers and traders — both Eskimo and white — made their way in their schooners in summer from as far east as Cambridge Bay. There they would replenish their stocks from the two large vessels which arrived — the Hudson's Bay ship which ordinarily put in an appearance late in the season but which on this occasion had been forced to turn back, and another, the S.S. *Patterson,* which sailed under American registry from Oakland, California, year after year. As a result, for a month in the summer Herschel Island became a place of large-scale activity where everyone would gather, and the police would have to be there to perform their usual duties and to collect customs dues.

I had gone to Herschel Island from Aklavik at the time of the mishap to the Hudson's Bay ship and, after making what arrangements I could to load the *St. Roch* with supplies, had remained there, as was usual, until the trappers and traders had sailed for the East. Then with the summer's business completed we returned to Aklavik to prepare for the winter's activities which soon would be there. As the doctor was traveling to Herschel Island, my wife had gone on his schooner in case some emergency arose as a result of her condition, while I went in the police boat with the others from the detachment and met her there. Now we made our way back separately in the same manner.

Mary's time had almost come and I was feeling some concern, of course. When we got back to Aklavik things would be better, I thought, for instead of the rough temporary quarters we maintained at Herschel Island, at least she'd have such comforts as we had at home and there would be the local mission where she could be looked after when her infant was born. Ordinarily, I would be with her for the next two months, for with the approach of the freeze-up in the in-between season when the ice was forming on the river and sea, traveling came to an end.

It was therefore with very mixed feelings that soon after I returned to Aklavik I read a wireless message from headquarters, Ottawa, which said that a lady botanist who had been traveling to Herschel Island on the Hudson's Bay ship had left the vessel somewhere along the Alaskan coast with the intention of trying to make her way on to the island, alone. She had made the long trip from England to study the flowers — there was a profusion there in the summer months — and evidently was not to be deterred from her purpose by any impediment. If the ship could not take her to Herschel she meant to get there on her own!

Something had to be done at once; she could be alone in a region where almost no habitation existed and might have a very hard time with winter a step round the corner. If she tried to get to Herschel on some Eskimo schooner she might find herself in a very precarious position indeed.

There was nothing to do but to go back to Herschel, even though there was only a chance in a thousand that she'd reach there. There was one trapper on the island named Bennet who could give her shelter, but this would be only of the roughest kind. If she *did* get to Herschel, unless I went to her help she'd have to remain until after the freeze-up, as there was no transportation farther on. No Eskimo schooner which had brought her from Alaska would have time to make the extra 150-mile trip to Aklavik and return.

It was very late in the season and if our schooner was delayed by bad weather it might be frozen in. If this happened the boat would be lost, and I and anyone I took with me would have a difficult time returning. We'd have to get to land and make our way back on foot the best way we could; with the rivers and lakes on the point of freezing, it might take as much as a month or six weeks.

The next day, one of the men from the detachment — Constable Parkes — and I set out for Herschel Island. All ordinary travel had ceased, and preparations were being made to haul the boats up on the riverbank where they would remain until spring. A few flakes of snow were beginning to fall, some small pieces of ice were already running down the river, and it was impossible to tell what the conditions would be when we reached the sea. If a gale blew up there'd be very little visibility and we could well lose our way on the coast. But we made our way down the river and soon the estuary was behind us with the Beaufort Sea stretching ahead, fortunately flat and calm. Somewhere out of sight beyond the horizon was Herschel Island, only a few square miles in extent, to the west. As the hours passed — daylight was getting limited now — we both watched the weather carefully for signs of a coming storm, for the Beaufort Sea close to the land is very shallow and if a boat is caught in the shoals it will break in pieces by being pounded up and down. The bays were all frozen — there was no refuge there.

Finally, after three days' travel, we reached the island and ran the boat close to shore. By this time there were three or four inches of snow on the ground but Bennet was waiting, having seen the schooner when it was still some distance out at sea. There was a few minutes' conversation. Had he seen the lady botanist? Had he heard anything about her? He knew nothing and it was now clear that she must be at some place in Alaska where we could not go.

We had done our best; if the person we were looking for was not at Herschel Island there was nothing to do but return. Only time would tell whether she was safe or what had happened.*

A thin skin of ice was beginning to form on the sea in patches as we made our way back. We headed out to sea, waiting no longer; every minute would count in our race to the estuary before the channel froze solid. But we could make only five or six miles an hour with our old, heavy-duty, two-cylinder engine and we had a long way to go — close to a hundred miles — before reaching the river. The coastline crawled by, flat and level with the water, the far-off mountains indistinct in the gray misty twilight covering the sea. Soon we passed one point jutting out, then another and another. And then, when we were half way home, it began to blow for the first time, the wind slowly rising and getting stronger. With the rising leap of the waves, there was nothing to do but to crash through the ice on some bay and stay there or we might find ourselves aground in the tumult of water and the shallows.

But the gods of chance seem to have an odd fellow-feeling at times for those who are gamblers, and now when things were beginning to get really bad they came to our aid. We found a bay half hidden by the gray mask of evening, larger than the others, with open water in its center. We ran through the narrow approach, stopped our engine, and let down the anchor, the wind wrapping around us and lashing at our parka-clad bodies with its wet, flying blanket. For the moment we were safe, but in a few short hours the bay would freeze over.

In the first light of dawn the sea had gone down. We prepared for departure. Parkes pulled over the flywheel with a heavy iron lever. Again! Then another try and several more in succession. Nothing. From all around the ice crept slowly toward us, as if intent on freezing us in.

* She finally arrived at Aklavik by dog team at the end of November, having stopped over with a trader in Alaska until after the freeze-up and having then been assisted by Eskimos, from point to point, along the coast.

An hour went by as Parkes worked at the engine. Another pull, then another — and suddenly it coughed once or twice and as suddenly subsided. There was hope. We flung ourselves at the flywheel, tearing it over. The engine, as though admitting defeat, barked in expostulation, and then began its normal roar as though nothing had happened. The sight of the flywheel going round was like a close glimpse of heaven.

Parkes took the wheel and without waiting an instant we steered for the mouth of the bay in which we'd been held prisoner. Now nothing remained but to find the narrow channel, the mouth in the estuary which would lead to Aklavik. For miles we scanned the shoreline carefully, searching, our hands to our eyes, trying through the half dark and mist to see where the sea ended and the river began. If we went past, we'd never have time to go back. And then suddenly we were in it, breasting our way up its current with the drift of the ice floating by, small pieces and bits, a white fugitive throng making its escape to the sea.

It was getting dark again by the time we turned the last bend of the river and saw the settlement with its houses before us. The long, stretching bank was empty of everything except for one waiting figure. It was Mary.

I learned afterwards that she'd spent most of the hours there in the frost and the cold, hoping against hope that although the probability seemed against it, the boat would return. It had been a narrow squeak! The next day we pulled the schooner from the water and the river froze over that night. The cold hand of the frost, which had played with us loosely, had tightened its fingers and now held the land in its grip.

It had been an anxious time for Mary, living alone in the house with each day getting shorter, the night closing in. The oil lamps were burning now with only an interval of two or three hours when the light brightened briefly, only to fade again as early evening came on. The dark days. To anyone who had been used to the longer hours of sunlight in the south it was like a great blackness slowly gathering, something that came down the sky, closing the door to where all vision had been. It hadn't been very cheerful for her getting up in the morning, lighting the fires, looking through the window, seeing nothing but the blackness, cooking a solitary meal as the house became warm and the cold inside went away. Then there'd been the long hours on the riverbank during the last three days, waiting and watching, for she had no way of knowing what had happened. Once in a while she'd go back to the house with the wind beating behind her as it swept in from the ocean, to stoke up the fires and rest for a moment and get the circulation back in her veins. Then she'd go back to the river, waiting, standing at its edge or sitting on an old stump of a tree which had been washed up. But not for long, for the cold would bind itself round her until she'd tear herself loose again by getting up and walking, up and down the riverbank, up and down.

It was a strange life for a young girl who'd been brought up in a city where everything she needed was close at hand. Here, at Aklavik, it meant continual improvisation and making the best of what we had. Even food was a problem. One day soon after freeze-up, two of our men shot three or four caribou in the nearby vicinity and as it was late and beginning to blow, left them out overnight until they could be hauled in the next day. The news was most welcome as it meant a change from the canned meat we'd been eating, and we looked forward to getting a share of the load. When it came, besides a leg or two it included a couple of livers — a delicacy — in which were a number of long, narrow grooves. As they'd been chopped from the animal's frozen body with an axe, they were still as hard as rocks and in their cracks a faint dusting of snow could be seen. Mary picked one up and looked at it curiously. She'd never seen a caribou liver before and spent some moments examining it closely, turning it over and looking at the marks. She ran her finger down the corrugations and then put it in a bowl by the stove to thaw out.

"Well, I suppose it's all right," she said, somewhat doubtfully. "It'll be a nice change to have something fresh for dinner this evening. It looks as if something's been scraping it though." She pointed to the liver. "What made the marks?"

I knew what the grooves were, and I'd have to tell her sometime.

"It's only the wolves," I replied, "They must have come in the night after the carcasses froze. They try to get at the livers — those are the marks of their teeth. When the liver's thawed out we can cut out the places they've gnawed. They'll be quite all right."

"You're joking. . . !"

"No, I'm not — it happens every so often. They're perfectly good. Just think of the poor old wolves, gnawing away, not getting anywhere. Probably starving, too. By the way they've been at them they must have blunted their teeth!"

She laughed, looking at me curiously, wondering if I was serious, only half believing. It was quite true though, and after performing some minor surgery on the liver, we ate it that night. There were a few scratches still left but those didn't matter, and after a time Mary came to accept this kind of thing as part of the new life she led.

There was not much in the form of recreation for Mary at Aklavik, either. We had a battery-operated radio receiver, but during the summer with the long hours of daylight there was no reception at all, and with winter closing in, occasionally one United States station could be heard but none from closer points. Sometimes we could get parts of broadcasts from England and would hear the booming notes of "Big Ben," the great bell on the clock tower of the Houses of Parliament in London, carrying its message across the roof of the world. There were few books to read except those we could get from the small police library or from our friends in the settlement, but Mary did not miss this. Looking after the house; cooking; doing all the washing by hand until we were able to get a manually operated machine with a handle which one pushed backwards and forwards — everything we hung on the line outside the building soon froze stiff and had to be dried again in the kitchen — and the many extra tasks she had to do under such unusual conditions, left her little time at all. It was extraordinary, I thought, how she adapted herself so cheerfully to her new situation. Very soon there'd be someone else in the family and while a child would be company when I was away, she would need all the resources she had to take care of it properly under these conditions.

October passed and November came along. Now the whole world was deep in its snowshroud, the temperature dropping far past the zero mark, the wind and the drift howling and buffeting past the windows and doors. Round the corners of the house the snowbanks lay heavy where the blizzards had eddied and whirled, leaving great mounds of white which grew higher and higher as night followed night and the winter went on. I dug a path from the kitchen door to the outhouse, but in no time at all the snow filled it in. It was much the same at the front entrance from which lanes led to the other buildings; the drift blew continually, inching along, spreading and coming to rest in their deep channeled trenches, wiping them out until nothing was there. The moon shone all day and all night, its silver disc staring down through the clouds which swept through the skies. The wind blew, sometimes hushed but more often tearing and screaming, striking with dagger points at anything that stood in its way. To leave the house meant forcing one's way at an angle with one's face turned to one side to shield eyes, nose, and cheeks from the tearing white claws of the storm.

But it was not always like this. Sometimes, when the wind dropped, there were gray days with scarcely a breath in the air. Then the silence dropped its veil on the land, the clouds stopped their racing and hid the stars above. Gradually the snow grew higher and higher, the shining dunes heavier and heavier until, joining together, they held the whole country in thrall.

It was on such a day, on November 29, that our daughter Beverley Ann was born at the mission. It was about half a mile away and Mary, without telling me where she was going — I was working in the office and she merely said she was going out to get some fresh air — had made her way to the building the previous afternoon. An hour or so later, when a messenger arrived to tell me where she was, I'd followed her steps through the snow.

The mission was a large, rambling structure — the biggest in the settlement — and just at that time some extra rooms were being added as hospital accommodation. As these were only in process of preparation, however, Mary was put in the ante-room or "parlor" as it was called, just inside the front door, and it was there at four o'clock in the morning that our daughter was born.

It was a week or more before Mary was able to get back for a few hours to the house. The weather was so bad that it was a hard, tough journey to make the trip from the mission. Bringing the baby home with the wind blowing and the snow beating down was quite out of the question, and so after an hour or two at the house she'd go back. Finally, the week before Christmas we brought Beverley back during a temporary lull in the weather, when for once the gales had subsided. It was one of those gray days when, in the calm and the stillness, the dark formed around like a cloud. Before, we'd been afraid that the sub-zero temperatures and the driving force of the wind might do some irreparable damage to her lungs.

Christmas at Aklavik was a gala occasion, a time of festivity for all. Mary had only been back from the mission for a few days, but notwithstanding this we'd asked all the men in to share a roast of caribou meat which we'd kept for our Christmas dinner. They came in their full dress uniforms with their scarlet jackets and sat round a couple of tables we'd pushed together and covered with a long white tablecloth. As there were no Christmas decorations available, a dozen paper roses which the sisters had made and given her as a present when Beverley was born took their place. For the first time that winter she put on a full length evening dress instead of the usual slacks and windbreaker she wore indoors, and which, as it had been left hanging in a cupboard in the lean-to, we'd found frozen to the wall. However, after prying it off with some difficulty, the use of a hot iron soon brought it back to its original condition, and with the caribou roast and some canned vegetables from our stores, in the warm glow of the coal-oil lamps round the wall we spent a most enjoyable evening. Next day, we knew we'd be back to normal again, wearing our usual winter clothing and bucking the wind and the snow.

Soon the New Year arrived, and as the dark days began to disappear and the light grew stronger, I knew that I'd have to go to Fort Norman to inspect the detachment. While the journey there would be made by plane, I'd have to return by dog team. It would take five or six weeks at least, as on the way back I'd have to look in on all the local residents and the river detachments en route. It would mean that Mary would be alone in the house with a two-month-old baby at the very worst time of year.

February came and the mail plane roared in early one afternoon. I listened to it as it went down the river and circled coming back. A short time before a plane had crashed on takeoff and with the poor weather conditions I wondered whether this one would make it down. Flying in those years was a hazardous business with no proper airfields or weather reports to tell the pilots what lay ahead. Their only safeguard was the fact that if they ran into poor visibility and had to, they could come down on some lake on their skis. There was a sudden hush as the pilot cut his engine and came in to land, and then the crescendo of sound took up its beat again as the plane taxied up to the bank. It would stay overnight at Aklavik before flying me south.

I finished my work at Fort Norman in seven or eight days and set out down the river with a dog team and an Indian, and a week or so afterwards got to Good Hope. After a short stopover — another week or so was required to dispose of police matters there — I went on to Arctic Red River, about two hundred miles away, camping in the snow or in old cabins, and ran for nearly two weeks twenty, thirty or thirty-five miles a day, depending on the condition of the trail, behind the dogs. I was concerned about Mary. I hadn't heard any news of her since I'd left Aklavik more than a month before and sitting round the campfires wondered what the situation was at home. I was making as fast time as possible, for there was one place ahead, north of Arctic Red River, where I knew that a trapper had a small battery-operated radio. If I could reach it in time I might hear a short-range broadcast from Aklavik which was put out once a week — *The Voice of the North* it was called — giving news.

The day of the broadcast when we woke in the morning it was blowing a moderate blizzard, but I felt we could make our way through; if we could get to the cabin where the radio was I might hear if anything important had happened while I'd been away. When the Indian guide followed me out of the old abandoned cabin in which we'd slept over-night and felt the storm blowing he looked down the river and then lost no time in going back in; as far as he was concerned, the weather was a break — we'd have to stay where we were in comparative comfort until it let up. But soon we set off again on the trail, changing around at half-hourly intervals so that each of us could get a rest from the deep snow ahead and from pumping our snowshoes up and down.

After two or three hours of this kind of travel the blizzard diminished by degrees and now we could make better time. Finally we reached the trapper's cabin, and that night he tuned in to Aklavik and I learned that all was well. Now it would not be far, only one more hard day and I'd be home. It was a pleasant thought; the journey from Norman had been a bad one with conditions as rough as they come.

Six weeks later I had to go to Herschel Island and see how the Eskimos were getting along on the coast. It was April now, and if there was any danger of starvation this would be the time when they would be running short. The dark days had gone and the sun shone brightly all day, only setting for an hour or so every night. It was getting warmer, too, and with the easier travel on the sea ice I thought that Mary could come along, at least as far as Shingle Point. I didn't want to leave her alone again so soon after my trip to Fort Norman, and there was an Anglican mission there where she could stay while I went on along the coast.

There were three of us who set out from Aklavik exclusive of Mary — a guide, one of our constables, and myself. We left one morning, having left Beverley at the mission, with my wife wrapped in an eiderdown robe in the toboggan I was handling while two other teams hauled the food and the rest of the load. After three days' traveling we reached Shingle Point approximately a hundred miles from Aklavik. There I left Mary while the rest of us went on to Herschel Island, a trip which took no more than a week there and back.

After visiting the Eskimos on the coast and looking after their affairs, we returned and picked Mary up and started off again for home. The sun was blazing down, the glare reflecting from the snow like a white, searing torch. With our faces hardened by the winter's storms this did not affect us, but with Mary it was different, and while we did not know it at the time, slowly and invisibly its rays were taking their toll. To complicate the situation, in one of the toboggans we also had an Eskimo girl with a suspected case of appendicitis, whom we were taking to the doctor. Since there was the danger of her appendix bursting, we were running behind the dogs all day and far into the night covering many more miles than was usual, which meant being exposed for hour after hour to the sun.

We had put the Eskimo girl in the toboggan Mary had been using on the trip to Shingle Point, and had borrowed a sled with runners from the mission in which to take Mary back. This was an unwieldy contrivance for conditions on the river because the snow was piled high and the runners sank in, making much harder pulling for the dogs. The others, with their toboggans, were in consequence far ahead and soon out of sight once we reached the deep snow, while I was pushing and straining behind the sled, helping the team and trying to catch up. It was very heavy work, the sled tilting and sometimes upsetting, and I was perspiring profusely, the sweat running in streams into my eyes. It was quite impossible to see anything at all with the snow flying and all I could do was hold on to the handles, pushing as hard as I could.

I was considerably surprised, therefore, when after one of these upsets the dogs suddenly took on a new lease of life, the sled jerking ahead and taking the load off my arms. I ran as fast as I could on my snowshoes behind them and after a few hundred yards, feeling much encouraged, called down to the sled to my wife.

"That's better," I said. "Now we're making real time..." There was no reply.

I still couldn't see anything, but after a while I brushed my eyes clear of perspiration and bent down, thinking she hadn't heard; it was unusual that she hadn't made some kind of reply or remark. I stopped the team for a rest and took a closer look at the eiderdown robe in the sled. It seemed a lot flatter. My wife wasn't there!

I was astonished. Where had she gone? She had been in the sled a few minutes before, now she was not. Then I remembered the sudden burst of speed the dogs had put on, and looked around. There, a quarter mile back by the side of the trail, was a figure floundering along in the deep, sticky snow, her legs sinking in to her knees at each step as she tried in vain to catch up. The last time the sled had upset she'd fallen out.

"Why didn't you shout?" I asked as she came up again to the dogs. I brushed off the snow which covered her from head to foot.

"I did," she replied, "but you didn't hear me, you were much too busy with the dogs! I was so surprised when I found myself in the snow that by the time I was able to get up and make any sound at all you'd gone quite a way on."

She got back in the sled and we ground on at our usual slow pace. With the runners sinking deep in the drifts there was a good deal of difference between an empty sled and one with an extra hundred pounds. All the dogs looked round from time to time in remonstrance.

"Were you frightened back there?" I asked, after we'd gone on for a while.

"No," she answered, her voice so muffled by the folds of the eiderdown that I could hardly hear what she said. "Not frightened ... I knew you'd have to stop sometime ..."

I said nothing. Later we caught up to the others who had pulled off the trail to make camp. They had the kettle boiling and the frying pan on the fire and in it was something to eat. After we'd had lunch and Mary had renewed the ice packs on the sick girl's stomach we all felt a lot better, and then there was a great deal of laughter and things were all right.

The day after we reached Aklavik — in time for the girl to

get proper care — we awoke in the morning and I saw that one of Mary's eyes was closed; the flesh around it had swelled during the night, sealing it shut. Then the other eye began to close up also and her forehead and cheeks to puff out until she was quite unrecognizable. She became entirely blind, her face resembling nothing more or less than a vegetable marrow. We were both worried sick — she'd lost all semblance to anything human and neither of us knew if the swelling would stay or go down. Fortunately, though, the doctor swiftly diagnosed it as a bad case of sun poisoning, and after several days in bed at the mission where she and the baby were looked after by the sisters the swelling gradually subsided and her face regained its normal shape. Of course, our greatest fears were about her sight and it was a tremendous relief when at last she could see again. The first thing she'd looked at was the baby, whom she'd only been able to feel for before. It had been bad enough for me, just waiting and wondering and thinking about her; for her it was a thousand times worse. That was the last dog team trip we made together — one such excursion was quite enough.

A couple of months later the river broke up, its blocks of ice tumbling to the sea. When this occurred there was always the danger of an ice jam forming and blocking the channel so that the water backed up; if this happened there was every possibility that the settlement would be flooded. But the river behaved itself that year, and it was only a matter of hours before the ice disappeared and in its place was the current flowing deep and free. We launched the boats and canoes, preparing for the different mode of travel we would use now that summer had come.

We had not seen any kind of fresh fruit or eggs — processed eggs brought in the previous autumn had long since grown too stale to eat — for a full nine months and were literally starving for something fresh to break the monotony of our diet. One day soon after the river had gone out we saw a visitor at our door. He was the district manager of the Hudson's Bay Company and had arrived on a smaller vessel which had reached Aklavik before the *Distributor* that year and brought us half a dozen fresh eggs, and — marvel of marvels! — two magnificent cantaloupes. Mary stared at them with an expression of unbelief in her eyes — it had been so long since she had seen anything like them. Then we ate them, savoring each mouthful. It was the same with the eggs, each one was to be cherished almost like gold until finally they were eaten, one by one. I watched Mary, pleased and half amused at her reaction to these unexpected gifts, thinking that she was learning the hard way, as I had, the worth of things of which one has been deprived.

That summer we had an unusual guest at the barracks — an Eskimo named Ahigiak who had been convicted of manslaughter at Coppermine, five hundred miles east, in Coronation Gulf. First rumors of the crime in a little-known area of the mainland had seeped into Cambridge Bay detachment; then these had to be investigated and what was left of the murdered man's body found; finally Ahigiak's whereabouts had to be discovered so that he could be arrested and taken to the nearest place to which a judicial party could be brought from the south.

The Eskimos like Ahigiak who lived far to the east were almost entirely removed from white men and knew little of their ways. There were three essential things in their lives — food, shelter, and a female companion to make sealskin boots and sew the skin clothing. Without a woman, a man was at a serious disadvantage, and in consequence when there was a shortage of women in any small Eskimo community it was not outside the bounds of possibility that, to even things up, someone might be killed.

Ahigiak was one of the more fortunate Eskimos who had a wife and family, but there were others in his area who did not. One, in particular, made no secret of his wish to take Ahigiak's wife for his own, and as there was only one method — in Ahigiak's opinion at least — of forestalling this, Ahigiak took the initiative from his rival and shot him.

After some long and difficult patrols and an investigation extending into many months, he was finally located and brought to Coppermine during the open water period, and a judge and counsel were flown in from Edmonton. An interpreter was found and a jury assembled from among the local inhabitants. He was found guilty, not of murder as originally charged, but bearing in mind the unusual circumstances, of manslaughter instead. He was sent to Aklavik, where he was to serve a five-year sentence for his crime.

The facilities for keeping long-term prisoners at the barracks were very limited, consisting as they did of one small hut with a cell which was seldom used. For Ahigiak's purposes, however, this was quite sufficient, and as the hut was warm and provided shelter he must have thought that, with the three regular meals he received, he was extremely well off. Certainly his existence as a prisoner was much more comfortable than anything he'd previously experienced in his stark and harsh life. He was put to work carrying wood and water or in any capacity in which he could be used.

Despite the comforts of his new life he certainly missed his wife and child. In consequence, although he could speak no English, whenever he came to our house Ahigiak would remain in the kitchen for a few minutes trying to converse with Mary in sign language. There was no doubt about what he was trying to say — that he had a daughter of his own somewhere far to the east on the barren lands and that he was pleased to see a white child, an experience he'd never had before. One day, when Beverley was older and Ahigiak had been at Aklavik for about a year, we saw him go running down the path outside the barrack square, a sight which caused some consternation as he'd never been seen in so great a hurry before. But we need have felt no concern. He was not trying to escape; he'd seen our daughter fall in a ditch and was on his way to rescue her! He picked her up, grinning, and returned full of smiles to present her proudly to Mary! Ahigiak and Beverley became great friends as time went on and I think that in some ways she took the place of his daughter. Later, in the third year, Ahigiak fell sick from tuberculosis and after Mary and I had returned to the south we were told he had died. We were sorry to hear that, for apart from the crime he had committed he was kind, good-humored, and cheerful. In a way he had been the victim of the conditions under which he lived.

Except for Ahigiak's arrival, the summer passed uneventfully. The *Distributor* came in and we were glad to see it steaming down the channel, carrying goods, supplies and newspapers sent by Mary's parents. We read them eagerly, starting at the latest issue, and then going back to the others to bring ourselves up to date. As soon as the sea ice broke on the coast — it was later than on the river — we went to Herschel Island in the schooner, leaving Beverley at the mission again to give Mary a rest, and stayed there until the trappers and traders from the East had come and gone. When the summer's business had been completed we returned to Aklavik. Already the dark days were approaching once again.

To understand the difficulty of raising a small child in the Arctic of those days one must realize that there were none of the usual refinements in the way of food; there were no canned fruit juices, no fresh milk, nothing beyond the rations which we used ourselves. Nevertheless, strange to say, our daughter thrived; she was nearly a year old now and lived exclusively on a diet of fish, cereal, highly flavored eggs — which had grown to smell worse and worse every day as the winter went on until, by spring, they had to be opened with considerable care in case they exploded — and some cans of condensed milk which were a part of the stock in the warehouse. Perhaps it was the oil in the fish, perhaps the cold, clear air of the North — there were few germs there — whatever the reason she prospered without any limitations to her health, without sickness of any kind.

September came and as the sun sank lower and lower, getting closer to the horizon each day, the twilight drifted down again on the land. As soon as the river had frozen I'd had to be away on one or two short trips by dog team, but these were only matters of a week or more, nothing to cause concern. Mary, after a year in the country, was used to it (once she had seen the ice go out on the Mackenzie she was no longer a "cheechako" but could consider herself a "sourdough") and took such absences as a matter of course. But it was difficult caring for a young child under such conditions and when I was away she had additional tasks which ordinarily would be mine. There was always the job of getting up in the very early hours of the morning to stoke the fire to keep the bedroom from freezing, then of lighting the kitchen stove, and sometimes when the weather was very cold of breaking the ice in the water barrel before the kettle could be filled. There was wood and water to carry, ashes to be dumped, and snow had to be gathered and carried inside and melted in the tub for the washing. Occasionally, she could get one of the men from the barracks to help her with some of the heavier tasks but by no means all the time.

There was another thing that was bad that second winter — we had no fresh meat. The caribou herd which had made its migration close to Aklavik the year before had chosen another route. We were short of vegetables too; the fresh supply sent down from Fort Simpson farther south on the river — at Aklavik none were grown as even in summer the frost was too close to the surface — had not lasted as we had expected for there'd been some loss from freezing. The absence of the caribou herd was a serious matter. No one seemed to know where they had gone, and in the huge expanse of the barren lands and the Yukon to find them would have been like looking for the proverbial needle in the haystack. After the freeze-up we'd only been able to get one toboggan load of meat from Fort McPherson — near where a few caribou had been shot in the mountains — but once that was gone we had lived mainly on bread which Mary made and some rice, and fish after the start of the year. Fortunately, there was a good supply of flour and more than enough fish — caught the previous summer and kept frozen in an ice house below the surface of the ground — to take care of all our needs. As soon as February came I knew that I would have to go to Fort Norman again, on the usual winter patrol.

The return journey from Fort Norman by dog team that year was just the same as the last. Storms, icy winds, and low temperatures never seemed to let up, but after a six-week absence I finally got back. For Mary, it had been a lifetime of experience under very tough conditions, and while she'd faced up to the hardships of the last two winters quite cheerfully I knew that a third would be too much. It was fortunate that when the ice went out in a few months' time our term of northern service would be ended and we would be going south.

But it was not to be so easy as that. With the passing of winter we were surprised to learn that I had been ordered to leave, not on the first boat of the year, as I had expected, but the last. This meant another trip to Herschel Island for the summer's work. It was an agreeable change, however, and with the knowledge that we would be leaving in August time passed quickly. For the first time we took Beverley with us to the island in the schooner. There was only one thing to mar the promise of the future. Some

Indians who had traveled over the mountains from the Yukon had brought measles to Fort McPherson and from there it had spread to the coast. The epidemic had struck the inhabitants of the delta with deadly results; because of the absence of contagious diseases in the North no immunity had been built up and, with only one doctor to look after the welfare of the community, everyone who was not sick had to get out and help.

Then there was another delay. Due to a washout on the railway between Edmonton and Fort McMurray, the supplies which were being transported to the *Distributor* at Fort Smith would be held up for a month. The vessel could not leave without them as they had to be taken down the Mackenzie for the northern posts. Now it would be getting close to freeze-up and there would not be much margin left. Each day I watched the river for those signs of smoke from the vessel's funnel which would first herald her appearance; then, one day, suddenly she was there, circling into the bank.

There was not a moment to be lost. Our lucky day was Friday, September 13, 1935. The lines were cast off and the ship commenced her return trip. The short northern summer was definitely at an end, there was thick snow on the ground, and darkness was descending earlier each day as the winter season advanced. Instead of traveling the full twenty-four hour period of daylight as the vessel usually did in July and August, it had to tie up each night when there was no visibility left. But to us this did not matter; we were going south at last; our tour of Arctic duty was over, and the storms and the blizzards, the long trips made by dog team, the rough living conditions for Mary were things of the past.

But every moment had been worth it. We knew now that if we'd been able to withstand the difficulties of the last two years together, no other experience would, in comparison, ever count. It had been a great education for both of us and something far beyond that — an adventure in which we'd won out in the end as we'd hoped.

More than a month later, we reached eastern Canada where we were to be stationed at Ottawa, the headquarters of the Force.

15

~~~~~~~~

The Brown Tide

IT WAS a long way from the Arctic coast to the capital city of Canada and an even greater distance in time — or so it seemed — since I had last been there as a recruit in 1923. Twelve years had gone by and, since Commissioner MacBrien had taken over command of the Force in 1931, a large number of changes had taken place and more were to follow.

The headquarters building was still on Rideau Street in downtown Ottawa, but it was soon to be replaced by a more imposing structure not far from the Houses of Parliament, about a mile away on the edge of the Ottawa River. When it was ready for occupation, it would be called the Justice Building and would be shared by the officials of that department and the Royal Canadian Mounted Police. In the meantime, though, with the added responsibilities of the Force, there was no doubt but that the present accommodation — a small group of offices over a store — was very cramped for our purposes.

Three years before, when I had left for the Arctic, the R.C.M.P. had just been getting into its stride where its new obligations were concerned — the general policing of the eastern and western provinces, exclusive of British Columbia, Ontario, and Quebec. Now it was fully operative, enforcing the Criminal Code and local laws in approximately half the settled areas of Canada, and in addition was functioning in a federal capacity from the Atlantic to the Pacific and performing its innumerable duties from the international boundary to the regions of the Pole. In less than four short years the Force had doubled. It now consisted of 2500 officers and men, and the number of detachments had also increased proportionately from approximately 200 in 1932 to more than 400 in 1935. From almost a question mark in 1923 when I had first joined — no one had seemed entirely certain as to what its future might be — it had found a new growth in a changed age of mechanization, its stature greatly increased in Canadian affairs. I was appointed as officer in charge of the Intelligence Branch on a Canada-wide basis and, as a part-time occupation, editor of the R.C.M.P. *Quarterly Magazine,* which had come into being during the last two years. To one who had been used to driving dogs and facing the storm and stress of the elements in an entirely different field of endeavor, these two tasks might have been more than enough to tax anyone's capabilities had it not been for a most unusual individual with whom I was to be associated and without whose help in the beginning I would not have found my feet as quickly as I did.

The Intelligence Branch, as it was then known, dealt with all matters involving the security of the state, and prominent in its operation was Sergeant Johnny Leopold — a short, dark man with deep brown eyes who was an expert in subversive activities. For more than seven years he had been a secret agent in the Communist Party in close association with its leadership, until one day in November 1931 he appeared in court in Toronto in his R.C.M.P. uniform and, by the evidence he was in a position to give, helped convict a group of eight persons active in that party's higher echelons, who as a result were sentenced to terms of imprisonment. An Austrian by birth, he spoke several languages, and I had first come in contact with him when I was a Corporal at Whitehorse in the Yukon, where he had been removed for reasons of safety before giving evidence at the trial at which he was subsequently to appear. There, since I was larger than he, I had been of some service to him in dealing with an oversized individual by whom he'd been attacked, and as a result a bond of friendship had been established which was to prove invaluable in the new sphere to which I had been assigned. Years later, we were to form an effective partnership which, with the help of others, was to be instrumental in running down a large espionage network.

The Intelligence Branch in 1935 was only a small department of headquarters, for although it had been operating on a minor scale since even before the Communist Party of Canada had come into being shortly after the first World War, its scope had scarcely been adequate to meet the new threat of Nazi world conquest which had cast its long, dark shadow over Europe. In 1935, the drums of the Nazis were already beating, their cadence muffled it is true, but nevertheless strong enough to give cause for apprehension. We in the Intelligence Branch began — as the months went on — to form an estimate of the danger to Canadian institutions if war should break out, and to ascertain the identity of possible enemy agents and potential saboteurs. I was well aware, for example, of the sabotage on the American seaboard in the 1914-1918 war, when German agents had inserted fire pencils in the holds of ships proceeding overseas with supplies, and the damage they had done.

This was not something which could be dealt with in a day, but required a full effort for months. However, by applying all our resources, we made such headway that, when war did in fact break out in 1939, we were able to take effective measures against those aliens in Canada who could otherwise have proved hostile to the Allied cause. Thanks to this surveillance and to the guarding of vulnerable points, and advice given to industry in regard to protection of plants and manufactories, no known act of sabotage was committed in Canada during the whole course of the war by enemy agents either from within the country or abroad.

Sabotage was not the only threat. Long before the German plan had started to take shape the Communists had been busy fomenting strikes and causing disturbances and unrest in any way they could. On a number of occasions, riots and disorder had occurred, with resulting serious damage to property, and so, besides keeping an eye on what the Nazi enemy might do, it was also necessary to know the Communist potential for harm should some unforeseen emergency arise. While naturally enough all Communist propaganda had been directed against the German threat in the years before the war, with the signing of the Hitler-Stalin pact shortly before the invasion of Poland, this trend reversed itself. Now the Soviet and Germany were allies and overnight the policy changed entirely. Fortunately, we knew those who might prove detrimental to the Allied cause and, before any material damage could be done, they too were gathered up and rendered harmless. Again, after the invasion of the Soviet Union by the German forces, they were released when another complete reversal of policy on the part of the Communists — this time in support of the Allied war effort — occurred.

I was not to see all this — at least from any headquarters standpoint — for, with the organizational procedures completed and after four hard years of work during which I had hardly a minute to myself, I was transferred for reasons of health — I had become run down and afflicted with a serious ear condition — to a quieter area where I was to engage in ordinary police activities for a change. It was the summer of 1939, just before the outbreak of hostilities, when I was moved back to Regina, this time to assume charge of the Sub-Division which looked after the enforcement problems of the area adjacent to the city, a district with a dozen or more detachments in a radius of about two hundred miles.

The four years I had spent in developing the scope of intelligence had, however, been most valuable in adding to my general information of what was going on not only nationally but in a much wider field as well. From studying the situation as I had, and watching the trend of events at home and on the continent between 1935 and 1939, it had become obvious that there were two major threats to the democratic way of life: the first, the Nazi aim toward world conquest; the other, the long-range menace of Communism. But at that time very few people were conscious of this. There was an immediate challenge to be met — the brown tide of the Nazis — and every effort had to be applied to getting ready. Although in 1937, 1938, and even the early part of 1939 an armed conflict had not seemed inevitable, the preparations for it in a security sense had to be extensive in case it came.

Regina was much as I'd remembered it when I'd left in 1932. It must have been June or July when I got there and, with my wife, took up quarters in one of the houses on the barrack square. In September, war was declared and after an interval of time — I was still under medical care — in common with a large proportion of other officers of the Force I asked to be released for the period of hostilities so that I could take my part. But the government, bearing in mind the First World War when, in 1918, only a few hundred men had been left to look after the internal interests of the country, wisely decided that the heavy responsibilities of the R.C.M.P. required the retention of all its members in Canada, and ruled that no leave could be granted to officers, non-commissioned officers or Constables for the purpose of proceeding overseas; and further, that no discharges would be granted — by purchase or otherwise — to N.C.O.'s and men with this or any similar purpose in view. It was pointed out that, with the requirements of internal security, intelligence and secret service, the guarding of vulnerable points of national importance, the police supervision of the large foreign population and subversive organizations, the registration of enemy aliens, and the carrying out under war conditions of the agreements with the six provinces regarding general police work, this decision was essential to ensure that Canadian interests were protected and given the attention they deserved. The only exception to this general rule was a representative unit recruited from the R.C.M.P., which would act as a provost corps and in the beginning would number about one hundred men.

Despite this general policy, the Force was to suffer certain losses from its strength in Canada, for soon after the outbreak of war, the R.C.M.P. Marine section — 33 ships and more than 200 officers and men engaged in peacetime in curtailing the incursions of liquor smugglers off the Atlantic coast — was taken over by the Royal Canadian Navy with most of their crews. With the added demand for men for the fighting forces, all recruiting for the R.C.M.P. was stopped, and as the war went on and men left at the end of their contractual obligations the strength began to fall again until those who had, perforce, to stay behind in Canada found themselves hard pressed to deal not only with their usual duties but also with the heavy responsibilities the war had imposed. Detachments which had previously numbered two or three men were reduced in many cases to only a single R.C.M.P. member, who in certain areas had to supervise a large foreign-born population and apply wartime emergency measures. The increased stress, with these depleted resources, was relieved only to some small extent by the recruiting of a number of ex-members who, either because of age or some other reason, were not eligible for the Army, Navy, or Air Force.

While men of the R.C.M.P. were to give their lives over-seas in the service of their country, casualties at the hands of criminals and murderers were also to be suffered at home. Shortly before the war, an experiment had been tried with police service dogs which could be used in tracking down criminals, and now, in Saskatchewan, we had four of these animals stationed at strategic points across the province so that they could be moved at short notice to any place where a serious crime had been committed. These dogs — which were entirely different from the sled dogs of the north — were highly trained in a tracking capacity, and when the section was first formed were mostly Alsatians. Besides being of use in trailing down murderers and criminals, they had already proved themselves on many occasions in finding children who had wandered away from their homes in the bush and who might otherwise have died from exposure or starvation. Each dog was controlled by only one man — the dog handler — whose orders it would obey with almost hu-man intelligence, standing guard or attacking at a word from its master. In searching for armed criminals in wooded areas they were worth their weight in gold. The work of a dog handler, who at all times had to be in the lead of the search party, was therefore exceedingly hazardous, as is shown by the circumstances of the tragedy that led to the death of Constable W. E. Rhodeniser.

On August 25, Nelson Sammy, an Indian of the White Bear Reserve, had shot and killed his wife, father-in-law, and mother-in-law, and had escaped into heavy bushland. Armed with a rifle, he was known to be a good shot and to have uttered threats against the life of any person who might get in his way. The only method by which he could be tracked down was with a police service dog, and Con-stable Rhodeniser, who was stationed at nearby Yorkton, was immediately sent for and with his dog Tell took up the search in the lead of the party. Nelson Sammy had put considerable distance between himself and his crimes, and it was evening before the search party began to close in on his hiding place. Although darkness was beginning to set in, it was decided that an attempt should nevertheless be made to arrest him before he did further damage, and the search party pressed on with Tell on the trail and Constable Rhodeniser immediately following.

In the blackness ahead Nelson Sammy was waiting. Suddenly, just as Tell barked, indicating that they were getting close to their quarry, the bushes ahead erupted in gunfire, and a bullet from the murderer's gun hit Rhodeniser before the others could go to his assistance. He had been fatally wounded. Although the Indian was captured soon after, the cost of the arrest had been high.

Up to and including Constable Rhodeniser's death there had been sixty-two members of the Force who had given their lives in the performance of duty. Their names are commemorated on a plain white marble monument which stands on the barrack square close to the administrative building in Regina and which was erected toward the end of 1935, just about when I was returning from Aklavik. Although the memorial is small and unassuming, the record speaks for itself and is there for all — recruits and visitors alike — to see. Despite its size, it is an impressive monument, vividly illustrating part of the drama of the settling of the West.

As editor of the *Quarterly Magazine* at Ottawa, on returning from the North I had read the names on the Honor Roll listed in the first issue of the publication in July 1933, for from the saga it disclosed one could learn not only the identity of those who had died but could also form an idea of the changes which had taken place during the different periods of the Force's work, first as the Northwest Mounted Police, then as the Royal Northwest Mounted Police, and finally in the last decade and a half as the Royal Canadian Mounted Police. If one uses one's imagination, the whole picture is there in short, graphic words; how, before the turn of the century when the Force was working to make the prairies safe for settlers, its members had died at the hands of half-breeds and Indians; then, during the following years as conditions changed, when arresting bandits and murderers; and lastly, as its scope and responsibilities broadened to the north, had sacrificed their lives in the Arctic.

Reading the Honor Roll, one can see the past wind out behind one. Between 1879 and 1897, the names include thirteen men killed by Indians and half-breeds, five drowned on different occasions on patrol when fording rivers or in lakes, and one who died in the course of his duties while trying to make his way through a blizzard. Of course, the names of those who met their deaths a few years later on the lost Fitzgerald patrol are there. In abbreviated terms, it provides a history in which the past and the present are shown, all through the years. "Killed by Indians near Battleford, N.W.T., on May 14, 1885, while on scouting duty." "Killed at Minchinass Hills, near Duck Lake, N.W.T., on May 28, 1897, while attempting to apprehend Almighty Voice, the Indian murderer of Sergeant Colebrook." "Drowned when fording the Bow River on the Blackfoot Reserve, N.W.T., on September 6, 1903, while on patrol." "Shot and killed by a burglary suspect while on night patrol in Frank, Alta., April 12, 1908." Or later in the century, "Killed near Tofield, Alberta, on April 23, 1913, while attempting to apprehend Oscar Fonberg, a suspected lunatic." "Drowned near the mouth of the Indian River, east of Herschel Island, Arctic Ocean, on August 18, 1924, while on special duty." These are just a very few illustrations to show an indication of the pattern of work and the type of danger encountered by our men in the various eras during which the Force changed and grew. The list goes on, however, to the present day, and every so often another name is added. Now it is approximately twice as long as it was in 1939, but bearing in mind the hazards which have to be faced it seems surprising that it is not considerably longer.

But now it was 1939, the beginning of the war years, and the R.C.M.P. was stretched to its limits in looking after the interests of the country. All over Canada, its members were working more often than not far into the night. I was engaged in routine matters of administration, overseeing the work of the Sub-Division and supervising the investigations of its members. I regained my health by degrees, was promoted to Superintendent, and was transferred in 1943 from Regina to assume charge of the Winnipeg Sub-Division of the Force. During my stay at Regina, there had been one event of importance — to my wife and myself, at least — another daughter, Mary Frances, was born on March 3, 1940.

Policing requirements in Manitoba were no different than they had been in Saskatchewan — it was simply a matter of trying to keep up, on a wider scale, with the pressure of duties. After the seven years I had spent in the North and the four subsequent years when I had been engaged in intelligence duties at Ottawa, I found that although we were hard pressed for time it was a change, at least, to be directing in regard to criminal matters. I was forty-three by this time and had been twenty-one years in the R.C.M.P., and while the first several years of service had been spent in areas which called for a full application of one's physical energies, the last eight had necessitated an equal degree of endeavor — and a good deal of adaptability — in applying all one's mental resources and abilities to the work.

But if from my personal standpoint the last four years, in comparison with what others were doing, proved uneventful, this situation was to change in the very near future, for in 1945 I was transferred back to my old appointment in charge of Intelligence at headquarters and there, the next year, was to find myself involved in a matter of tremendous significance. Of all the curious changes and trends that I had encountered during the whole course of my career, this was to prove without question quite the most strenuous challenge and struggle.

Sometimes I wondered in the after years whether all that I'd gone through in accumulating experience had not been pointed toward meeting the problems of endurance with which I was soon to be faced in this particular task.

16

~~~~~~~

Igor Gouzenko

IN 1945 I had been back in Ottawa about a year. The war was over; the atom bomb had been dropped on Hiroshima approximately a month before. The office of the Director of Criminal Investigation had fallen vacant due to the retirement of the Assistant Commissioner in charge, and I had been temporarily assigned to that work also until some more senior officer could be transferred. It was a busy spot; the telephone never seemed to stop ringing, and what made it worse was that I still had to oversee the work of the Intelligence Branch where Leopold, now an Inspector, was taking my place. One never knew what the call might be about. It might be a summons from the Commissioner,* or about some crime, or something to do with the secret service end of the work. There were people to interview, meetings to go to, memoranda to dictate, and the usual hundred and one things on which an opinion had to be formed and a decision made — sometimes at very short notice — before some other question came up. Now, in a flash, the pressure of duties was to be greatly intensified by the appearance of Igor Gouzenko.

H. Montgomery Hyde covers the initial stages of the

* Commissioner S. T. Wood had taken over command of the R.C.M.P. in 1938, on the death of Commissioner MacBrien, and had been responsible for the operation of the Force during the difficult war years.

case in *Room 3606*,* a biography of Sir William Stephenson, the head of the British Secret Service section which during the war had its offices in New York.

Late on the night of September 6th, 1945, William Stephenson, who happened to be on a routine official visit to Ottawa, called on Mr. Robertson, Under-Secretary of State in the Canadian Department of External Affairs, at his private residence. With him he found Mr. Thomas Archibald Stone, Counsellor in the Canadian Embassy in Washington. Earlier that day Stephenson had heard a story to the effect that an employee of the Soviet Embassy had been in touch with the Department of Justice through the R.C.M.P., offering to furnish information, and he wanted to know if Robertson knew anything about it. As a matter of fact, Robertson did. He told Stephenson that the head of the Intelligence Branch of the R.C.M.P. had informed him that a man who had given his name as Gouzenko and said he was a cipher clerk in the Embassy had made such an offer, and the Intelligence officer had asked for guidance as to what action to take. The Under-Secretary had in turn consulted the Prime Minister, Mr. MacKenzie King, with the result that the R.C.M.P. were instructed to do nothing for the time being for fear of the diplomatic repercussions which might arise from a false step ("Too hot a potato," the Prime Minister remarked), although this was not to prevent the R.C.M.P. from keeping a watch on the Russian.

There was no doubt about it; Igor Gouzenko, a cipher clerk at the Soviet Embassy (who also held the rank of Lieutenant in the Red Army), had gone through a frightening time. His adventures had begun the previous evening when he had left his office and shortly afterwards had approached the newspaper building of the Ottawa *Journal*. He was in a bad predicament. He knew that before long his absence would be discovered together with the disappearance of certain secret papers he had taken from the embassy, and it was essential that he find someone immedi-

* *Room 3606* by H. Montgomery Hyde. Published by Farrar Straus in New York, 1963.

ately who would listen to his story. It was night as he made his way up in the elevator to what he thought would be the obvious instrument — a newspaper — to disclose what he knew. On the first visit he had hardly made his appearance when he was engaged in conversation by a woman in the elevator who appeared to recognize him, whose face was familiar, and whom he thought he might have met at one of the embassy functions. He was apprehensive too, for, as he says in his own story published in *Cosmopolitan Magazine* for February 1947, he could not be sure, knowing the manner in which the N.K.V.D. (Russian secret police) operated, that one agent at least might not be planted in the Ottawa *Journal*. In this event news of his presence at the newspaper office would soon be passed to the embassy with disastrous results to himself. He decided to leave and returned later that night in a second attempt to contact the editor.

On the latter occasion he was no more successful. The editor had gone, and finally, when he got in touch with one of the staff who would listen, it was suggested that he contact the R.C.M.P. By this time he must have been desperate, for he decided to try to see the Minister of Justice — although it was now close to midnight — and with this purpose in view went to the Justice Building where the Minister had his office, only to be told by the night guard to return the next morning. It was a natural enough reaction on the part of the night guard — he could hardly disturb the Minister, who would probably be at home and in bed, at the behest of someone he took to be merely some excited foreigner.

As there was nothing further he could do at this late hour, Gouzenko went home. After a few hours' rest, he set off again the next morning, accompanied by his wife and young son, to meet with no better success, being passed from one office to another — including that of the Minister of Justice where he tried to contact the Minister without result, although he was able to get in touch with two of the Secretaries. To those who could take in its significance, he must have seemed like a large load of dynamite — undesirable in one's immediate proximity! Finally, having exhausted all channels which, as far as he knew, might be open to him, disheartened and at a loss to know what next to do, Gouzenko and his wife returned to their apartment to await events which they knew would not be long in forthcoming. His disappearance would have become known to the N.K.V.D.

On our part, Leopold and I had been quite as busy. Word had been passed to us about what this strange figure was doing — he'd talked to another R.C.M.P. officer in a different department during the course of his travels — and we'd been to see the Under-Secretary of State for External Affairs. Following the interview, we had placed plainclothesmen on Gouzenko's trail to see where he went. It was an unprecedented situation. While, from what we'd heard, Gouzenko's purpose seemed genuine, we'd not seen him ourselves and, because he was an official of a foreign government, we could not take the initiative in meeting him. It did not take much imagination, though, to realize what might happen. Undoubtedly the agents of the N.K.V.D. would attempt to make a search of the downtown apartment where Gouzenko lived as soon as they discovered he was missing, and if they tried to remove him from the building by force — presumably Gouzenko would resist them — an excuse would be provided for us to step in; from there we could decide where developments might lead. With this in mind and quite unknown to Gouzenko, we stationed detectives round his apartment. Without being aware of it, Gouzenko was well protected, for the Soviet agents, if they appeared, would have only one objective — to remove him to the embassy together with the documents — and if this was attempted they could be stopped immediately. We would then know for sure that something was seriously wrong, that the papers Gouzenko had in his possession were definitely important, and that he was not some crackbrained individual traveling around with an unfounded story. If this plan of action may seem unnecessarily cautious, it must be remembered that the situation in 1945 was not just what it now is when it is not regarded as entirely unusual for persons to change sides. Gouzenko was the first individual to try to seek asylum in Canada; we had just concluded a war in which the Russians had been our allies; and while we in the Intelligence Branch and a few others knew of the threat that was lurking round the corner — the pattern whereby, as time went on, the Communists would attempt to achieve their final objective, world domination — most of the people of the North American continent were quite unaware of the fact that once the German threat was handled, another and larger danger would arise. From a security standpoint it was tremendously important. So far it had not been possible to gain any positive proof of Russian activities which could be publicly laid on the table, for quite apart from the fact that the war had immersed us in an all-out effort in other directions, the Communist undercover network was of so secret a nature that there was not enough evidence to point this out definitely. If Gouzenko had anything in his possession of value it might close the gap! Gouzenko, from all outward appearances, was going to a great deal of trouble for some purpose of his own.

Things worked out much as we'd expected. Night had come and Gouzenko and his family were back in their apartment, wondering in a considerable state of apprehension, no doubt, what the next few hours would bring. It had been a very bad day, nobody had come to his help, and the prospects were dismal, for as far as he was aware, all his efforts had been in vain — he was caught in the maelstrom in which he and his family must now be sucked down. Early that night, looking out of his window, Gouzenko saw two men sitting in the park across the street whom he naturally took to be agents of the N.K.V.D. but who were in reality R.C.M.P. plainclothesmen. Later he saw another man who was watching the back of the building from the areaway. It was a reasonable enough supposition — he knew nothing of the very definite interest we were taking in his welfare.

Soon he had a visitor. An embassy official arrived at the apartment, knocked and banged at the door with his fist and, after calling Gouzenko's name, went away. In desperation, Gouzenko climbed from the balcony of his apartment to the adjoining one in which a Sergeant of the Royal Canadian Air Force was living. After hearing Gouzenko's version of what was happening — that he was in danger from the N.K.V.D. — an offer was made to put him and his family up for the night. In the meantime, however, while Igor was talking to the Sergeant, Anna Gouzenko had contacted another neighbor directly across the hall, and while the R.C.A.F. Sergeant left on a bicycle to summon the city police, the family moved, on the other neighbor's invitation, into her suite. Soon two members of the city police arrived and, on contacting Gouzenko, told him that the building would be kept under observation for the rest of the night. At a prearranged signal with the light in the bathroom — it would be kept on and if it was turned out it would mean there was trouble — they would move up to the apartment and take such action as might then be required. All this time our men had been watching the apartment, but so far nothing had occurred to warrant their entering the picture.

At about midnight, four officials from the embassy arrived and knocked at the door of Gouzenko's apartment, and through the keyhole from across the hall he recognized them. The R.C.A.F. Sergeant, having returned, heard the noise, came out, and told them that there was no one at home. After thanking him politely, the visitors departed — to make their way back surreptitiously almost at once and break in the door. In the meantime, Anna Gouzenko had been signaling with the bathroom light to the city policemen, and in a few minutes they arrived, finding the lock to Gouzenko's apartment broken and the Russians making a search of his possessions inside. Although they were not arrested — as officials of the embassy they claimed diplomatic immunity and nothing in any case was to be gained by attempting to restrain them — the events of the night had confirmed that Gouzenko was important in the eyes of the embassy, and if this was the case it was reasonable to believe that the documents he had could be of considerable value. Further, as there were now definite grounds to show that he and his family might be in danger — the forced entry of his apartment had proved this — there was justification for giving him temporary protection at least. Accordingly he was placed under close guard by the city police overnight.

Although it was now long past midnight, I had been kept in touch by telephone with what was happening, and it was arranged that in the morning Gouzenko would be brought to R.C.M.P. headquarters so that we could see what he had. Having obtained approval of this course of action from higher authority, I waited impatiently in my office early that day wondering just what the documents might be, what Gouzenko would have to say. If the papers were valueless and we had no definite information, we would have nothing but his word — nothing to back up any allegations he made. It would not in any sense constitute proof, and it was reasonable to suppose that the Russians would deny any accusations he made. It was quite possible that they would imply that Gouzenko was suffering from mental delusions — that he was sick and that, in his own interests, they wanted him back before he did himself some kind of harm. If this kind of representation were made, it might precipitate a really bad position. We would have an official of a foreign government on our hands without any real knowledge of the truth of what he said. The break-in of Gouzenko's apartment could be explained away by any one of a number of reasons — he had stolen something from the embassy or made threats against his own life; or he was under orders to return to the Soviet Union with his family and as a Russian national they felt they controlled his affairs.

It would be an entirely different thing if the papers he carried showed some situation which was definitely detrimental to Canadian interests. Then almost any chance would be worth taking — we would be justified in holding him until we got to the root of what it was. Leopold and I waited, wondering.

I will not forget my first meeting with Igor Gouzenko. Leopold and I were waiting anxiously in the Director's office that morning when Inspector Williams — the officer in charge who had been actively engaged in looking after Igor and Anna Gouzenko's interests during the night — brought him in. I saw at once that here was a person who had passed through some hell of his own. I had an immediate feeling of sympathy, a knowledge that he was so bereft of any kind of help in his precarious position that I should try to do everything for him, not just as a cog in the huge wheels of government but as an ordinary human individual as well. Afterwards, when I had time, I thought it might have had something to do with Jack Spratley, whom I'd met in the wilderness so many years before, and who had leaned over a metaphorical precipice to help someone in distress, and who had been so great an influence in the pursuit of the thing I'd been searching for so long. At all events, here was someone who had a wife and child — someone who was hanging by his fingertips to his own particular cliff, struggling, never knowing whether help would come or what the next few moments would bring. My whole mind, apart from this feeling of sympathy, was fixed on the documents. Would they stack up?

I cannot describe Igor Gouzenko for obvious reasons,

but that he had courage and resolution was immediately apparent as, notwithstanding the tribulations he'd suffered, his manner was composed as he took his place in the hard-bottomed chair. His eyes flickered to Leopold for a moment and then came back to mine.

"I understand you want to see us," I said. "What about?

He told us his story, how he'd left the Soviet Embassy two evenings before; that he knew that there were a number of spies operating against the interests of Canada; that he felt the public should know. I found it difficult at times to understand his full meaning, but obviously he was sincere and his general purport was plain.

We listened, not saying much, for his disclosures indicated a very serious state of affairs. Secrets about the atom bomb together with other top-secret information had been passed to the Russians by Communist sympathizers within the country who were in important positions of trust. It was breathtaking to hear him, but I was still on edge — unless proof was forthcoming it was just one man's word. I wondered if it could really be true. It sounded incredible!

Time was passing — fifteen minutes or so — but nothing had been said about the documents. Finally I could stand it no longer and asked, "What about the documents — I hear you've got some papers to show us?"

There was a short pause as, turning from one of the others to whom he'd been talking, Gouzenko looked at me squarely. Then he put his hand in the inside pocket of his coat and produced a thick envelope and handed it over. I took it and passed it to Leopold after taking the contents out and examining them cursorily — most of the papers seemed to be in Russian.

"We'd better get some of these translated right away," I said.

Leopold took the papers and left the office to give them to the Russian translator who was waiting.

We went on with the conversation, getting as much information as we could. As far as I was concerned, I was thinking of all the vast possibilities that Gouzenko's appearance had opened up. We had to be sure that what he said was true. We were on our way, though — at least we had the papers, and there was something about Gouzenko which made me feel that we would not be disappointed in the end.

Soon the information we were waiting for came back. It was fantastic! About four of the documents had been translated and they showed that there was an agent in the Department of External Affairs and one in the United Kingdom High Commissioner's office, both of whom had been passing secret information to the Russians. Besides this, a scientist whose identity — he was described by a code name — was not disclosed until later had supplied particulars about the atom bomb, at that time an ultra top-secret project! It was enough. The other documents would have to wait until we had time to translate them. The immediate necessity was to look after Gouzenko. If the other documents were as startling as the first few had been, it was obvious that from a security standpoint we would have an enormous quantity of information in our hands.

But to get Gouzenko and his wife and small child out of town and hide them had, among others, one serious complication. Anna was six months pregnant and I could see the difficulties we'd be in if she suffered a miscarriage. We'd have to take them to some place where their whereabouts would be secret except to the two or three men who would be detailed to guard them — those and a handful of others who of necessity had to be informed. If the Russians became aware of what we were doing, it would certainly mean that the agents in the spy system would be alerted, and there were a great number of leads which would have to be followed up before we were ready. Even if a single newspaper reporter got an inkling of what was going on, unless he could be prevailed on to keep quiet the whole case might be blown before it got started.* It would be big news. It was one thing for one or two people to have heard that a mysterious individual was wandering around town with some extraordinary story, but quite another if word leaked out that we had judged him important enough to place him in hiding. It was awkward enough as it was, for the embassy officials would know that Anna was about to have a baby and we'd have to find a hospital which she could enter under some other identity. They might well be on the lookout for a woman in her condition who spoke only Russian, and there was no knowing at all where their agents might be.

Things had to be done very quickly. By that afternoon, a few of Gouzenko's and his family's possessions had been gathered up from their apartment, and they were on their way to the woods and a small, lonely cabin, a sufficient distance away to ensure that they'd not be discovered. Although they were later moved from place to place in the interests of safety — places where the curiosity of neighbors would not be aroused — in the full six-month period which it took to follow up the leads in the documents and to complete our arrangements, not a single leak occurred in Canada as to what was going on.

As soon as this immediate requirement had been looked after, we went to work on the documents, translating them one by one. Very soon it was seen that a large espionage network existed and that included in it were a number of scientists and persons in positions of trust who had been passing secret information to the Russians, but as their identities were hidden by code names considerable time was required for our small expert staff to find out who they were.

Six months — from the time we first saw Gouzenko in September to February of the next year when the raids were made and the agents arrested — under these trying circumstances can seem a long time. One point that caused particu-

* Much to the credit of the Ottawa *Journal*, bearing in mind the significance of the case, no publicity was given to Gouzenko's visit to the newspaper.

lar concern was the fact that those whom we knew to be spies could not even be followed. One inadvertent error which might lead to a single agent's suspecting that someone was trailing him could mean that this would be reported to the Russians and the whole network aroused. In the end, apart from taking steps to have those agents whose identity we knew moved under one pretext or another to less vulnerable positions where they would not have access to secret documents and would thus be rendered harmless, we left them to themselves. But it was a thing which kept me awake, sleepless at night, wondering if we'd made the best deduction we could. It was with indescribable relief that I found, as time went on, that not a single one had disappeared.

All this, of course, required a great deal of work, extending as often as not to twelve or fourteen hours a day, weekends included, and this was to continue for most of the close to two-year period which it took to finish up the case. To add a bizarre touch to the proceedings, somewhere about halfway through the investigation I was struck by a car when driving home from work. It was quite late at night and I had got out of the car to go to the assistance of a woman who was being beaten by two men armed with a club on one of the dark city streets. As I crossed the road, suddenly I received a terrific blow in the back which hurled me through the air for several feet before I landed on my chin. After a few seconds during which I must have lost consciousness, I awoke to see two great blazing lights staring at me from a scant twelve inches away, the headlights of the car which had hit me. Intent as I'd been on reaching the scene of the disturbance and crossing the road at a diagonal away from the oncoming traffic, I'd failed to see a car approaching from behind. Its radiator had struck me square in the back, breaking off a large piece of the grill. Covered with blood from the wound in my chin and with my suit ripped in tatters, I picked up the piece of metal as possible future evidence and then drove on home while a city policeman who had arrived on the scene dealt with the two men who'd been engaged in the fracas. Apart from a few very bad bruises and having to stay in bed for a couple of days, I felt no ill effects and put my good fortune down to the fact that where the car had struck me I was very well muscled from driving dogs in the North. On the impact, instead of breaking any bones or suffering other injury, I had been shot through the air like a rubber ball bouncing. One of the spectators of the accident had been very excited. "You ought to be dead, you ought to be dead! I can't understand it," he had kept repeating — and except for some act of providence and a good set of muscles, I suppose he might well have been right. Anticlimatically it turned out that the accident had been a coincidence and my own fault for not keeping an eye on the traffic; with only a single purpose in mind — to deal with the disturbance — I'd not been paying sufficient attention. At all events, the driver of the car had been in no way to blame.

Slowly but surely, we were weaving our net round the agents, gathering up the information which had been given us and fitting in the odds and ends of details which would later establish without doubt that what Gouzenko had told us was correct. While we ourselves were entirely satisfied in regard to his story, we knew that when prosecutions were entered even with the documents in our possession we would have a fight on our hands. Then, from another angle of the case, a further complication arose — in December, Anna Gouzenko had her baby. First, we had to find a doctor out in the country who could be completely trusted not to mention anything of what he'd been told. Then we had to enter Anna into a hospital under an assumed name while one of our men who could speak Russian posed as the father, visiting the hospital, walking up and down the corridors and expressing concern in broken English for his putative wife and child while Igor was kept in hiding a considerable distance away. But the plan went through, no suspicion was aroused,

Anna finally returned to her husband with her child and we waited for what would happen next.

The decision came in February 1946, when a Royal Commission was appointed consisting of two judges of the Supreme Court of Canada, to hear the evidence and investigate the facts. By this time we were ready. The identity of a sufficient number of the agents was known to warrant action being taken and, under special authority of an Order in Council enacted in October 1945, on the morning of February 15, in a number of closely timed raids, they were picked up. The detention of the suspects came completely unheralded, not only to the general public but to most of our headquarters staff and presumably to the Russians as well; after weeks of concern about not shadowing the agents, the course we'd adopted had paid off.

On February 15, the day of the arrests, nothing seemed certain. We had gone as far as we could in the investigation and now had to await what the Royal Commissioner proceedings would disclose. One officer, with an adequate staff, had been appointed to look after the interests of Gouzenko, Inspector Leopold assisted the Royal Commissioners, and two other officers had been specially selected to deal with the initial questioning of the suspects and to tie in any additional leads which might come up. One atomic scientist had left Canada for England during the earlier stages of the case — in the ordinary course of his business — and had been accompanied, quite unknown to himself, by one of our undercover operatives on the same plane. On arrival there he was pointed out to a British secret service member who by previous arrangement was waiting at the airport. Later, after those who were active in the spy ring had been arrested in Canada, the scientist was taken into custody and on being convicted was sentenced to ten years in jail.

I had to correlate all the different angles of the case, giving direction for the safety measures of Gouzenko, maintaining contact with the government and keeping in touch with those who were engaged, each within his own separate sphere, in all their different tasks. It was like trying to lead a group of mountaineers roped together along the side of a precipice — a single mistake could mean that all might be swept down. Then, as a sidelight, during the six-month period between the appearance of Gouzenko and the detention of the agents, my wife began to have serious doubts about my behavior. I could of course tell her nothing and, after working at the office until very late at night, would pace the floor of the bedroom through the early hours of the morning, smoking innumerable cigarettes and trying to decide where a certain course of action might lead or whether some other course would be best. The seal was finally put on her doubts when, on one occasion, I left the house and went to the office at three o'clock in the morning to check on some matter I was worried about and felt needed attention. When I returned an hour or so before dawn she was much concerned; nothing she could visualize could warrant my doing this and yet I could not explain.

As matters turned out, there had been little cause for anxiety. When questioned by the Royal Commissioners, some of the agents admitted what they had been doing quite freely. Of those later arraigned in the Canadian Criminal Courts, nine were convicted on charges involving the passing of information to a foreign power,* while eight were acquitted and went free. As a further result of the investigation, one other individual was sentenced for making an untrue or misleading statement to procure a passport and, in common with the others, paid the penalty for his crime.

Out of this case came an awakening to the threat to the northern hemisphere which up to that time had been realized by only a few.

* Including the only Labour Progressive Party (previously the Communist Party) member in the House of Commons and another accused, the National Organizing Secretary of the Party.

One of the main concerns all through the investigation had to do with the future of Gouzenko and his family once the main issues had been disposed of and the trials had come to an end. What would he do? He had no financial resources, no status as a Canadian citizen, not even a vocation in which he could be employed. Besides, it was obvious that, after everything had been concluded, it would be necessary for him to take up an entirely new life — one in which his true identity would be hidden so effectively that Igor Gouzenko would disappear and another figure emerge in the pages of the present as they turned one by one from the past. It was no easy matter to create such a person when there were such obstacles as a foreign accent, for although Gouzenko's speech and diction were excellent by now, it was still fairly obvious that he came from some European land. I had grown very attached to Igor and Anna as the months went on — I admired their intelligence, resolution, and courage — and felt that this very important question must be settled.

The main difficulty was a financial one, but after considerable negotiation this was removed by the sale of his story to *Cosmopolitan Magazine,* for which he received a substantial sum, and when I heard that the deal had gone through I breathed a sigh of relief. Then a public-spirited citizen in Ottawa contributed quite a large amount to his welfare and, for the time being at least, his financial troubles were eased.

One day Igor and I discussed his future. We had been talking in the garden of a house in which he'd been hidden, and the question came up. While at that time I was by no means certain of his specific talents I suggested that he might turn his hand to writing a book. He was doubtful, but I had not been wrong in estimating his capabilities. Later, long after the whole matter had faded into the background, he produced a novel, *The Fall of a Titan,* which became a Book of the Month Club selection and a best seller. In the flyleaf of the copy he sent me, he wrote an inscription. Nine years had passed and I was an Assistant Commissioner in charge of British Columbia at the time. It read:

> To Assistant Commissioner Rivett-Carnac
>
> *Your vision, your great confidence and thoughtful-ness made it possible for my family and myself to live and to work in free Canada.*
>
> *When I wrote this novel I often thought about you, and these thoughts were of deepest gratitude.*
>
> *With respect and admiration,*
>
> Igor Gouzenko

The Royal Commission sums up very effectively the value of what Igor Gouzenko did: "In our opinion Gouzenko, by what he has done, has rendered great public service to the people of this country and has thereby placed Canada in his debt."

I think that Gouzenko appeared at a critical period when the North American continent was peacefully sleeping, and at the risk of his life and buffeted by the winds all around him, took it by the shoulder and shook it awake. It seems a miracle now that the small candle-flame he carried was not snuffed out, surrounded as it was by a gale of such potency and force as to pass all understanding. At least, in the beginning. Then, as time went on, the faint light grew stronger, becoming a torch, a conflagration, which none could miss seeing. His story ran round the world as though a tocsin was ringing. People dressed hurriedly and looked out of their windows, aware at last that some small figure was shouting. At first nobody believed what he said; some shrugged it off; others who were frightened hid their heads in the blankets. But these were only a few and in the mind of the world there grew a great sense of awareness. People were awake at last to the threat in the distance. As Gouzenko said himself, "I am glad that I found the strength within myself to take this step and warn Canada and the other democratic countries of the danger which hangs over them."

Igor and his wife were very brave people.

For me the case had a somewhat ironic ending. One morning, close to its finish, I awoke doubled up with pain. The hospital authorities notwithstanding a series of examinations could find nothing wrong. All I could do was sleep day and night, full of narcotics. I knew what the trouble was — my body had called a natural halt when the mind could go no further. When I was better I was sent on a special mission to the continent, during which I slowly recovered. Then on my return I was moved immediately to Regina, this time to be Assistant Commissioner in charge.

The successful conclusion of the case had not, of course, in any sense been due to one man's efforts; in common with everything accomplished by the Mounted Police it had been a unified achievement brought about by the untiring work and efficiency of many officers and men. As far as my own part was concerned, beyond the inquiry itself I had gone a long way in the pursuit toward knowledge — I had done something for others, had stretched out a helping hand to save four people from destruction. It gives me a pleasant feeling to think of them, secure somewhere in the life they have chosen when at one time they hung from the chasm's dark edge by their fingers.

17

Western Horizons

YOUTH is the time for excitement. Then, as the years go on, things simmer down. One is older, more experienced, but much of the fire is gone. Dog teams, elephants, the roar of the battle, the sense of adventure and physical encounter have all disappeared like notes faintly heard from some distant orchestra.

But there are still challenges to be met from an office chair. Not so much physical but relating to things of the spirit instead — which still have to be met and disposed of as they come at you one by one. In a sense, the espionage inquiry had been such a challenge, a battle fought from within the confining walls of a room. Now, I had to take on a larger command. For Regina, in those days, was the biggest Division of the Force, responsible not only for the policing of the Province of Saskatchewan, but having under its aegis the Training Division as well. As the train traveled west through Ontario and Manitoba, I wondered how it would feel to go back to where I'd started as a Corporal nearly twenty years before and where later I'd been given my breaking in as a very junior officer when I'd returned from the Yukon.

It was a time for rejoicing in 1947; the war had ended,

families had been reunited, and as far as the R.C.M.P. was concerned our men who had left to serve overseas were back in the ranks, doing their work almost as though nothing had happened. Many of them had held commissions while on active service, but now in most cases they returned to the positions they'd held. The Force was resuming its old march again, commencing another era in which it would broaden, spreading east and west in its scope. It was a late summer day when I got to Regina with my wife and two daughters, with the same golden wheat waving on the flat, level plain, and after the strain of the last two years it was good to see that yellow sea stretching away in the distance, with hardly a break in its pattern.

Before, when I'd been in Regina, the work had been much less confining and much of my time had been spent in traveling around. Now, while I could occasionally get away to inspect some Sub-Division or detachment, I had the training establishment as well as law enforcement to supervise. Since 1932, there had been two Divisions at the "Depot," one to look after the policing end of affairs and another to train the recruits, each operating separately with a different officer in charge. While the same framework was continued with an officer remaining in command of the Training Division, the whole, for purposes of administration, now was placed under my control.

A year passed, then another, with nothing of moment occurring as far as I personally was concerned. It was largely a cut and dried proposition; the "Depot" had been in existence since before the turn of the century and matters ran smoothly. A touch here and there at the right moment was all that was necessary to keep the machine operating properly. Recruits came and went exactly as they had in the old days and, looking out of my window, I could see them formed up in squads as they always had been, marching up and down.

Out in the field our men were working under their usual high pressure, investigating thefts, holdups, and murders, all the crimes found in country districts or towns. There were seven Sub-Divisions in the province, each with a large number of detachments. Some, in addition to federal and provincial requirements, performed municipal duties as well. However, of all the cases investigated in those years, one stands out. It combined most of the aids available to a modern police organization; radio, police cars, a tracking dog, and airplanes were used, and helped effect the arrest of a murderer who, two thousand miles east, had shot down one of our men.

On May 25, 1950, as Constable Alexander Gamman was walking down the street returning from a routine duty he had been performing in Montreal, he saw an armed man run out of one of the local branches of the Bank of Toronto, closely pursued by the manager, who shouted to Gamman that a holdup had occurred. On the point of making his getaway the bandit turned and fired his pistol at the manager, who fell wounded to the pavement. Constable Gamman, in uniform but unarmed, attempted to grapple with the gunman, who fired three times at him, one bullet taking deadly effect. The bandit made off on foot, escaping into the streets of the city, and disappeared.

Three weeks passed and notwithstanding the efforts of the city police and R.C.M.P. investigators in the eastern areas of Canada, no sign of Gamman's murderer could be found. Due, too, to the general excitement in the bank at the time of the holdup there was not much in the way of a description of the bandit except for two salient points — the bandit was a *big* man and he had a gold tooth. Besides this it was believed that he'd been wounded at the time of the holdup, as bloodstains were found close to the scene of the crime.

The scene now shifts to Saskatchewan nearly a month later, to Moose Jaw, about fifty miles west of Regina. There, a Canadian Pacific Railway policeman accosted a man he found getting out of a boxcar, and the man held him up with an automatic pistol. After threatening the policeman the man had disappeared in the night. It had been dark and the policeman had not been able to see him properly, at least not enough to describe him; he said, however, that he was a *big* man. As he was armed with an automatic pistol, it was reasonable to assume that he might be wanted for some serious offense he'd committed elsewhere. Unless this was so it seemed unlikely that he would have produced the weapon when he probably could have made his escape without resorting to such an extreme.

Without a moment's delay the full resources of the R.C.M.P. went into operation. The radio network alerted all detachments to the south and west of Regina, patrol cars were warned to be on the lookout for the fugitive, and a tracking dog was obtained. Twenty-four hours passed without any sign being seen of the bandit and then at noon of the second day he was traced to a point southeast of Moose Jaw near the United States boundary. He had been given a lift there by two persons in a car, who, of course, were not aware of his identity. He had been dropped off so many miles south that even with our men and the police dog on his trail, he was far enough ahead for the pursuing members to know he would cross the international boundary before they could catch up. As a result the Sheriff's officers in Montana and the state highway patrol were warned that he would soon cross the line, and a few hours later he was captured at gunpoint on the United States side. On being handed over to our men at the border he was found to be suffering from a bullet wound in the thigh — he was in fact the murderer of Constable Gamman and had accidentally shot himself in the leg during the struggle with Gamman — and when questioned admitted his part in the Montreal murder. It had been a very long chance with practically nothing to go on but the lucky seven had turned up once again.

And so the work went on, the usual day-to-day activity of any large law enforcement agency. The year previous to the murder of Constable Gamman, Newfoundland far to the east had joined Confederation, becoming another province of Canada, and had contracted with the federal government to have the R.C.M.P. look after its policing. Now, in 1950, the Force was responsible for the provincial policing of the whole of Canada excepting British Columbia, Ontario, and Quebec. That same year British Columbia on the shores of the Pacific followed suit. The biggest area of any to be taken over, it would be a difficult job entailing the total reorganization of policing facilities.

At that time, in British Columbia, the R.C.M.P. was engaged solely in enforcing the federal laws, and had its local headquarters in Vancouver, a majority of the work having to do with investigations concerning the anti-drug laws. Within the province there were only a few detachments in comparison to the other areas in which the Force was maintaining the provincial laws. These detachments were spread out at considerable distances, their duties having no connection with the Criminal Code or local statutes, which were a responsibility of the Provincial Police. I had been in Saskatchewan in 1928 — though only for a short time — when the R.C.M.P. had taken over the same obligations for that area, and had a general idea of the difficulties. Another organizational structure, similar to that which had become standard in the seven other provinces, would have to be built.

On August 15 the changeover was made; the headquarters of "E" Division, as it was called, was moved to Victoria, the capital city of British Columbia on Vancouver Island; and Assistant Commissioner A. T. Belcher — who had been appointed to commissioned rank in 1931, at the same time as I — took over charge. Then, eight months later, when he was promoted to Deputy Commissioner and transferred to Ottawa, I was sent to British Columbia.

It was late in March 1951 when I heard of the transfer. Orders reached me at Bismark, North Dakota, where my wife and I were snowed in on our way back from Ontario after a short period of furlough in eastern Canada. After a few days at Bismark, the weather cleared sufficiently for the roads to be plowed, and we reached Regina very soon after, where our effects were packed up once again and we left for the coast.

Victoria, the garden of the Pacific, lies about eighty miles from Vancouver, the largest city in British Columbia, and is separated from the mainland by the Juan de Fuca straits. As our Canadian Pacific vessel steamed into the harbor on an early spring day, the great bulk of the Empress Hotel loomed up before us, with the majestic dome of the Parliament buildings rising high on the right. It was a complete reversal from the blizzard conditions on the prairies which we'd experienced only a few days ago. Here, flowers were in bloom, the buds breaking out on the trees in profusion, with daffodils and bluebells rising in a panoply of gold and blue from the green of the grass in the parks' open stretches. A moderate breeze fanned the city. It had been nearly twenty years since I'd been away from the snow country; Victoria, gaily caparisoned as it was and bedecked in spring raiment, was a welcome change. Far on the mainland, a range of mountains raised their heads high in the sky, and to the south another range — the Olympics — formed sugarloaf cones, their peaks snow-encrusted, on the United States side. We were surrounded by the burnished steel-blue of the sea all around us, the mountains beyond hiding rivers and lakes and the teeming activity of cities and towns on the mainland, dotted here and there over an area eight hundred miles long and roughly four hundred miles wide. Out of sight though it was, there, I knew, was a hive of industry working, a vast mountain country busy with every kind of commercial venture — lumber, coal, fruit orchards, pulp mills, fishing, ship building, and mining, to mention only a few. The province which had first come into being nearly a hundred years before was one huge business enterprise, thrusting and surging; and now the R.C.M.P. was here to police it and my job was to build together two law enforcement agencies into one.

There were a multitude of misunderstandings and confusions to clear up. The members of the provincial police who had joined the ranks of the R.C.M.P. were highly proficient in regard to local requirements but knew very little or nothing of the federal work, while our men who had been accustomed to dealing with federal laws were unfamiliar with what the provincial police previously had to do. At first it was like having two entirely separate organizations marching side by side, both with a common purpose but with practically no knowledge of the problems which accrued each to each. There were not even enough uniforms to go round — some of the provincial police wore their old uniforms. Gradually, step by step, month by month, the pattern grew clearer, and where doubt and confusion had existed, things settled down.

In Regina, where the R.C.M.P. had been functioning for many long years, the forms of procedure were well laid out and everyone knew what to do. Here, in British Columbia, there was little precedent to follow and we had to improvise.

It was a challenge to build and to form, requiring an all-out endeavor. Evening would come and I would go home exhausted, never at rest, my mind digesting the things that had happened, trying to come to some conclusion as to what course might be best, putting in a word or two of encouragement here and there, sometimes — though not very often — of reproof. For that was one of the things I'd learned the hard way in the ranks — I'd been part of it all and knew what the men were up against, the difficulties they had, and the manner in which their problems could perhaps be overcome. It had been an invaluable education, indispensable now in these latter years of my service when it could be applied. Criticism, I knew, could kill all endeavor where the burdens were heavy, while just a word or two of praise would in most cases spur a man on. They were the important ones, the men in the field — without them nothing could be done. And yet, at the helm as I was, I had my own function — never to appear disturbed, never to show anxiety whatever the occasion, always to be calm. In the turmoil of involvement, one had to sit like a rock unshaken by any storm which might be blowing, the center on which matters revolved. And then at night one could throw off this false identity and lie awake — as I suppose most people do — wondering just how far he'd been wrong.

Gradually the foundation was finished, the walls went up, the roof went on. Now, after a year or two, we were approaching one single identity of knowledge, a mechanism in which the various units all operated as one. "E" Division — now the largest Division of the R.C.M.P. — was functioning at last in exactly the same manner as the other Divisions to the east.

During those years — five altogether — in which I was stationed in British Columbia, literally thousands and thousands of cases were successfully solved by the hundreds of men on detachments, north, south, east and west. Although most of these might, to greater or lesser degree, be regarded as routine irrespective of the amount of investigation required, one or two stand out particularly. In one — or so it seemed to me — it was almost miraculous that the R.C.M.P. member concerned managed to escape with his life.

It was on April 3, 1956, that four masked bandits held up the Royal Bank of Canada at Coquitlam, a town in the vicinity of Vancouver. They carried an arsenal of weapons — a .32 caliber revolver, a .38 caliber weapon, and a sawed-off shotgun. While three of the bandits held up the bank, another waited in an escape truck nearby, with a submachine gun. Fortunately, during the course of the holdup, although he was facing three men armed with weapons, the manager of the bank was able to trip an alarm, and Constable H. M. C. Johnstone, of Maillardville detachment, made immediately for the bank. He entered the premises and confronted the bank robbers, two of whom fired their guns before Johnstone could discharge a shot in return. Although hit in eight places, Johnstone was able to give such an account of himself during the course of the action that the bandit armed with the sawed-off shotgun fled panic-stricken while the other two were able to get through the door and make their escape from the bank.

Despite Johnstone's wounds, he was still able to get up and pursue the bandits outside, where, in a further exchange of gunfire, he killed the leader of the gang while the other two were taken into custody by members of the R.C.M.P. who had arrived. The fourth man, who had been in charge of the truck, managed to make his escape temporarily but was captured soon afterwards. Constable Johnstone, who had sunk to the pavement with his back against the wall of the building during the final stages of the battle, subsequently recovered and was promoted to Corporal in recognition of his act. Later, he was awarded the George Medal, for great bravery, by Her Majesty the Queen.

In another bank robbery attempt a man named Henry Seguin held up the Canadian Bank of Commerce at Williams Lake, more than two hundred miles north of Vancouver, on December 15, 1952. Seguin lay in wait for the manager when he left the bank, late at night. Forcing a pistol into the manager's side as he was about to enter his car, the bandit ordered him to return and open up the vault. Before this could be accomplished, however, he was disturbed by two employees who had returned to pick up some parcels, and in the ensuing excitement the manager was shot in the leg while Seguin escaped.

Immediately the members of Williams Lake detachment

took up the pursuit of the criminal and next morning tracked him to where he was lying in wait. In the battle that started with Seguin opening fire on the police, the bandit was wounded by a shot in the chest. He was lodged in a local hospital under guard and his fingerprints sent to headquarters, Ottawa, where, through the nationwide facilities of the R.C.M.P. Identification Bureau, his prints were found to be identical with an individual wanted for murder in Ontario. He was returned there for trial, and though found guilty and sentenced to be hanged, managed to cheat the gallows by swallowing poison, which he had concealed on his body, a day or so before the final processes of the law were to take place.

Finally the reorganization was complete. My own area of work, which of course had been purely administrative, came to an end and I was moved to Ottawa to become one of the two Deputy Commissioners of the Force. I was coming close to the end of my service, having completed thirty-three of the thirty-five years allowable, a period in which I had engaged in most of the activities of the R.C.M.P. from one end of Canada to the other. In the latter stages, British Columbia had been a rewarding experience, for with the help of the officers and men I had been able to build something. The Commissioner in a letter was kind enough to include words to the effect that the establishment of "E" Division in the form in which it had been left would always be looked upon as one of the major accomplishments in the history of the Force, a pleasant testimonial which made my efforts seem very much more than worthwhile.

18

~~~~~~~~~

The Top of the Mountain

O F COURSE I had never expected to become Commissioner. In the beginning I had been glad enough
to find a haven which provided board and lodging. It was
nice to know, when I first joined the R.C.M.P., that there
would be breakfast, lunch and then dinner every day —
not a cloud-piercing ambition, I suppose, but quite a great
height at the time. If this seems a curious statement to
make, and if you haven't actually had the experience of
getting down almost to the bottom rung in the ladder of
life, try to imagine it. It cuts you off square with the
ground, flush with the earth, and suddenly where you stood
there is nothing. It teaches you what is most important in
being — that all at once you've disappeared, that you have
no more worth than a straw, that you're so unimportant
that you can hardly be seen, and that if you are to force
your way upwards again, it can be done only by sheer
fighting. Whether it's "good for you" I can't say. All I can
do is speak from one man's experience. In the sense of
perspective, it's very illuminating.

And it has its reward, for you never forget it. It strips
away all the false trappings of everyday living — perhaps
it's the very first glimmer that leads to some kind of meaning, a clarity of vision regarding the troubles of others.

Probably, it's the birth of metaphysical thinking — things become noticeable which I know, in my case at least, would have stayed hidden. Had it not been for this, Jack Spratley might have seemed someone quite unimportant, Igor Gouzenko a cog without flesh-and-blood meaning.

But it wasn't like that. As time passed and ever so slowly I grew to maturity, everything that came within focus had to be closely examined, not so much for what appeared on its surface but for what lay deep down, almost unplumbable but there in its mystery if you searched hard enough for it. You knew what man was now, half beast, half god, his feet forever floundering on the chasm's steep sides, searching — just as you were — for fulfillment, the lodestone of gold at the top of the mountain. Apparently, in some unfathomable way, if you were to get there yourself you had to reach down and help him, feel for him blindly with hands of compassion. And yet, on the other hand, there was the battle — the struggle for survival — for if you loosened your grip you might fall to destruction. It was a contradiction in terms on a knife-edge, a rallying point of the mind from which you never quite knew where you'd go — whether you'd be strong enough to seize in your hands this thing of the spirit having no substance, this paradox, this question eternal to which there must be some kind of answer at the end of all searching. I had come a long way through the wilderness now, hunting the forests of life, climbing the cliffs to each pinnacle, trying to find it.

There was a new headquarters of the R.C.M.P. when I returned to Ottawa, a great, gray, rectangular stone building that stood in an open space near the edge of the city. Before, in 1947, when I'd left there, all administration had been dealt with from the Justice Building, but as the Force had grown, more and more space had been needed. Now, it numbered about five thousand men, with close to a thousand additional civilian staff posted across Canada from one end to the other. When I had joined in 1923, the Force comprised about eleven hundred men. The headquarters building seemed to be a personification of this, its size and appearance overshadowing the ghost of its predecessor, the small set of offices on Rideau Street in the downtown area. In one's mind's eye, one could see it, lodged in only a corner of this new and imposing vast structure. Over the main door, a huge crest of the Force stared down on the entrance way, the eyes in its buffalo head surveying all visitors.

Inside, the cold, stone passages vanished to right and to left flanked by their offices, and then went out of sight behind right-angle corners. Beyond, they continued, I knew, for many hundreds of feet in either direction, for here, in the entrance hall, I was at the headquarters' center. From the outside, it was an imposing edifice of four or five stories, long and narrow rather than broad, creating on first sight a monastic impression. It had in fact been intended for a big Roman Catholic seminary before the R.C.M.P. had taken it over.

Immediately to the right of the entrance hall was the Commissioner's office, and to the left another large room for the use of the Assistant Commissioner in charge of administration. My office, I found, was directly opposite the Commissioner's and adjacent to that of the other Deputy Commissioner. The rest of the building — the various floors filled with hundreds of men — took in all branches of headquarters, to deal with criminal investigations, intelligence, supply, treasury, etc., all divided into their various work areas and subsidiary units. Besides the Commissioner and the two Deputy Commissioners, the officer establishment at that time consisted of three Assistant Commissioners* — in charge of supply, criminal investigation, and administration — and a number of Superintendents, Inspectors, and Sub-Inspectors, all of whom were responsible for the sec-

* Later increased to four.

tions they looked after with the staff at their disposal. My job, in common with that of the other Deputy Commissioner, was to deal with certain aspects of administration not handled by the Commissioner, and to spend much of my time inspecting the Divisions of the Force across Canada. It meant traveling around with an Inspector, a male stenographer, and a senior N.C.O., looking into the books and records at each of the places visited, and discussing with the local officer in charge any problems which arose. Then after an absence of several weeks — we would inspect two or three Divisions in succession — we would return and report on conditions so that the Commissioner could act, if he chose, on any recommendations we submitted. It was a well-defined and established procedure, largely repetitive in nature, and merely a matter of going over the same thing in all the cities, towns and detachments we visited, looking into the files and trying to find methods by which efficiency could be improved. When we returned, the other Deputy Commissioner would take over in his turn and I would remain at headquarters in an administrative capacity until he came back and it was time to set off on my rounds once again. It was a tedious job which only had features of real interest once in a while, but it served a good purpose in keeping the headquarters staff close to what was going on in the field in a personal way, and had an additional advantage inasmuch as a senior officer from the staff could, from time to time, get a look at what was going on in the widely separated Divisions.

This went on for a year. It was getting close to the end of 1957, and in July 1958 I was to retire at my maximum period of service. However, I was asked to stay on for another year and I agreed to do so. The senior Deputy Commissioner left and on his departure I found myself the second ranking officer in the Force, a position in which I was required to take the Commissioner's place when he was absent from Ottawa. Occasionally this would be for extensive periods, and during such times the responsibility of being in charge of the R.C.M.P. automatically devolved on me until he came back and took over.

In this way — in these interim intervals — I was able to get a very good idea of what it meant to have the reins in my hands, and later this experience was to be highly advantageous. I did not find it too difficult; I was now at the top of the pyramid, the last man to rule on all major decisions. It was a high-pressure job with a large orbit of responsibility, but with an experienced and competent staff I didn't have much trouble. There were, of course, a great number of questions to settle from all parts of Canada, for the Force was now responsible for policing nearly all the provinces. Only Ontario and Quebec still retained their provincial forces, but even there the R.C.M.P. enforced the federal statutes. The only vestiges of its past as the Northwest Mounted Police and the Royal Northwest Mounted Police were in the reputation it had gained, the traditions which had been handed down, the uniform with its scarlet serge jacket, and the horses which were still kept at Regina and Ottawa for ceremonial purposes. These latter remained, forming a physical link with the early days, but their onetime purpose of transportation had given way to airplanes, patrol cars, and ships with which the modern force was now equipped. The time when only a couple of character references were required to join had gone by, and very close scrutiny was given to every prospective recruit. These were a different type, too, who joined on a career basis, sometimes straight from school — the pay was better, the marriage regulations less stringent, and while the competition was severe, for anyone who applied himself there was a good chance of getting on. Among other things, radio and teletype now linked the land, supplying instant communication, and only in the far North were there a few places which, by comparison with the past, could still be regarded as cut off.

It was late in 1958 when something happened which broke the pattern of my work. Crawley Films, a local company, decided to produce a series of half-hour television scripts about the R.C.M.P. and required someone to act in an advisory capacity. The sequences were to be developed in the Ottawa area, a composite effort on the part of Crawley Films, the Canadian Broadcasting Company and the British Broadcasting Corporation. Since the C.B.C. had an interest in this production and someone with an overall knowledge of the work was required to undertake the task, I was delegated to get the business under way.

It was an interesting vocation in which I now found myself, and an enlightening one, too. I had, of course, not the vaguest conception of what would be required; the movie industry was a completely foreign sphere. The head office was on the outskirts of Ottawa and from there it was planned that the interior shooting would be done in the studio, some thirty miles distant in the Gatineau country on the other side of the Ottawa river in Quebec, while the exterior scenes would be taken in the low-lying hills of the district and at points nearby. My task was to look over the scripts and to attempt to make them as nearly authentic as possible and then be present at the filming to answer the many questions which would continually arise. I soon found that this schedule left no time at all to carry on with my usual police duties.

It was late in the autumn when I began to look over the few scripts which were ready and to try to get them into shape for when production would begin. It soon became apparent that in my advisory capacity I had little control over the subject matter of the half-hour sequences, my main functions being to give advice and point out things which did not conform to R.C.M.P. procedure; for while the script writers were fully qualified in their own field, they naturally knew nothing about police work and when questions arose they came to me for the answers. These were of unlimited variety. What type of uniform would be worn on a given occasion? What would be said? Was the script correct from the standpoint of action? The questions ranged throughout the large miscellany of duties performed all over Canada, and required a knowledge of the work carried on not only in the southern areas of the country but in the northern regions as well. Sometimes, by reason of the unfamiliar paths the script writers trod, the detail of explanation became extremely involved, but they and the officers of Crawley Films were most accommodating and receptive to suggestion and we got along very well. I much enjoyed my association with all those I met. It was a new form of endeavor and about as far as one could get from the routine, run-of-the-mill work to which I'd been accustomed and the freedom of thought expressed by my new literary companions was often highly refreshing. It was a pleasant change to mix with them on their own ground and to be accepted mainly for what one was as an individual and only in part for what one represented. All through the latter years of my service in command positions I'd had to conform to what was recognized as standard behavior, always presenting a front to comply with a formalized pattern, being one person inside and on the outside another. Now I found this unconstrained atmosphere intellectually stimulating — it was like being caught by the hand and dragged, never quite knowing where I was going, over imaginative fields which previously I'd never set foot on. It was reasonable enough — these were the people who let their minds range in spheres of original, creative invention. I was the braking influence, the person more solidly attached to the ground on whom they depended to act as an anchor.

I had no idea of the long hours of work involved in the film business or the amount of painstaking care required to produce a very short picture. Work started at an early hour of the morning — just after sun-up — so as to take advantage of every bit of light for the outside scenes, and then, when evening came, quite often the interior episodes were shot in the studio. To me, it always seemed to be a race against time — a week was allowed for each picture and in that time it had to be completed; unless this was done, the actors who had been engaged for the following sequence the next week would remain unemployed, sitting around, with consequent hurt to the budget. Almost every scene had to be shot and reshot until it was perfect, quite a bit of the time in the snow and the cold under very uncomfortable conditions.

I was enjoying this new type of life with the film company and knew it would take a long time to complete the thirty-nine sequences scheduled. Accordingly, as there seemed to be no point in remaining with the Force — when all my time was taken up on these other activities — I thought I might as well retire and obtained permission to do so. I was already close to six months over the maximum time period, and there were others in the R.C.M.P. who could take my place without any kind of disruption. Besides, notwithstanding the long hours and discomforts, there was something about the film industry which was appealing — it was new, it was exciting. I think what I enjoyed most was to see something form itself each week when before there'd been nothing. It was creative and, for better or worse, everything was original.

It was not to last for long. Winter was coming to an end, the days were drawing out, and the month of March was in more than full stride when I was called back to headquarters. It came as a cataclysmic surprise to everyone, but to no one more so than myself. An emergency situation had arisen, brought about by a disagreement the Commissioner had had with the government, as a result of which he'd sent in his resignation. The difference related to a large and dangerous strike of woodworkers in Newfoundland. There'd been a savage riot in the Grand Falls area, one of the local constabulary had been killed, and a call had come in for reinforcements. A contingent of men had been gathered together in eastern Canada to send to the scene of the trouble, but at the last moment the government decided that this was not necessary. Commissioner Nicholson,* feeling as he did that help for the R.C.M.P. establishment was essential, sharply disagreed and said he could carry on no longer. As a result, the Commissioner's appointment fell vacant.

The news of the Commissioner's resignation hit like a bombshell! I was still on leave from the Force, having been given the usual period of furlough at the end of my service and, while I now had no actual connection with the R.C.M.P., for paper purposes I was still on the staff.

Within a few days I was called to see the Minister of Justice and offered the appointment. The year before I'd been in the hospital with coronary trouble and I was by no means sure, with the added burden of work, just what might happen. But it was an emergency, and I thought that if I returned temporarily for a while I could handle the affairs of the Force until another officer was moved in from the provinces and was given an opportunity to familiarize himself with what was required from an Ottawa standpoint. I knew all the officers and quite a number of the men and was well known by them in the various provinces in which I'd served. If the government thought that I was the person who should accept this responsibility, then obviously I should do so and do the best that I could.

But while these were the considerations of duty, of course there were personal considerations as well. It was a great compliment. Looking back through the years, there was considerable satisfaction in the thought that, although I'd started right at the bottom, if I got to the summit it might prove something valuable — that a person could come to

* Commissioner L. H. Nicholson had taken over command of the R.C.M.P. on Commissioner S. T. Wood's retirement in 1951.

a new world, unarmed and defenseless, a stranger, and then either by luck or good judgment, climb the rungs of the ladder, one by one, to the top. It had been done in other vocations, I knew, but never in the Mounted Police. It was a tremendous opportunity to be seized without question, the end of an immigrant's odyssey in all things material, and in this sense at least I would have come to full growth.

The year that followed was a hard one — I was back in the collar again, pulling with all my strength at the load. Apart from the problems that had to be solved in the office, there were speeches to be made at large gatherings to which I'd been invited both in Canada and the United States. There were the Divisions of the Force across Canada to be visited and inspected, flying from one to the other in an R.C.M.P. plane. There were all the security arrangements to be made for a Royal visit by Her Majesty the Queen and His Royal Highness Prince Philip, and after that a tour of the western Arctic by aircraft; as it was a quarter of a century since last I'd been there it was necessary to bring myself up to date with the changes that had occurred. Finally, there was a trip to England and Paris to discuss police matters with the British authorities and to attend a conference with the members of Interpol at which the heads of most of the world's police forces were assembled. In its concluding stages I was elected one of the two vice-presidents of the organization — an appointment previously held by my predecessor, Commissioner Nicholson — and although this reflected no particular credit on me, it was a very fine testimonial to the police force I represented and the country from which I came.

When I came back from overseas, my heart began to act up. The doctors said that I could only undergo minor strain or tension — if I persisted it might lead to unwelcome results. I'd done what I'd set out to do, there was someone else to take over, and, bearing all considerations in mind, there was no point to be served in staying any longer. And so, at the end of nearly thirty-seven years' service, for the second time I retired.

On April 1, 1960, I handed over to my successor, Commissioner C. W. Harvison, and walked down the steps of the great, gray, stone building for the last time, profoundly thankful that, with all that had gone before, I was still on my feet. It was the end of the pursuit that I'd started nearly fifty years previously. I was grateful to be alive and even more thankful for all that I'd learned.

The cold, stone eyes in the buffalo head guarding the entrance stared at me blankly as I turned from the past and went on.

Epilogue

~~~~~~~~~~~~~~~~~~

WHAT does man pursue? It seems a long time now since I asked myself this question at the beginning of this book. There are different goals, of course, I know, but peace was the underlying thing I'd searched for as the years passed by.

In these chapters, I've tried to trace the trail I followed, the markers as I found them upon this hidden way. It had been a hard journey through the wilderness in which I'd traveled half across the world and picked up life's lessons as I went along.

Perhaps, these come very easily to some — I cannot tell; only that from my youth there was an emptiness, and I had to find these things I searched for, one by one. Strength in adversity; kindness; a sense of values and of beauty, too, were what I'd looked for as I'd journeyed on.

But, far past these — a home.

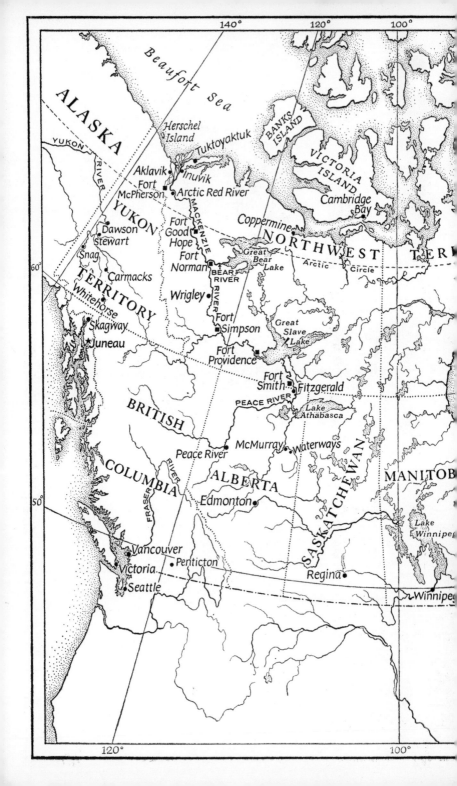